Authorware 5
Attain

AUTHORIZED

macromedia®
PRESS

Authorware 5 Attain Authorized
Macromedia, Inc.
Orson Kellogg

 Published by Macromedia Press, in association with Peachpit Press,
a division of Addison Wesley Longman.

Macromedia Press
1249 Eighth Street
Berkeley, CA 94710
510/524-2178 • 800-283-9444
510/524-2221 (fax)
Find us on the World Wide Web at:
http://www.peachpit.com
http://www.macromedia.com

ISBN 0-201-35411-X

Printed and bound in the United States of America

 Printed on recycled paper

9 8 7 6

CREDITS

Producer
Karen Tucker, Macromedia

Instructional Designer, Author, and Programmer
Orson Kellogg

Production
Rick Gordon, Emerald Valley Graphics
Myrna Vladic, Bad Dog Graphics
Debbie Roberti, Espresso Graphics

Editor
Judy Ziajka

Editor, Revision
Lisa Theobald

Indexer
Karin Arrigoni

Thanks to the following people:
The AWARE List, Marjorie Baer, Andrew Chemey, Christine Cobaugh, Greg Daigle,
Tom Dinger, Darci DiNucci, Ronni Eloff, Joe Ganci, Paul Gilbertson, Brian Herring,
Andy Keith, Luiz Lanna, John McGehee, Tyson Norris, Patrick O'Connor, Kate Reber,
Jeff Schick, Jeff Schwamberger, Ed Skwarecki, David Swenson, Fran Taylor, Christian
Vescia, Kevin Wallace, Jamil Zainasheff

ABOUT THE AUTHOR

Orson Kellogg designs and develops instructional and marketing interactive media.
His work—on behalf of such companies as Autodesk, Oracle, Hewlett-Packard, Sun,
and Symantec—has won three awards from the Society for Technical Communication.

table of contents

intro
duction

Authorware is a powerful and flexible tool for developing all kinds of interactive multimedia. Authorware is perhaps best known as an authoring tool for computer-based training (CBT), mainly because it makes it easy to handle a wide variety of media and precisely track and respond to users' actions. But what makes it so good for CBT also makes it the perfect tool for other media-rich, highly interactive projects such as interactive magazines and catalogs, performance-support applications, and educational games. And when you combine its CBT features with an expanding list of Internet capabilities—including several new features in version 5—Authorware becomes a powerful tool for creating Web-based training (WBT) that looks, feels, and performs very much like what has been possible only when delivered on CD-ROM. This book is designed to help you get started using this exceptionally powerful and versatile tool.

Authorware 5 Attain is one of three components in the Macromedia Attain Enterprise Learning System that provides an integrated solution for developing and delivering interactive learning over intranets and the Internet. The other components are Dreamweaver Attain and Pathware. Dreamweaver Attain is an HTML authoring tool with special features for creating Web-based learning content. Pathware is software for training administration and management. You'll find a trial version of Dreamweaver Attain on the CD-ROM that accompanies this book.

This Macromedia Authorized training book introduces you to the major features of Authorware 5 Attain and guides you step by step through the development of several Authorware projects. The 18 lessons in the book are profusely illustrated with screen captures to help you check your progress through each project. By the end of Lesson 18, you should be able to build Authorware projects that feature text, graphics, sounds, digital movies, and nine kinds of interactivity. You'll learn to distribute your Authorware pieces on floppy disks, CD-ROM, or the Internet.

These are the 18 lessons:

Lesson 1: Authorware Basics
Lesson 2: Creating a Simple Piece
Lesson 3: Adding Motion and Sound
Lesson 4: Introducing Interactions
Lesson 5: Hot Spot Interactions
Lesson 6: Text Entry Interactions
Lesson 7: Enhancing Interactions
Lesson 8: Hot Object Interactions
Lesson 9: Target Area Interactions
Lesson 10: Perpetual Pull-Down Menus
Lesson 11: Distributing a Piece
Lesson 12: Introducing Variables
Lesson 13: Using Variables for Branching
Lesson 14: Integrating Digital Movies
Lesson 15: Introducing Frameworks
Lesson 16: Building Framework Pages
Lesson 17: Navigating with Hypertext
Lesson 18: Enhancing Frameworks

Each lesson begins with an overview of its content and learning objectives. A series of short tasks teaches important Authorware skills broken into bite-sized units. Most lessons also include:

Tips: Shortcuts for carrying out common tasks and ways to use the skills you learn to solve common problems.
Boldface terms: New vocabulary that will come in handy as you use Authorware and work with multimedia.
Menu commands and keyboard shortcuts: Alternative methods for carrying out commands in Authorware. Menu commands are shown like this: Menu › Command › Subcommand. For example, the Save command on the File menu is shown like this: File › Save. When a keyboard shortcut is available, it is listed with the first step in which it can be used; a plus sign between the names of keys means you press the keys simultaneously: for example, Ctrl+S.

2

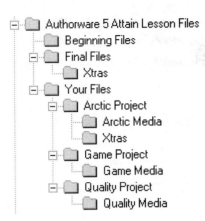

The Beginning Files folder contains prebuilt Authorware files you can use to start your work in most of the lessons. The Final Files folder contains a completed Authorware file for each lesson. The Your Files folder is where you'll save your work for the three projects you develop.

Appendix A provides a quick reference to shortcuts you can use for common commands in Authorware. Appendix B lists other learning resources you can use to expand your Authorware knowledge.

All the files you need are included on the enclosed CD-ROM. An installation program on the CD will copy the files to your hard drive and create a set of folders you can use to hold your own work. The Authorware 5 Attain Lessons folder, which will be created on your hard drive, contains three subfolders: Beginning Files, Final Files, and Your Files. The Beginning Files folder contains a set of prebuilt files you can use to begin most of the lessons. The Final Files folder contains a completed version of the Authorware file for each lesson. You can use these files to preview each lesson's results or to compare against your own work.

A folder named Your Files contains three folders that store your work for the three main projects in this book—Game Project, Arctic Project, and Quality Project. Within each project folder is a media folder that holds the media files needed for that project.

The instructions in *Authorware 5 Attain Authorized* are designed for multimedia developers, graphic artists, instructional designers, illustrators, Webmasters, technical writers, and anyone else who wants to become a developer of interactive media and is new to Authorware. Although intended for Authorware beginners, the instructions assume that you are familiar with Windows basics, such as choosing items from menus, opening and saving files, and using a mouse.

Finally, the instructions in this book assume that you already have Authorware 5 Attain installed on your computer and that your computer meets the system requirements listed at the end of this Introduction. If you don't own Authorware 5 Attain, you can

3

install the time-limited training version provided on the enclosed CD-ROM. This version has all the capabilities of the full product, but after you install it, it will work for 45 days only. See the ReadMe file on the CD for installation instructions and information about other software included on the CD.

Welcome to *Authorware 5 Attain Authorized*. We hope you enjoy the lessons in this book.

WHAT YOU WILL LEARN

By the end of this book, you will be able to:

- Create interactive multimedia applications using text, graphics, sound, and digital movies
- Use media elements that you import into Authorware and external media elements that are linked to your pieces
- Create and modify text using the built-in text tools and Authorware text styles
- Apply screen transitions and path animations to enhance visual elements
- Create interactions that let users trigger responses by pressing keys, entering text, clicking buttons, or clicking objects on the screen
- Create interactions in which users drag objects to locations you define
- Create navigation structures that allow users to navigate to multimedia content by moving forward and backward among pages or by searching for text they enter
- Create hypertext that lets users click a word or phrase to display additional information
- Use Authorware's built-in system variables to expand the functionality of your pieces—for example, by storing information that users enter and then later displaying it to them
- Prepare a piece for delivery on CD-ROM
- Prepare a piece for delivery over an intranet or the Internet

MINIMUM SYSTEM REQUIREMENTS

Intel Pentium processor

Windows 95, Windows 98 (or later versions), or Windows NT 4

16+ MB of RAM

CD-ROM drive

640×480, 256-color display (higher resolution and color depth recommended)

50 MB of free hard-disk space for Authorware 5 Attain (plus 15 MB for the lesson files)

SoundBlaster-compatible sound card

QuickTime for Windows support

Authorware basics

LESSON 1

Authorware provides a unique combination of simplicity and power for producing and publishing interactive information. You can quickly assemble simple yet effective multimedia productions by dragging and dropping icons along the Authorware flowline. As you deepen your knowledge of Authorware and explore its more sophisticated capabilities, you can create virtually any kind of interactive application you can

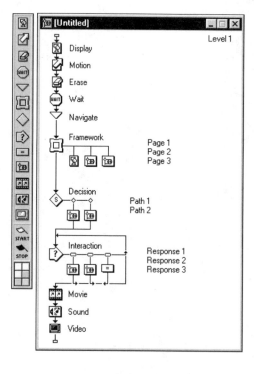

Dragging icons to a flowline is the way you create powerful interactive applications with Authorware. In this illustration nearly every Authorware icon has been used to create an application that incorporates text, graphics, sound, video, and several kinds of interactivity. This lesson introduces you to basic Authorware features— the tools you'll use to create your own interactive applications.

imagine, combining a rich array of media with compelling interactivity—to enhance learning and deliver information. With Authorware Web Player, you can distribute your work over the Internet as well as on CD-ROM.

This lesson is a get-acquainted session, designed to introduce the basic Authorware components. In this lesson you won't build a project. You'll simply take a guided tour through Authorware. In later lessons you'll learn to use most of the tools introduced here.

note *Before beginning the lessons in this book, make sure you have installed Authorware 5 Attain or the time-limited version of Authorware 5 Attain and that you've installed the lesson folders and lesson files for this book. You can install the Authorware time-limited version and the lesson folders and files from the accompanying CD-ROM. For installation instructions, see the ReadMe file on the CD.*

WHAT YOU WILL LEARN

In this lesson you will become familiar with the basic Authorware components used to:

- Assemble and view the structure of an Authorware piece
- View and manipulate the visual elements of a piece
- Control the playback of a piece
- Add graphics, motion, sound, and digital movies to a piece
- Create text and simple graphics

APPROXIMATE TIME

It should take about 30 minutes to complete this lesson.

LESSON FILES

Final Files\03_Final.a5p

GETTING ACQUAINTED WITH AUTHORWARE

Authorware enables you to produce a wide variety of interactive applications. Its icon-based authoring techniques provide an efficient and easy-to-understand way to build complex multimedia productions: To create an Authorware piece, you drag and drop **icons** onto a **flowline** to outline the structure of your piece.

In this first task, you will get acquainted with the basic Authorware interface.

1] Start Authorware 5.

You can start Authorware 5 from the Windows Start menu (Programs > Macromedia Authorware 5 > Authorware 5) or by locating the Authorware folder in Windows Explorer and double-clicking the Authorware icon.

When you start Authorware, the New File dialog box appears, asking you to select a Knowledge Object for the new file.

A new feature in Authorware 5, **Knowledge Objects** provide an interface that helps you create sophisticated interactivity. A Knowledge Object is an encapsulated section of an Authorware file along with a wizard that guides you as you select options for how the section of the file is used.

Using Knowledge Objects, an inexperienced Authorware user can create complex interactions. In addition, experienced Authorware developers can create their own

8

Knowledge Objects to accelerate the pace of certain tasks or to hand off portions of an Authorware project to less experienced developers.

Because this book's purpose is to help you learn to work directly with Authorware and to thoroughly understand how Authorware works, you won't be using Knowledge Objects here. Therefore, to work with the examples in this book, you need to prevent this dialog box from appearing each time you start Authorware.

2] In the New File dialog box, click the box labeled *Show this dialog at startup* to remove the checkmark. Then click the None button to indicate that you don't want to use a Knowledge Object for this file.

The Knowledge Objects window is displayed on the right side of your screen. This window lists all the Knowledge Objects included with Authorware. If you had built your own Knowledge Objects, you could include them in this list.

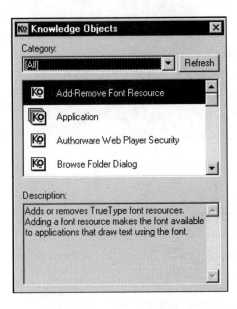

3] Click the "X" in the upper right of the Knowledge Objects window to close the window.

What you now see is the main working environment you'll use for all the lessons: the Authorware **Design window**. From here you'll assemble the elements of interactive media on the flowline. Across the top of the window is the **menu bar**, and below it is the **toolbar**. The **icon palette** containing the tools you'll use to build your pieces is along the left side of the Design window.

9

tip *If the toolbar does not appear, choose View > Toolbar to display it (or press Ctrl+Shift+T).*

ICON PALETTE MENU BAR TOOLBAR

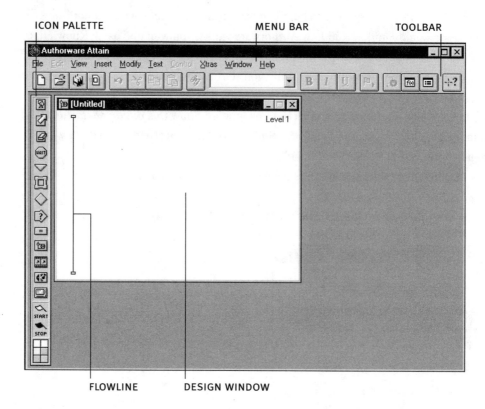

FLOWLINE DESIGN WINDOW

4] Open the menus to see the available commands.

Many commands can be activated by using keyboard shortcuts as well as via the menus. Keyboard shortcuts, which you can use to activate a command without using the menu, are listed next to the corresponding command name.

The menus you see reflect the **Macromedia user interface standard**. By designing menus and other interface elements to be consistent from program to program, this standard makes it easier for you to use different Macromedia applications together.

5] Move your cursor slowly across the toolbar buttons.

The buttons on the toolbar provide shortcuts for the most common functions, such as saving a file, running a piece, stopping a piece, and changing the appearance of text. When you pause the cursor over a button, a **Tooltip** appears and describes the button's function.

6] Move your cursor slowly over the tools in the icon palette.

Tooltips also appear here to remind you what each tool does.

TOOLS IN THE ICON PALETTE

 Display icon. Displays graphics and text on the screen.

 Motion icon. Moves graphics, text, or digital movies across the screen to locations and at speeds you select.

 Erase icon. Erases objects displayed on the screen.

 Wait icon. Pauses the flow of activity on the flowline for a duration you set or stops the activity until the user clicks the mouse or a button.

 Navigate icon. Sets up a navigation link to a location you specify or the user chooses.

 Framework icon. Creates a paging structure for navigation consisting of a series of icons that users can navigate among. Navigate icons always lead to an icon within one of these paging structures.

 Decision icon. Directs activity along one of several paths depending on conditions you set.

 Interaction icon. Directs activity along one of several paths depending on how the user responds.

 Calculation icon. Contains expressions you create that work with and extend beyond the capabilities of the other tools in the icon palette. An expression can be as simple as assigning a value to a user-created variable that controls what the user sees. Expressions can also perform powerful tasks such as retrieving information from a user's hard drive or a Web site.

 Map icon. Contains a series of icons that you group together to organize the flowline into manageable chunks. Each map icon contains its own flowline.

 Digital movie icon. Plays digital movies.

 Sound icon. Plays digital sounds.

 Video icon. Plays video from videodisc or videotape, commonly called analog video.

Start and stop flags. Mark the beginning and end points of a section of a piece that you want to run without running the entire piece.

Icon color palette. Applies colors to icons you select to help you visually identify and organize the content in your piece.

GETTING ACQUAINTED WITH THE DESIGN AND PRESENTATION WINDOWS

You'll do almost all your work in Authorware in one of two windows. In the Design window, you assemble the content along the Authorware flowline using the tools in the icon palette. When you run a piece, the **Presentation window** opens to show you how your piece will appear to users. In the Presentation window, you also create text and simple graphics and manipulate all the visual elements in your piece. You will often move between these windows as you create, review, and revise your pieces.

To better understand the differences between the Design and Presentation windows, in this task you will open an Authorware piece and switch between the two windows.

1] Choose File › Open › File (Ctrl+O). In the Select a File dialog box, locate the Final Files folder. Then select 03_Final.a5p and click Open.

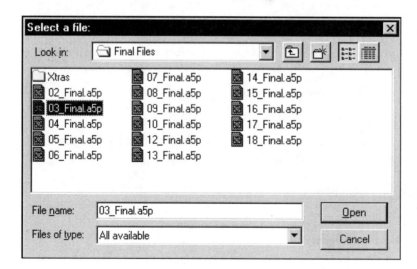

The Design window appears, displaying a series of icons from the icon palette along the flowline. Each icon either contains media, such as text or graphics, or represents an action that is performed on one of the media elements. When you author a piece, you drag icons from the icon palette to the flowline in the order you want their content to be displayed. You can literally design the structure of a piece just by placing icons along the flowline and then later add content to the icons.

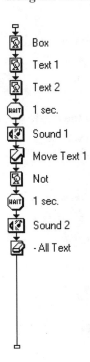

Box
Text 1
Text 2
1 sec.
Sound 1
Move Text 1
Not
1 sec.
Sound 2
- All Text

2] Choose Window › Control Panel to open the Control Panel (Ctrl+2).

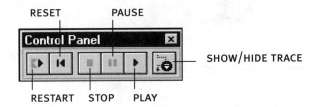

You use the **Control Panel** to play back an Authorware piece or a section that you're working on.

You can click the buttons on the Control Panel to restart a piece from the beginning, to reset a piece to the beginning for debugging, and to stop, pause, and play your work. The Show/Hide Trace button on the right expands the Control Panel into a Trace window, where you can trace the flow icon by icon to debug a piece.

The Control Panel is available only when the flowline contains at least one icon.

3] Drag the Control Panel to the upper right of your screen.

Now the Control Panel is available without covering up anything in the main work area of the Authorware window. If your screen resolution permits, one good place for the Control Panel is above the main window area, to the right of the toolbar.

4] Click the Restart button on the Control Panel to play the piece from the start.

The Presentation window opens, and a short sequence plays back. You will be building this simple production in the next two lessons.

tip   *You can also open the Presentation window by choosing Window > Presentation (Ctrl+1). You can close the Presentation window and switch back to the Design window using the same command. With sufficiently high screen resolution, you can view both windows at the same time and use your mouse to select the window you want to work in.*

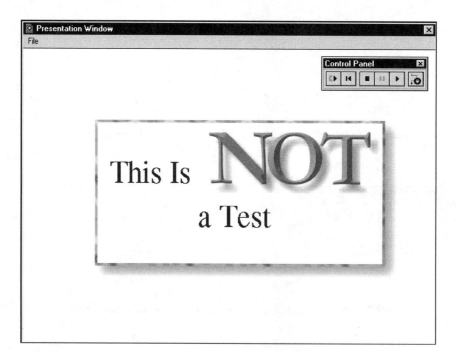

5] Return to the Design window from the Presentation window by clicking the Stop button on the Control Panel.

FOLLOWING FLOWLINE LOGIC

One key to learning Authorware is understanding the flowline. The activity in an Authorware production proceeds downward along the flowline. At places where the flowline structure is horizontal rather than vertical, the flow proceeds from left to right. To see how the flowline structure works, you will explore its organization in the Authorware piece you opened in the preceding task.

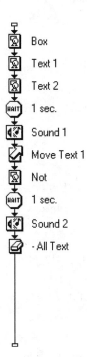

Box
Text 1
Text 2
1 sec.
Sound 1
Move Text 1
Not
1 sec.
Sound 2
- All Text

The flow begins with the first icon, a display icon entitled Box. This display icon contains an image of a rectangular frame that was created in a graphics program and imported into Authorware.

 To preview the contents of an icon, right-click the icon.

As soon as the image in the Box icon appears on the screen, the flow continues down the flowline to the second display icon, *Text 1*, which contains the first line of text, and then to the third display icon, *Text 2*, which also contains text.

When display icons are arranged one after another with no pauses or other factors affecting the time when they appear on the screen, the time between the display of the first and succeeding icons is usually undetectable. That's why the contents of the first three display icons appear at the same time.

The fourth icon, labeled 1 sec., is a wait icon; it pauses the piece for 1 second. The fifth icon, Sound 1, is a sound icon, which plays a sound file. The sixth icon, Move Text 1, is a motion icon; this moves the first line of text across the screen while the sound plays.

The seventh icon, Not, is a display icon containing the word "NOT," which is another graphic imported into Authorware. This is followed by another wait icon, 1 sec., which again pauses the flow of activity for 1 second. Then a sound icon, Sound 2, plays while an erase icon, - All Text, erases all the text on screen.

GETTING ACQUAINTED WITH THE TOOLBOX

Whenever you stop a piece to add or modify content in a display icon, the **toolbox** appears. You use the tools in the toolbox to create text and simple graphics and to arrange graphic elements on the screen the way you want users to see them.

In this task, you will open a display icon to see the tools in the toolbox that appears.

1] In the Design window, click the second display icon, Text 1, to select it. Then choose Edit › Open Icon (Ctrl+Alt+O).

The Presentation window opens, displaying the contents of the icon—in this case, the words "This Is." At the same time, the toolbox for this display icon opens. The toolbox title bar always indicates the name of the currently selected icon.

2] Move your cursor slowly over the tools in the toolbox.

Tooltips again remind you what each tool does.

THE TOOLBOX

 Pointer. Selects and moves objects.

 Text tool. Creates and modifies text.

 Straight Line tool. Draws horizontal, vertical, and 45-degree diagonal lines.

 Diagonal Line tool. Draws lines at any angle. To make a line horizontal, vertical, or angled at 45 degrees, hold down the Shift key while drawing.

 Ellipse tool. Draws ovals and circles. To draw a circle, hold down the Shift key while drawing.

 Rectangle tool. Draws rectangles. To draw a square, hold down the Shift key while drawing.

 Rounded Rectangle tool. Draws rectangles with curved corners.

 Polygon tool. Draws multisided objects.

3] Choose File › Close › All (Ctrl+Shift+W) to close the 03_Final.a5p file.
When Authorware asks you whether to save changes, click No.

MULTIMEDIA DEVELOPMENT TIPS

Developing interactive multimedia is a complex process. Here are a few tips to keep in mind as you work on your Authorware projects.

Save under different file names. Make a habit of saving your piece under a new file name on a regular basis—daily, for example, or before you make major changes. That way, you'll have an earlier version to return to if you discover multiple problems in a newer version or simply change your mind about a series of revisions you make.

Back up your work. Make frequent backup copies of your Authorware files using tape, magneto-optical disks, or other removable media. Store these backups in a safe place. For especially large or important projects, store backups in a separate location from where you author the files.

Test early and often. During development, don't wait till you're almost done before packaging and running the piece on computers that are similar to your intended platform. If your piece needs to run on a 486 PC with Windows 3.1, for example, try out a prototype of the piece on such a machine before getting too far into development. Remember that the performance, video driver, and screen resolution of your audience's computers will usually differ from your own.

If your piece will be distributed on the Web, design it that way from the start. Maximize the performance of your Web pieces by keeping a few principles in mind:

- Use the smallest possible media files. For images, instead of creating BMP files, use JPEG, GIF, and PNG. For sound, instead of using WAV files use Shockwave Audio for music and Voxware for voice.

- Test your piece in each kind of browser that your users will have. Different browsers behave in different ways.

- Design your Web pieces to put more emphasis on interactivity—which requires little bandwidth—rather than on large graphics and long sounds.

For cross-platform development, test early and test often on the Macintosh. Avoid surprises late in development by running pieces that you develop for the Macintosh using the Authorware Mac Player (expected to be available in early 1999). For more information, see the Authorware 5 Attain Developers Center at the Macromedia Web site (*http://www.macromedia.com*).

Allow time for reviews, revisions, and QA in your schedule. Developing interactive multimedia requires the same cycles of testing, quality assurance, and revisions as any software development project. Build time for these activities into your production schedule.

WHAT YOU HAVE LEARNED

In this lesson you learned about these basic Authorware components:

- Design window for assembling and viewing the structure of an Authorware piece [*page* **8**]
- Icon palette for adding text, graphics, motion, sound, and digital movies to a piece [*page* **11**]
- Presentation window for viewing and manipulating the visual elements of a piece [*page* **12**]
- Control Panel for controlling the playback of a piece [*page* **13**]
- Toolbox for creating text and simple graphics [*page* **16**]

creating a simple piece

In this lesson you'll begin assembling the simple piece you examined in the previous lesson. You'll start by importing a graphic and creating text. As in all Authorware projects, you'll build the piece icon by icon, placing the icons along the flowline in the order you want them to appear and adding content or functionality to each one.

You'll work here with three display icons. The first display icon will contain an imported graphic. The second and third display icons will each contain a line of text that you create using tools in Authorware. By using separate display icons for each

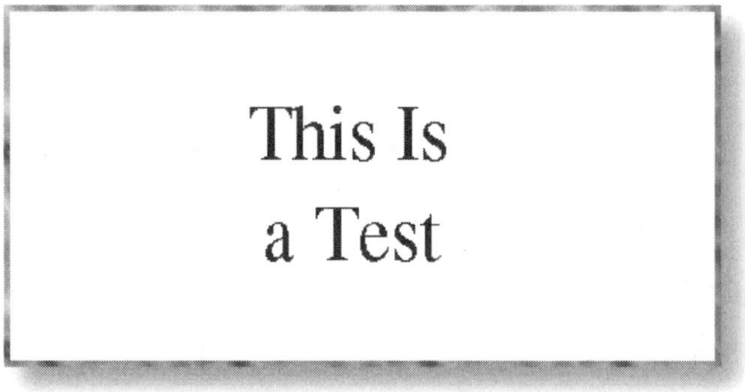

This Is
a Test

As you develop the piece shown here, you'll perform some of the most important tasks in crafting interactive media, beginning with importing a graphic, creating text, and applying screen transitions to the images on the screen.

text object, you make it possible to perform an action on one line of text without affecting the other. In Lesson 3 you will animate the first line of text while leaving the second line in place.

WHAT YOU WILL LEARN

In this lesson you will:

- Set global properties for a piece, such as the size and position of the Presentation window
- Place icons for text and graphics on the flowline
- Import a graphic
- Create text using the font, size, color, and graphic mode you select
- Apply a transition to enhance the impact of text

APPROXIMATE TIME

It should take about 1 hour to complete this lesson.

LESSON FILES

Media File:

Your Files\Game Project\Game Media

Beginning File:

Beginning Files\02_Begin.a5p

Completed Project:

Final Files\02_Final.a5p

SETTING FILE PROPERTIES

The first step in beginning the piece is to open the Beginning file and set its file properties.

1] Open the 02_Begin.a5p file in the Beginning Files folder.

This opens the Design window, where you will begin your work for this lesson. You can create two kinds of files in Authorware. The first is an **Authorware piece**, which has the .a5p file extension. The second kind, a **library**, is used for holding content that's used in several places in a piece; it has the .a5l file extension. You'll work with libraries in later lessons.

2] Choose File › Save As. In the Save Files As dialog box, locate the Game Project folder inside the Your Files folder.

You'll save the 02_Begin.a5p file under a different name so you can use the Beginning file again if you want to review the lesson later.

3] Enter the file name *02_Game* in the File Name box. Then click Save.

Authorware automatically adds the .a5p file extension when it saves the file.

> **note** *This Authorware file contains no text, graphics, or other media. It does contain a custom color palette that's needed to display the graphics you'll use in this lesson. In Lesson 13, you'll learn more about custom palettes.*

> **tip** *If your computer is set to 16-bit color or higher (instead of 8-bit color, 256 colors), you don't need to use a custom palette for this project. Instead of opening 02_Begin.a5p, you can simply start a new file.*

4] Choose Modify › File › Properties to open the File Properties dialog box (Ctrl+Shift+D).

You can use this dialog box to set a number of options that affect the performance and appearance of the entire piece. It's a good idea to at least review the default settings before beginning production. Changing these global settings late in production can be costly because much of your work may have been based on them. For example, if you change the Screen Size setting after creating artwork, you might have to redo the artwork to fit the different resolution.

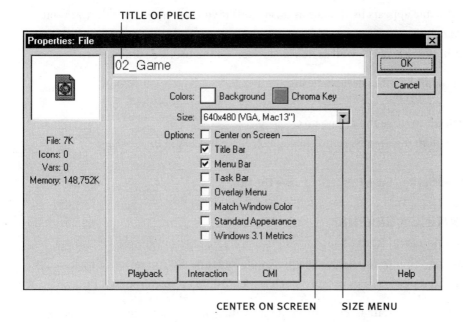

CENTER ON SCREEN   SIZE MENU

5] Open the Size menu.

You can choose from a variety of standard monitor resolution settings. You can also select Variable (at the top of the list), which allows you to drag the edge of the Presentation window to select a custom size for your piece.

tip *Design for the lowest resolution your users will have. Because it's usually difficult to predict what the lowest resolution will be, your best bet is to choose a relatively common resolution such as 640 × 480 pixels. If your Presentation window is set to a higher resolution than the user's, the bottom and right edges of your graphics or text will be hidden from that user.*

6] Select 640 × 480 (VGA, Mac 13").

This is a good standard size that works for any Windows user and any Macintosh user with a 13-inch or larger monitor.

7] Under Options, click the Center on Screen box.

If a user's resolution is set higher than the Presentation window size, this setting will display the Authorware production in the middle of the user's screen.

8] Click the text entry box at the top of the dialog box and drag to highlight 02_Game. Enter the title *Authorware Game.*

The file name appears by default in this box. But you can enter any title you want here. When you distribute your Authorware piece as an application, your title will appear in the title bar as well as next to its icon on the user's desktop.

You'll accept the other default settings.

9] Click OK to close the dialog box.

You'll explore the options in this dialog box again in Lesson 8.

10] Choose File › Save (Ctrl+S) to save the file.

IMPORTING A GRAPHIC

Authorware provides a toolbox you can use to create text and simple graphics in display icons. For most multimedia pieces, however, you'll use images that have been created in a graphics program such as Photoshop or Macromedia's Fireworks.

In this task you'll start assembling content by dragging a display icon from the icon palette and putting content in it by importing a graphic.

1] Drag a display icon from the icon palette to the flowline.

You drag icons from the icon palette to assemble the structure of a piece. You will place the first graphic used in this piece, a rectangular box, in this display icon.

DISPLAY ICON

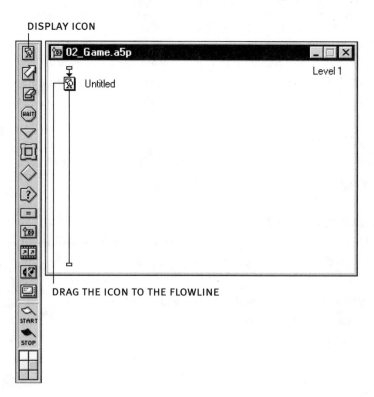

DRAG THE ICON TO THE FLOWLINE

2] Replace the default icon name, Untitled, with the name *Box*.

If you click elsewhere on the screen before typing a name, click the icon again to select its default name. Then type the new name.

To import a graphic, you first need to open the display icon that will contain it. You'll do that in the next step.

Box

3] Double-click the Box display icon to open it.

Authorware opens the Presentation window, where you can position and adjust the visual elements in your pieces. The toolbox is also displayed, with the icon name in its title bar.

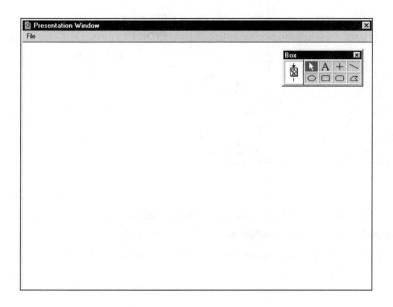

You will now import a graphic into the Box icon.

4] Choose File › Import (Ctrl+Shift+R) to import a graphic.

The Import Which File? dialog box opens.

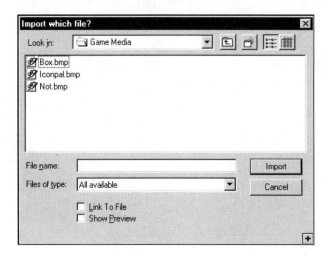

5] Click the Show Preview box.

The dialog box now includes a preview window. When you select a file, you can use the preview window to see whether it's the one you want before you import it.

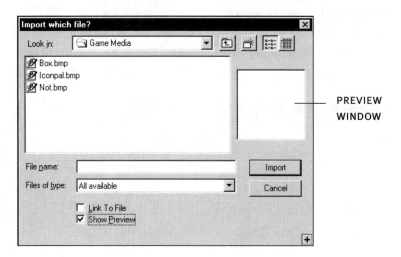

PREVIEW
WINDOW

6] In the list at the top of the dialog box, locate the Game Media folder. The Box.bmp file name will appear in the window below. Select this file.

When you select this file, its name appears in the File Name box and a thumbnail image appears in the preview window.

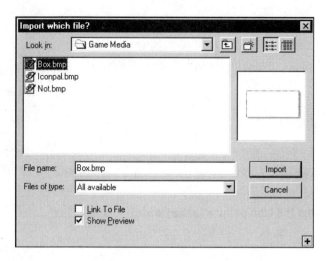

7] Click Import to import the graphic into Authorware.

The image—a box—appears in the center of the Presentation window.

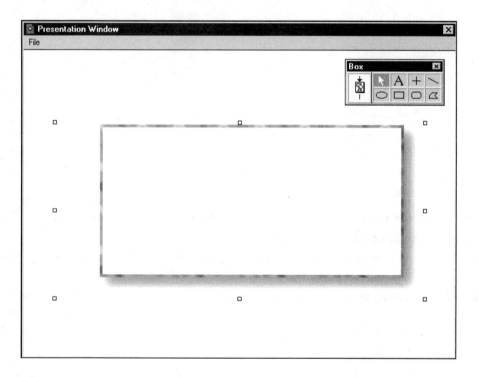

8] Choose File › Save (Ctrl+S) to save your changes.

Now you will add some text to the piece.

CREATING TEXT

In this task, you'll use the Text tool to create a line of text. First you'll need to create another display icon to hold the text. Then you'll display the two icons together so you can align the text with the Box graphic.

1] Switch back to the Design window.

To do this, press Ctrl+1.

This shortcut toggles between displaying and closing the Presentation window.

2] Drag another display icon from the icon palette to the flowline. Name it *Text 1*.

Box

Text 1

3] If the Control Panel isn't already open, choose Window › Control Panel. Then click the Restart button to play the Authorware piece.

The piece starts at the beginning. The Box display icon displays the graphic you just imported. Then the piece pauses at the Text 1 display icon, and the toolbox opens. Authorware is waiting for you to add content to the Text 1 icon.

tip   *One efficient authoring approach is to string a series of icons along the flowline for one section of a piece. Give the icons descriptive titles but no content. Then run the piece and fill in the content as you move from icon to icon. Every time Authorware encounters an icon that doesn't contain content, the flow stops and Authorware pauses so you can add content. When you've finished adding content to an icon, you can close the icon and Authorware will move down the flowline to the next empty icon.*

The content of the Box icon is displayed on the screen, and the Text 1 icon is open. You will create some text to place in the Text 1 icon.

4] Click the Text tool in the toolbox and then click somewhere near the center of the Box graphic.

The text margins and paragraph ruler appear, indicating the default width for the text you'll enter. Before typing anything, however, first select a text font and size.

PARAGRAPH RULER

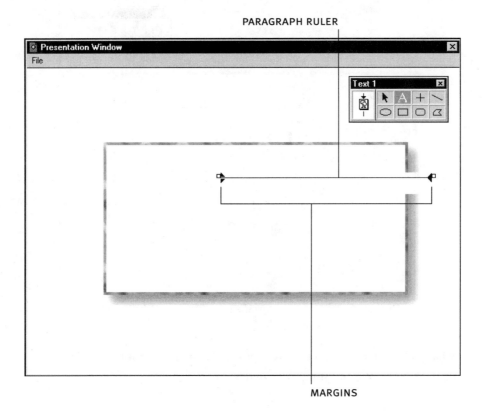

MARGINS

CREATING A SIMPLE PIECE

5] Choose Text › Font › Times. (If Times does not appear in the list of fonts, select Other and then select Times from the list of fonts and click OK.)

When using the Text tool to create text, you generally should limit your font choices to fonts that are standard on your users' computers. The safest bets are Times, Times New Roman, and Arial.

6] Choose Text › Size › 36.

You can specify sizes in preset increments, or you can choose Other and enter a size by typing it.

7] In the text field, type the following: *This Is*

You'll align this text later.

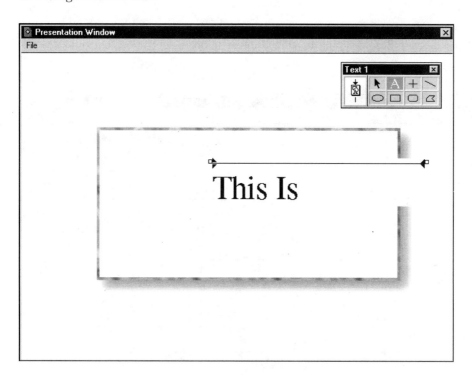

You now have a line of 36-point Times text positioned within the Box graphic. You can make this text more interesting by changing its properties.

SETTING TEXT PROPERTIES

Now you'll change the color of the text and make it transparent against the background image. To do this, you'll use the Pointer tool and Authorware's **Inspectors**. The Inspectors are tools that let you set various properties for the graphics you create with the tools in the toolbox.

1] Click the Pointer tool in the toolbox to select the entire text object.

Handles appear around the text object.

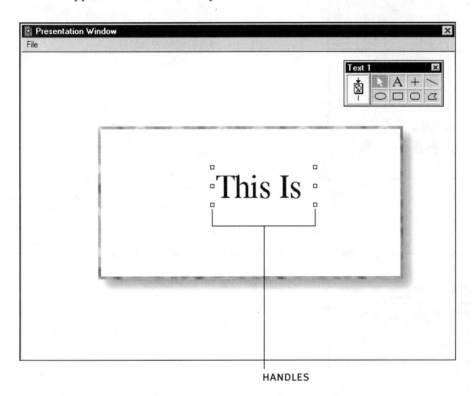

HANDLES

After you create text or graphics using the tools in the toolbox, click the Pointer tool when you want to manipulate the object further. In this case, you want to change the color of the text.

2] Choose Window › Inspectors › Colors (Ctrl+K) to display the Colors Inspector.

Use the Colors Inspector to set colors for the text and graphics you create in the toolbox.

> **tip** *You can also double-click the Ellipse tool in the toolbox to open the Colors Inspector.*

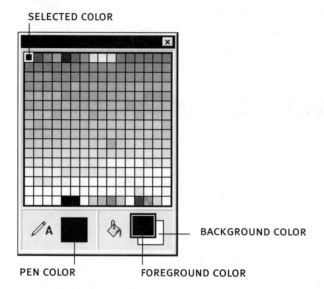

SELECTED COLOR

BACKGROUND COLOR

PEN COLOR

FOREGROUND COLOR

3] Click the Pen color chip. Then find the bright blue swatch in the palette and click it.

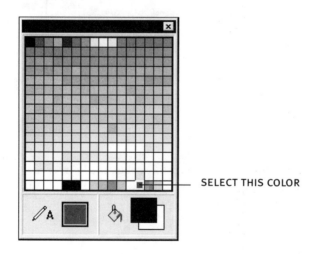

SELECT THIS COLOR

The pen color chip shows the color you selected. In the palette, the selected color has a white border. You use the pen color chip to set the color of the text, lines, and borders of objects you draw using the toolbox.

The text is now blue.

4] Close the Colors Inspector by clicking the close box at the upper right.

If you have space on your screen, you can leave this Inspector open and move it to one side so it is readily accessible for future use.

Now you will change the appearance of the text against the background of the Box graphic.

5] Choose Window › Inspectors › Modes (Ctrl+M).

The Modes Inspector appears. This tool provides six options that affect the appearance of text and graphics on the screen. The most commonly used options are Opaque, Matted, and Transparent.

 tip *You can also double-click the Pointer tool in the toolbox to open the Modes Inspector.*

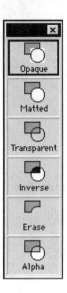

If you choose the Opaque option, the image completely covers the background. The Matted option is similar to Opaque, except that white areas around the outside of the image are transparent. The Transparent option makes all white areas of the image transparent. If you choose Inverse, any colored areas in the image are displayed in the color that is the inverse of the background color beneath them. If you choose Erase, the image shows the background color in place of all colored areas.

33

The Alpha option takes advantage of the alpha channel that some graphics programs allow you to include in graphics files. An alpha channel stores transparency information. Using the Alpha mode with an image that includes an alpha channel can cause the image to blend with the image behind it.

6] Click Transparent in the Modes Inspector.
This setting allows background images to show through the text.

7] Click the close box on the Modes Inspector to close it.
If there's enough space on your screen, you can leave this Inspector open and move it to one side if you prefer.

8] Save your work.

CREATING A SECOND LINE OF TEXT

You need one more line of text to complete this part of the project. You could create another line of text within the same display icon. Instead, however, you'll create the second line in a separate display icon. This will allow you to create an animation in the next lesson that involves only the first line of text.

1] Choose Window › Presentation to return to the Design window.

2] Drag a display icon to the flowline below the other two display icons and name it *Text 2*.

Now you'll run the piece from the start to display the content of the first two icons and open the Text 2 icon so you can add content.

3] Click the Restart button.

The piece stops at the Text 2 icon, and the toolbox opens.

4] Click the Text tool. Then click just below the first line of text to begin entering text.

Notice that whenever you use the Text tool, the text margins are displayed.

5] Enter the following text: *a Test*

This new line uses the same font, size, color, and mode as the text you created in the previous display icon. Authorware retains the previous settings, although you can change them if you want.

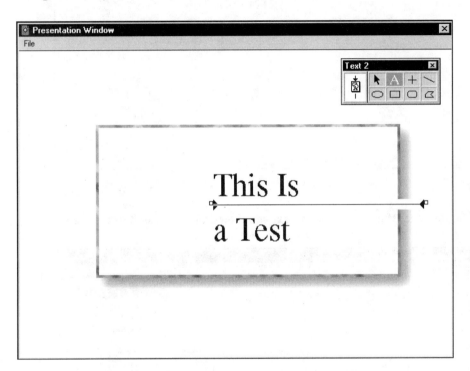

ALIGNING OBJECTS IN SEPARATE DISPLAY ICONS

You created two separate lines of text in two display icons. If both lines are not perfectly aligned over the graphic, you can align them now.

1] Click the Pointer tool in the toolbox.

2] Double-click the first line of text to select it.

The first line of text has handles around it, and the title bar of the toolbox reminds you that you're now working on the Text 1 icon.

3] Drag the first line of text so it's approximately centered in the box.

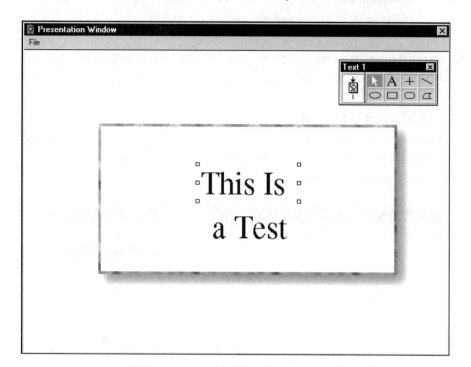

4] Double-click the second line of text and then drag to center it under the first line.

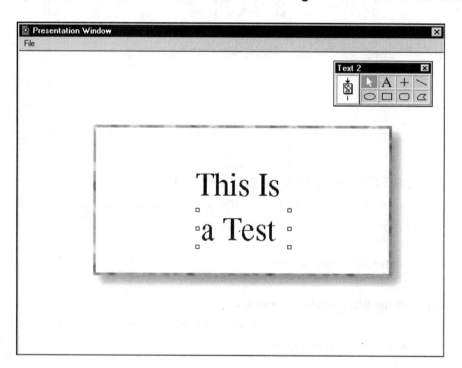

If you accidentally double-click the Box graphic instead of the text, the text will disappear behind the box. Just run the piece from the beginning again by clicking the Restart button in the Control Panel and then double-click the second line of text.

tip *Use the arrow keys on your keyboard to precisely align selected objects. When an object has handles around it, pressing one of the arrow keys moves the object up, down, left, or right by 1 pixel.*

5] Save your work.

Now you have two lines of transparent blue text within an image. This is nice, but you can do still more to make this piece more effective.

SETTING SCREEN TRANSITIONS

Screen **transitions** are visual effects that vary the way objects are displayed and erased on the screen. Skillful use of transitions can add impact and drama to information. Authorware provides you with numerous transitions to choose from. In addition, Authorware includes a number of transition **Xtras**—extensions to the product created by Macromedia and other developers.

In this task, you will apply a transition to both lines of text you created in previous tasks.

1] Double-click the first line of text to select it.

Handles appear around the text.

2] Choose Modify > Icon > Transition (Ctrl+T) to open the Transition dialog box.

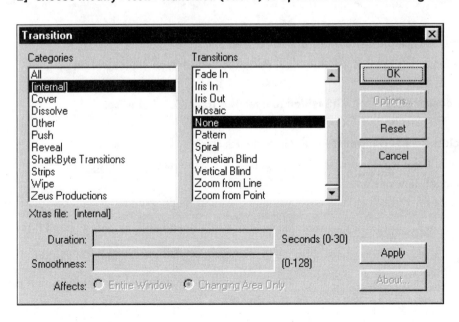

37

You use the Transition dialog box to select transitions and set their duration and smoothness. For this task, you'll use one of Authorware's built-in transitions.

tip   *Authorware includes the Director Transitions Xtra, which contains the entire set of Director transitions for use in your pieces.*

3] In the Categories list, make sure Internal is selected. In the Transitions list, select Iris Out.

This transition will display an image on the screen as though it were viewed through the expanding aperture of a camera. For this task, you do not need to change the default settings for duration and smoothness.

4] Click Apply to preview the transition in the Presentation window.

You may need to move the dialog box to one side to see the effect of the transition.

5] Click OK to close the dialog box.

You're going to use the same transition on the second line of text as well. First though, you'll see how the transition looks when applied to only the first line of text.

6] Click the Restart button to play the piece from the beginning.

As the flow moves down the flowline, Authorware displays the box, then the first line of text using the Iris Out transition, and then the third line of text with no transition. Now you'll apply the same transition to the second line of text. By using the same transition on two adjacent display icons, you cause Authorware to display both images at the same time using the transition.

7] Double-click the second line of text to select it.

Again, note that the toolbox title bar reminds you which icon you're working on.

8] Choose Modify › Icon › Transition to open the Transition dialog box.

9] Select the Iris Out transition again and click OK.

Now you'll see what happens when you apply the same transition to two display icons that follow one another on the flowline.

10] Restart the piece again.

To do this, click the Restart button or choose Control > Restart (numeric keypad 1 or Ctrl+R).

The first and second lines of text appear on the screen at the same time using the Iris Out transition. The transition affects them as if they were in the same display icon.

11] Save your work.

WHAT YOU HAVE LEARNED

In this lesson you have:

- Used the File Properties dialog box to specify global settings such as the size and position of the Presentation window for a piece [*page* **22**]
- Started assembling a piece by placing display icons on the flowline to contain text and graphics [*page* **24**]
- Imported a graphic into a display icon [*page* **26**]
- Used the Text tool in the toolbox to create text [*page* **28**]
- Used options on the Text menu to select a font and size for text [*page* **30**]
- Used the Colors Inspector to select a text color [*page* **31**]
- Used the Modes Inspector to make text transparent against a background image [*page* **33**]
- Applied the Iris Out transition to text using the Transition dialog box [*page* **37**]

and sound

adding motion

LESSON 3

In this lesson you'll complete the piece you began in Lesson 2 by adding a simple animation that moves an object along a straight path. You'll also add screen transitions and two sounds and remove images from the screen. To do all this, you'll work with several new icons on the icon palette.

Sound, animation, and screen transitions can work effectively together in Authorware to produce interesting effects with very little effort. In this lesson you'll see how simple it can be to assemble such effects.

When you finish this lesson, your piece will display the opening text and then move the first line to the left as an additional word moves onto the screen from the right and a sound plays; the new word will appear to be pushing the first line of text out of the way. Then, after a pause, the text will slowly be erased with a transition while another sound plays.

This short, simple opening is part of a game designed to test Authorware knowledge. In future lessons you'll build additional sections of this game.

WHAT YOU WILL LEARN

In this lesson you will:
- Add pauses to a piece
- Animate an object
- Practice importing a graphic
- Use a screen transition
- Add two sounds that play along with on-screen activity
- Erase objects

APPROXIMATE TIME

It should take about 30 minutes to complete this lesson.

LESSON FILES

Media File:
Your Files\Game Project\Game Media
Beginning File:
Beginning Files\03_Begin.a5p
Completed Project:
Final Files\03_Final.a5p

ADDING A PAUSE

So far you've used three display icons to display a graphic and two lines of text, all of which appear on the screen at the same time. In a few moments, you'll use a motion icon to move the first line of text to the left to make room for a graphic of another word. First, however, you'll add a pause to the flowline by using a wait icon.

The wait icon can be used in two ways: to pause a piece for a duration you specify or to stop all activity until the user interacts with the piece by clicking the mouse or pressing a key. Here you'll use it to add a 1-second pause.

1] In the Beginning Files folder, open 03_Begin.a5p. Save it as *03_Game.a5p* in the Game Project folder.

Alternatively, you can use the file you worked on in the previous lesson and save it as *03_Game.a5p*.

2] In the Design window, drag a wait icon from the icon palette to the flowline below the Text 2 display icon. Name the wait icon *1 sec*.

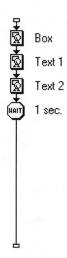

3] Double-click the wait icon to open the Wait Icon Properties dialog box.

The default settings display a Continue button on the screen and allow the user to continue the piece by clicking the button or pressing a key on the keyboard. The title of the wait icon, 1 sec., appears in the box at the top. You want to use the wait icon to pause for a specific time period, so you need to change the settings.

ICON TITLE   PRESS A KEY TO CONTINUE

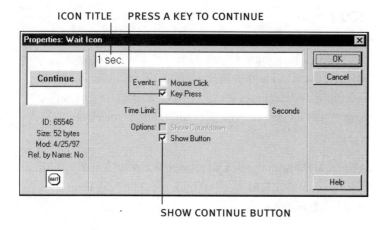

SHOW CONTINUE BUTTON

4] Click the boxes for Key Press and Show Button to remove the checkmarks.

Next you'll enter the duration you want.

5] Type _1_ in the Time Limit box.

You can also enter fractions such as 1.2 in the Time Limit box. If you don't enter any
number, Authorware will ignore the wait icon and pass immediately to the next icon
on the flowline.

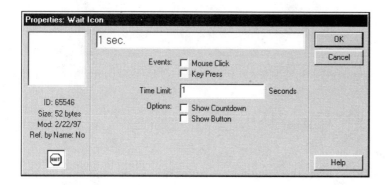

6] Click OK to close the dialog box.

After the images in the three display icons are displayed, the flow will pause for 1
second before the next action occurs—which you're about to create.

7] Save your work.

USING A MOTION ICON

Using the Authorware motion icon, you can create five kinds of **path animation** for objects in an Authorware piece. The simplest form, Direct to Point, moves an object along a straight line from one point to another in the length of time you specify. You can also use the motion icon to move objects along a curved path you create or to move objects along a path based on user responses or information such as the user's score on an interactive test.

In this task you'll use Direct to Point animation to move the line of text *This Is* to the left. When you introduce the graphic of the word *NOT* in the following task, it will look as if *NOT* is pushing *This Is* out of the way.

1] Drag a motion icon to the bottom of the flowline and name it *Move Text 1*.

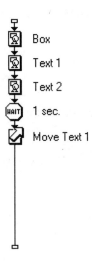

2] Restart the piece.
When the flow of activity reaches the motion icon, Authorware stops and opens the Motion Icon Properties dialog box.

44

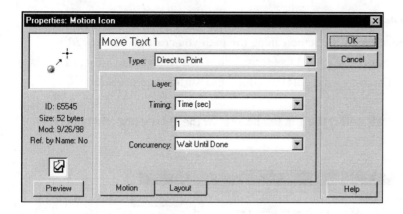

3] **In the Presentation window, click the first line of text, *This Is,* and drag it to the left until it almost touches the edge of the frame.**

You might need to move the Motion Icon Properties dialog box out of the way.

Authorware records the path you create when you drag the object.

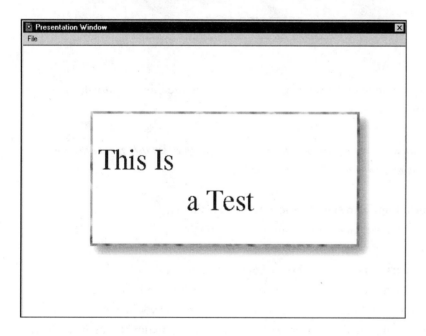

45

4] Click the Preview button to see the animation you just created.

This Is should move across the screen along the path you created. The speed at which it moves, however, is a bit slow for the animation you want to create. The motion occurs in 1 second—the default timing that Authorware provides.

5] On the Motion tab, select the *1* in the box below the Timing box and type *.1* over it.

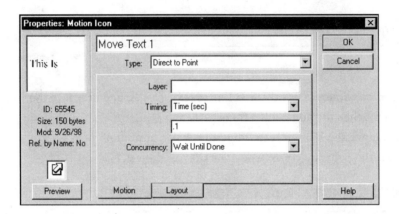

This assigns a duration of 0.1 second to the animation; the line of text will complete its movement in 0.1 second.

> **tip** *You can also choose Rate (sec/in) in the Timing drop-down list, again entering .1; the object will move at a rate of 0.1 second per inch.*

6] Click Preview again to see the effect of the new timing.

The text should move more quickly now.

7] From the Concurrency menu, choose Concurrent.

This setting allows the flow to continue down the flowline while the animation is occurring. You want the flow to continue so that the graphic you'll add in the next task will seem to appear almost at the same time as the animation. If you had selected Wait Until Done, the flow would not move to the next icon on the flowline until the animation was completed.

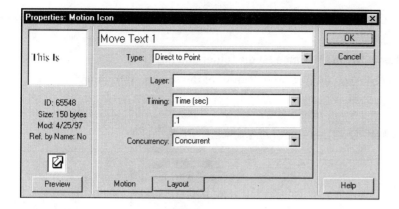

8] **Click OK to close the dialog box.**

9] **Save your work.**

IMPORTING A SECOND GRAPHIC

In Lesson 2 you imported the Box graphic you've been using in this lesson. In this task you'll import a graphic of the word *NOT* that will appear on the screen as soon as the *This Is* text moves to the left.

1] **Switch back to the Design window.**

To do this, choose Window > Presentation (Ctrl+1).

2] **Drag a display icon from the icon palette to the flowline below the motion icon. Name it *Not*.**

You'll import the graphic into this icon.

47

3] Restart the piece. When the piece pauses at the *Not* icon, choose File › Import.

4] Locate the Not.bmp file in the Game Media folder and import it.

The image of the word *NOT* appears in the center of the screen, in front of the two lines of text.

5] Drag the new graphic so that its baseline is about even with the baseline of the first line of text you created and its right edge is close to the right inside edge of the frame.

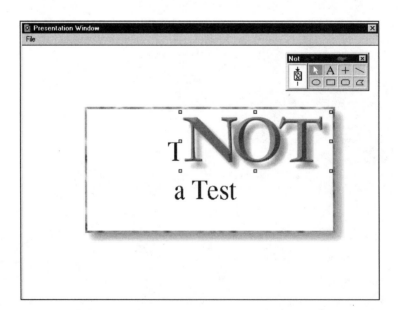

The **baseline** is the imaginary line that runs along the bottom of letters. The bottom of the letters in *NOT* should be about even with the bottom of the letters in *This Is*.

Remember to use the arrow keys for precise alignment.

tip *To constrain the movement of an object vertically or horizontally while you drag it, hold down the Shift key while dragging.*

6] Save your work.

USING A SCREEN TRANSITION

Some screen transitions come close to simulating animation: for example, making objects look as if they move onto the screen from the side or top. In this task, you'll use the Push Left Transition to make *NOT* look as if it's moving in from the right side of the screen.

1] With *NOT* selected, choose Modify › Icon › Transition.

The Transition dialog box opens.

2] Under Categories, select Push. Under Transitions, select Push Left.

Notice that when you select the Push category, the name of the file containing this transition appears below the Categories list. Push Left is one of the Director transitions available in Authorware through the Director Transitions Xtra.

3] Enter *.1* in the Duration box.

This is the same duration you used to move the line of text. As a result, *NOT* will appear to be pushing *This Is* out of the way as it enters the screen.

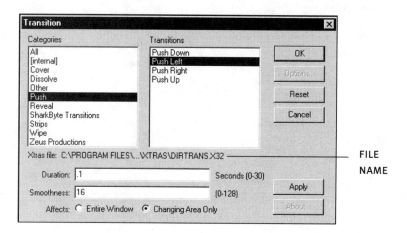

FILE
NAME

4] Click OK. Then restart the piece to review the entire sequence of activity.

> **tip**   *If you decide you want to change the animation you created for Text 1, you can do so easily. Switch to the Design window and then double-click the motion icon to open its dialog box. Drag the line of text across the screen in the direction you want. The new path will be saved, and the time setting will stay at 0.1 second unless you change that as well.*

5] Save your work.

IMPORTING AN AUDIO FILE

You can make the simple sequence you've created a little more interesting by adding a sound that complements the animation. In this task, you'll insert a sound that plays while the line of text moves to the left. In Authorware you can often give the effect of synchronized sound and animation by using sounds whose duration matches an animation or transition. You'll start this task by inserting a sound icon before the motion icon so the sound will play along with the animation.

1] Drag a sound icon to the flowline between the wait icon and the motion icon.

To make sure the icon is inserted between the two existing icons, drag it just to the right of the flowline so it's between the *1 sec.* and *Move Text 1* icon titles. When you release the mouse button, the icon will click into place on the flowline.

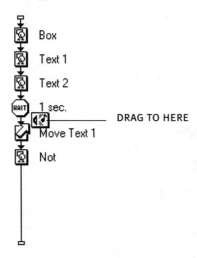

50

LESSON 3

2] Name the sound icon *Sound 1*.

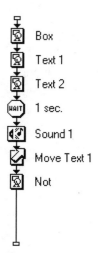

Box

Text 1

Text 2

1 sec.

Sound 1

Move Text 1

Not

3] Double-click the sound icon to open the Sound Icon Properties dialog box.

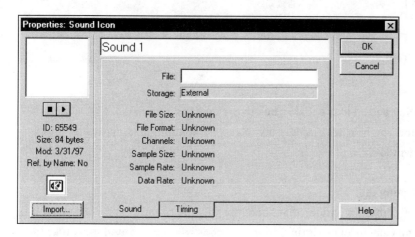

This dialog box provides options for importing and playing sound files.

4] Click the Import button.

The import dialog box opens.

51

5] Locate and select the Sound1.wav file in the Game Media folder for this lesson. Then click Import.

The Sound Icon Properties dialog box now displays information about the sound, such as its file size, file format, and sample rate. The sample rate is the number of times per second that the sound recording software produces a digital representation of a sound wave. Higher sample rates produce better fidelity but also result in larger sound files.

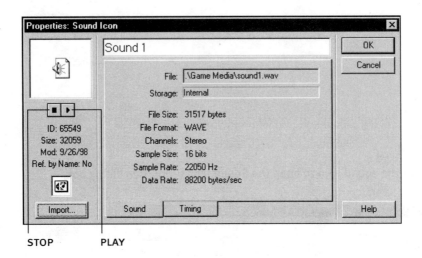

STOP   PLAY

6] Click the Play button in the dialog box to preview the sound.

The brief sound you hear will accompany the movement of *This Is* in the Presentation window.

7] Click the Timing tab.

The Timing tab provides options that affect the way the sound plays. For now, you'll change only the Concurrency setting, which controls whether a sound must play to completion before the activity on the flowline continues, or whether the activity continues while the sound plays.

8] From the Concurrency menu, select Concurrent.

Now while the sound plays, the animation of the line of text will also run. If instead you had chosen the Wait Until Done setting, the sound would play completely before the animation begins.

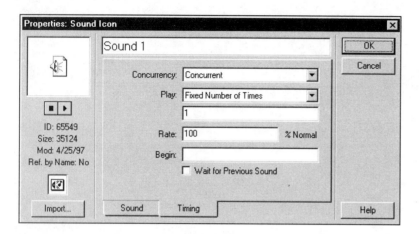

9] Click OK to close the dialog box. Then restart the piece.

When you run the piece, the sound should play at approximately the same time that the line of text is moving across the screen and *NOT* is appearing.

tip   *For more precise synchronization of sounds and images, you can use two Authorware functions: SyncPoint and SyncWait. See Authorware online help for details.*

ERASING IMAGES WITH A SCREEN TRANSITION

To complete this part of the project, you'll use the erase icon to remove all text from the screen and apply a transition, which removes an image from the screen. Then you'll add one more sound to accompany the transition.

1] Switch back to the Design window.

2] Drag an erase icon to the bottom of the flowline and name it – *All Text*.

Using the minus sign in a name is a way of reminding yourself that this icon removes content.

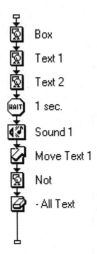

Box
Text 1
Text 2
1 sec.
Sound 1
Move Text 1
Not
- All Text

3] Run the piece.

When Authorware encounters the erase icon, it stops and opens the Erase Icon Properties dialog box, where you can select an erase screen transition and indicate which objects you want to erase. Notice that the instruction in the dialog box tells you to click the objects you want to erase. Before you do this, you'll select a screen transition.

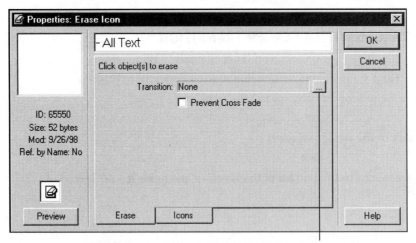

CLICK TO OPEN THE ERASE TRANSITION DIALOG BOX

4] Click the Transition button to open the Erase Transition dialog box.

You'll use one of the transitions to erase all the text.

5] Under Categories, select Internal. Under Transitions, select Mosaic.

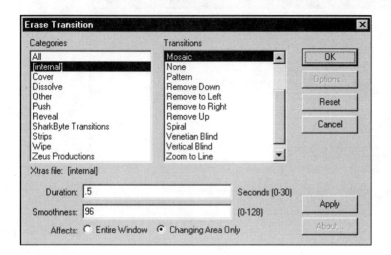

This transition will remove the image from the screen in small square blocks.

6] Click OK.

Notice that when you select a transition, its name appears in the Transition box.

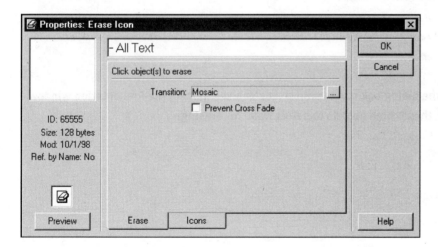

7] Click the Icons tab. Be sure Icons to Erase is selected for List.

THESE OPTIONS ERASE OR RETAIN
THE ICONS THAT YOU SELECT

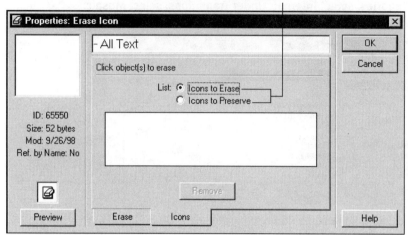

You can have Authorware either erase only the selected icons or only the unselected icons. Here you'll tell Authorware to erase the icons you select.

> **tip** *Erasing everything except the icons you select can produce unintended results. You might erase an object that you want to keep on the screen but that's hidden behind other objects at the time you select this option.*

> **tip** *To erase everything on the screen, choose the Icons to Preserve option without selecting any icons.*

8] Move the dialog box to one side so you can see most of the Presentation window. Then click these three objects to select them for erasing:

The Text 1 icon, "This Is"

The Text 2 icon, "a Test"

The Not icon, "NOT"

As you click each object in the Presentation window, you see the erase transition applied to that object and then its icon title appears in the list of erased icons in the Erase Icon Properties dialog box.

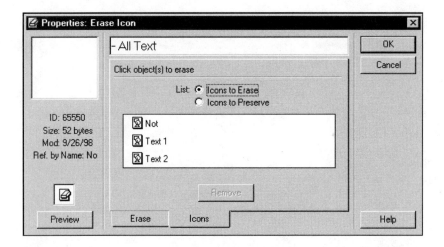

9] **To see the erase transition applied to all three objects, click the Preview button.**

10] **Click OK and then run the piece.**

The animated sequence plays, and then all three objects are erased with the Mosiac transition. However, the text doesn't stay on the screen very long before it's removed. In the next task, you'll insert a 1-second wait icon before the erase icon to give users a little more time to read the text before it disappears.

ADDING ANOTHER PAUSE TO THE FLOWLINE

To display the text on the screen a little longer, you'll add another 1-second pause in the flowline. The easy way to do this is simply to copy the wait icon that you placed on the flowline earlier and paste it where you need it.

1] **Select the *1-sec.* wait icon you placed on the flowline earlier.**

57

To do this, click once on the icon. It will be highlighted.

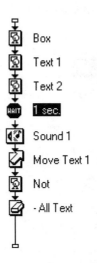

- Box
- Text 1
- Text 2
- 1 sec.
- Sound 1
- Move Text 1
- Not
- - All Text

2] Choose Edit › Copy (Ctrl+C) to copy the icon.

3] Click the flowline between the Not display icon and the erase icon.

The paste hand appears, indicating where the copied wait icon will be placed when you paste it.

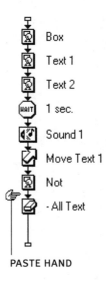

- Box
- Text 1
- Text 2
- 1 sec.
- Sound 1
- Move Text 1
- Not
- - All Text

PASTE HAND

4] Choose Edit › Paste (Ctrl+V).

A copy of the 1-sec. wait icon appears on the flowline before the erase icon.

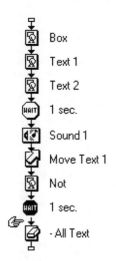

Box

Text 1

Text 2

1 sec.

Sound 1

Move Text 1

Not

1 sec.

- All Text

5] Run the piece again. Then save your work.

The 1-second pause makes the whole sequence work better. You'll often use the wait icon to insert pauses in the flowline when you're fine-tuning the timing of your pieces.

ADDING ANOTHER SOUND

This part of the project could be considered complete at this point. However, there's one other small touch you can add that will make this piece a little more engaging to users: a sound that plays while the erase transition is clearing the text from the screen. In this task, you'll insert a sound before the erase icon and set it to play concurrently with the erase operation. You'll use a sound that complements the transition taking place on the screen.

1] Switch back to the Design window.

2] Drag a sound icon to the flowline between the second 1 sec. wait icon and the – All Text erase icon, and name it *Sound 2*.

To make space for more icons on the flowline, you might need to enlarge the window by dragging the lower edge of the window downward.

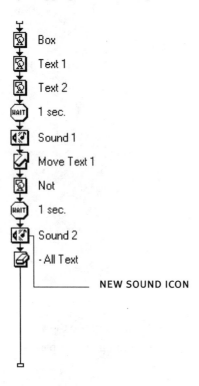

Box
Text 1
Text 2
1 sec.
Sound 1
Move Text 1
Not
1 sec.
Sound 2
- All Text

NEW SOUND ICON

3] Double-click the Sound 2 icon to open the Sound Icon Properties dialog box. Then click Import.

4] In the import dialog box, locate the Sound2.wav file and import it.

The Sound2.wav file is in the Game Media folder.

When the file has been imported, information about it is displayed in the Sound Icon Properties dialog box.

5] On the Timing tab, select Concurrent from the Concurrency menu.

The sound will play while the objects are being erased.

6] Preview the sound by clicking the Play button. Then click OK and restart the piece.

This time the complete sequence includes a transitional sound that plays while the transition is erasing objects from the screen.

> **tip**   *Look for opportunities in your pieces to "pseudo-sync" short sounds with transitions and Authorware path animations. The key is using sounds whose nature and duration match the visual effect.*

7] Save your work.

ON YOUR OWN

Experiment with different settings for the animation and transitions in 03_Game.a5p. First save the file with a new name to preserve the file you've completed for this lesson. Then use the new file to experiment with using a different path for the text. Try other types of transitions and vary the duration and smoothness settings for the transitions.

WHAT YOU HAVE LEARNED

In this lesson you have:

- Used the wait icon to pause a piece for a duration you set [*page* **42**]
- Used the motion icon to move a line of text across the screen [*page* **44**]
- Imported a graphic [*page* **47**]
- Applied a screen transition [*page* **49**]
- Imported two sound files that play concurrently with two on-screen activities [*page* **50**]
- Used the erase icon to erase objects with the Mosaic transition [*page* **53**]

interactions

introducing

LESSON 4

The heart of Authorware is **interactivity**—the capability of an application you create to respond according to what a user clicks on the screen or what keys a user presses. Authorware allows you to build 11 kinds of interactions without writing code or scripts.

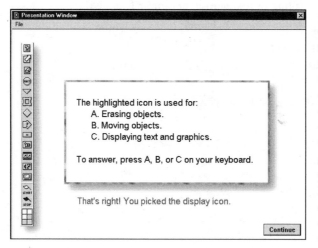

Interactive games such as this Authorware quiz program can be effective teaching tools. This application performs a different action depending on the key the user presses. Keypress response interactivity is the hallmark of many educational applications and is widely used in kiosk presentations and marketing applications as well. In this lesson, you'll see how easy it is to create interactive applications as you begin assembling the elements to create an Authorware game.

The core tool for creating interactivity in Authorware is the **interaction icon,** a powerful icon that incorporates the characteristics of several other icons. The interaction icon can contain images, like a display icon. It can branch to different paths, like a decision icon. It can pause activity until a user responds, somewhat like a wait icon. And it can remove objects from the screen, like an erase icon.

In this lesson, you will preview three kinds of interactions that you'll be creating over the next three lessons. Then you will build a simple example of the **keypress interaction,** which branches down different paths depending on which key a user presses.

WHAT YOU WILL LEARN

In this lesson you will:

• Practice importing graphics
• Define and apply two text styles to ensure consistent appearance of text
• Use an authoring technique for viewing the contents of several display icons while you create content in another icon
• Create and modify a simple graphic
• Create a keypress interaction, which responds when a user presses keys that you define

APPROXIMATE TIME

It should take about 1½ hours to complete this lesson.

LESSON FILES

Media Files:
Your Files\Game Project\Game Media
Beginning File:
Beginning Files\04_Begin.a5p
Completed Project:
Final Files\04_Final.a5p

GETTING ACQUAINTED WITH INTERACTIONS

This task introduces the three kinds of interactions you'll be creating over the next three lessons: keypress, hot spot, and text entry.

1] Open the 07_Final.a5p file in the Final Files folder.

This file is the full version of the project you'll start building in this lesson and you'll complete in Lesson 7.

2] Run the entire piece.

The opening will be familiar. After the text is erased, however, a question appears on the screen to test your Authorware knowledge. The question calls for you to press a key on the keyboard.

3] Try each response: A, B, and C.

Authorware provides a different response for each key you press. When you type the correct answer, C, a Continue button appears on the screen. This is a **keypress interaction**.

4] Click the Continue button to move on.

Another question appears, demonstrating a different kind of interaction—a **hot spot interaction**. This time you are asked to indicate the correct answer by clicking a certain area of the screen. You'll build this hot spot interaction in Lesson 5.

5] Try clicking several places on the icon palette before clicking the correct tool, the erase icon.

When you click the correct item on the screen, the Continue button appears again.

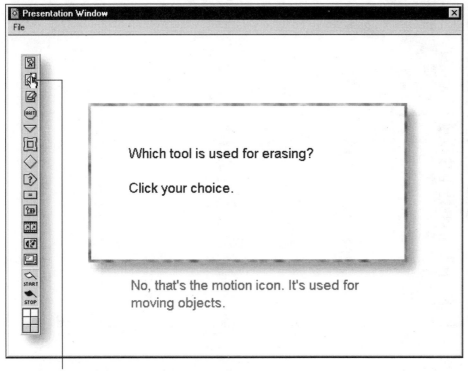

Which tool is used for erasing?

Click your choice.

No, that's the motion icon. It's used for moving objects.

THE USER HAS SELECTED THE WRONG
ICON RESPONSE TO THE QUESTION

6] Click Continue to leave the hot spot interaction and move on.

Now you see an example of a third interaction type, a **text entry interaction**. The question here calls for you to type your response in a text entry field and then press Enter so Authorware can determine whether you entered the correct answer.

7] Try typing what you think is the correct answer and then press Enter.

When you enter incorrect responses, you get one kind of feedback. When you enter the correct response—navigate—you get different feedback. If you enter the wrong answer three times, the correct answer appears, and you don't get another chance to respond. You'll build this text entry interaction in Lesson 6.

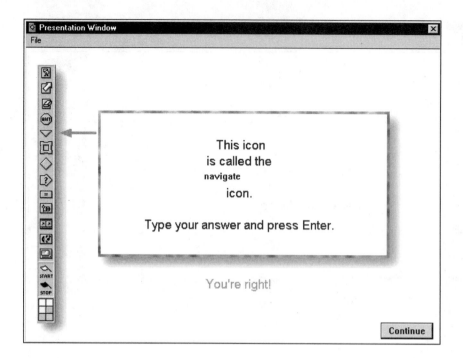

8] Choose File › Close Window (Ctrl+W) to close the file.

Now that you've had a preview of what you'll be building, it's time to get started.

OPENING A FILE AND IMPORTING A GRAPHIC

Before setting up the keypress interaction, you're going to import the image of the Authorware icon palette. This graphic will be used in each of the next three lessons.

1] Open 04_Begin.a5p in the Beginning Files folder and save it as *04_Game.a5p* in the Game Project folder.

Alternatively, you can use the file you worked on in the previous lesson and save it as *04_Game.a5p*.

2] In the Design window, drag a display icon to the bottom of the flowline and name it Icon Palette.

This display icon will contain the image of the icon palette you saw in the preceding section. Because this display icon will precede the interaction icon on the flowline, the image of the icon palette will be displayed on the screen during all the activities that occur as part of the interaction. Similarly, the Box image will also remain on-screen since this display icon, too, will precede the interaction icon. When you create a display icon, its contents remain on-screen unless you specifically erase them.

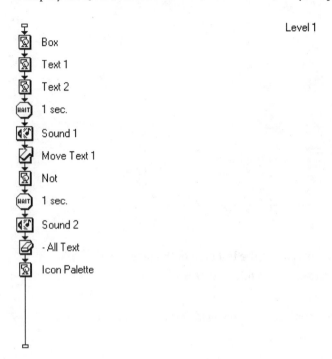

Level 1

Box
Text 1
Text 2
1 sec.
Sound 1
Move Text 1
Not
1 sec.
Sound 2
- All Text
Icon Palette

3] Double-click the Icon Palette display icon. Then choose File › Import to open the import dialog box.

4] Locate the Iconpal.bmp file and import it.

This file is in the Game Media folder.

When you import a graphic, Authorware places it in the middle of the Presentation window. You'll need to reposition it to make room for the text you're going to create.

INTRODUCING INTERACTIONS

tip *Click a point in the Presentation window before importing or pasting a graphic to indicate where you want it placed.*

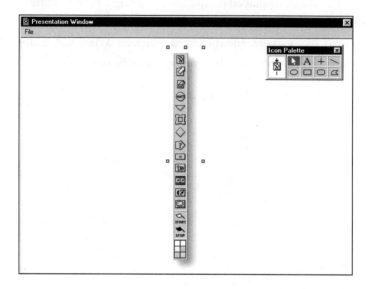

5] Drag the image of the icon palette to the left side of the screen so it's in approximately the position shown in the following illustration.

tip *To constrain movement vertically or horizontally while dragging, hold down the Shift key.*

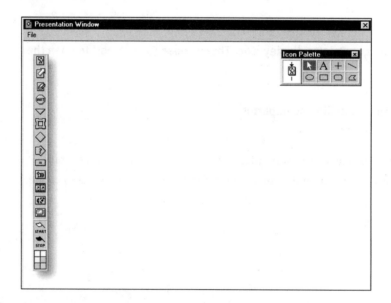

6] Save your work.

DEFINING A TEXT STYLE

Using **text styles**, sets of text attributes that you define, can save you a great deal of production time and ensure consistent use of fonts, point sizes, and colors throughout a project. In this task, you'll create two text styles that you'll use several times throughout the next three lessons. The first style will be used for questions. The second style will be used for the feedback displayed when the user responds to a question.

1] Choose Text › Define Styles (Ctrl+Shift+Y) to open the Define Styles dialog box.

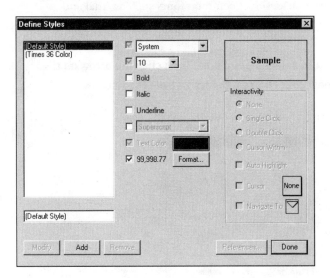

You can use this dialog box to create text styles and **hot text**, which is text linked to other content in a piece. You'll create hot text in a later lesson.

When you create text using other than the default style, Authorware records your new text settings in parentheses in the styles list in this dialog box. For example, because you created 36-point blue Times text in Lesson 2, Authorware lists *(Times 36 Color)* in the styles list. To convert a parenthesized listing into a style that you can apply to other text, overwrite the parenthesized name with a name you enter and click Modify.

tip *The Default Style text style is the starting point for other text styles that you define. All styles are based on it. To make it easier to define a group of related styles for a project, you can create your own default style in the Define Styles dialog box and then create named styles based on this style. For example, you can select (Default Style) in the styles list and then change the font from System to Arial. Then any font based on Default Style will use Arial.*

2] Click the Add button.

Authorware adds a style to the list named New Style. After you define the characteristics of this style, you'll give it a name of your own choice and save it.

3] Click the top check box to select a font. Then click the arrow in the font selection box to view your choices. In the list, select Arial.

The font menu lets you choose any font installed in your system. Not everyone has the same fonts, however. To ensure that the text looks the way you intend on whatever computer your users use, select common fonts such as Arial and Times Roman.

4] Click the second check box to select a point size. Then click the arrow on the point size selection box to view your choices. Select 14 from the list.

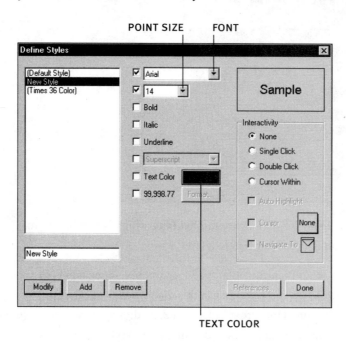

5] Click the Text Color check box. Then click the black color swatch to choose a text color. In the palette that appears, click the bright blue color shown in the following illustration. Then click OK.

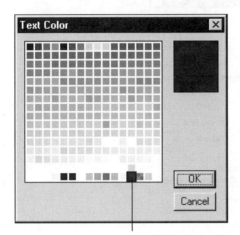

SELECT THIS COLOR

The word *Sample* at the upper right of the Define Styles dialog box shows how your text style will look.

6] Select New Style in the text entry box at the lower left of the dialog box and then type *Question*.

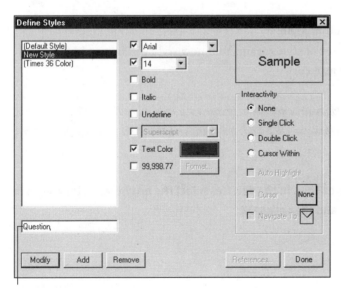

ENTER NEW STYLE NAME

7] Click Modify to save your style name.

The name Question replaces New Style in the list.

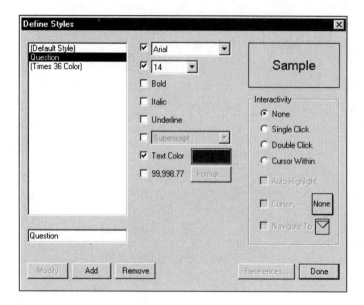

DEFINING A SECOND TEXT STYLE

While the Define Text Styles dialog box is open, you'll also create a variation on the Question text style to use to provide feedback. In this task, you'll change the color of the Question text style and save the change as the Feedback text style.

1] Click Add to create another style.

New Style appears in the list of styles again. Your new style will be just like the Question style except for its color.

> **tip** *To make it easier to create a new style, first select a style in the list that's similar to the style you want to create. When you click Add, the characteristics of the selected style will be available for you to use as the basis for your new style.*

2] Click the Text Color color chip. In the palette, select the bright red color shown in the following illustration and then click OK.

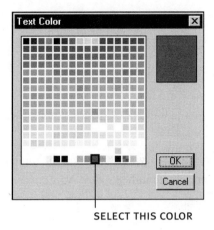

SELECT THIS COLOR

Now the color chip and Sample text are red.

3] Select New Style in the text entry box at the lower left of the Define Styles dialog box and type the new name: *Feedback*. Then click the Modify button.

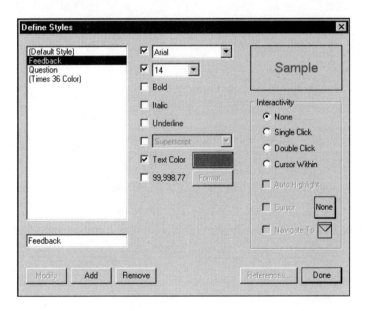

The Feedback text style appears in the styles list. You'll use this style for giving feedback to users after they respond to a question.

4] Click Done to save your new styles.

Now that you've created two styles, you're ready to use them to create text for the interaction.

5] Save your work.

PREPARING AN INTERACTION

In this task you'll perform the preliminaries for creating a keypress interaction. You'll add an interaction icon to the flowline and select options to indicate how Authorware responds when the flow exits the interaction.

1] Switch to the Design window and drag an interaction icon to the flowline below the Icon Palette display icon. Name it *Keypress*.

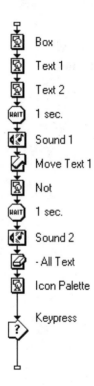

Box
Text 1
Text 2
1 sec.
Sound 1
Move Text 1
Not
1 sec.
Sound 2
- All Text
Icon Palette

Keypress

2] With the Keypress icon selected, choose Modify › Icon Properties (Ctrl+I).

The Interaction Icon Properties dialog box opens. You can use this dialog box to set numerous options that control the appearance and behavior of interactions, including the tracking of user responses. In this case, you'll specify what happens when the user exits this interaction.

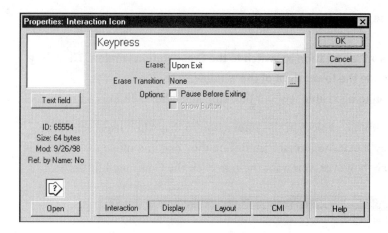

On the Interaction tab, the Erase setting controls when Authorware erases the text and graphics displayed in the interaction—that is, the content you add to the interaction icon.

In this case, you'll use the default Erase setting, Upon Exit. The question will remain on the screen until one of the response icons leads out of the interaction.

3] For Options, select Pause Before Exiting and Show Button.

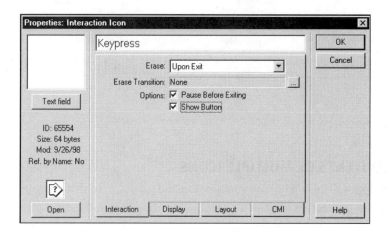

To get an idea of what these settings mean, remember the preview of the interactions you saw earlier in this lesson. Each time your answer was correct, a Continue button appeared on the screen. To move down the flowline, you had to click the Continue button. Pause Before Exiting causes the flow to stop as the flow exits the interaction. The user must then press a key or click the screen to continue. When you select Pause Before Exiting, the Show Button option becomes available. With Show Button selected, the user must either click a Continue button or press a key to continue.

4] Click OK to close the dialog box.

5] Choose Window › Presentation to switch to the Presentation window. Then drag the Continue button to the lower right of the window.

You want the button to be visible without blocking any other elements on the screen.

You're going to set up the choices in this interaction so that when users select the correct answer, they'll exit the interaction. Before they exit and move to whatever is next on the flowline, however, you want them to click the Continue button.

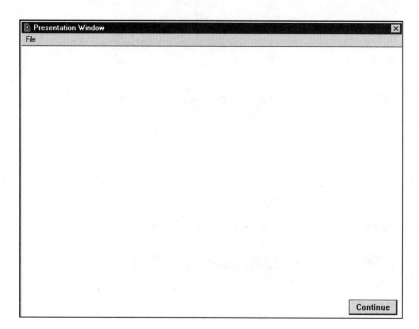

6] Save your work.

VIEWING THE CONTENTS OF MULTIPLE ICONS

An interaction icon, like a display icon, can contain text and graphics. In this case, you'll create text in the interaction icon for a question that users respond to by pressing a key.

First, you'll use an important Authorware technique that lets you selectively view the contents of several display icons while creating text or graphics in another icon. Instead of having to restart the piece every time you need to add text or graphics, you will select specific icons in the Design window whose content you want to see. To do this, you hold down the Shift key while you double-click each icon. Authorware will then display the content of every icon you select in this way, so that the contents of all of the icons appear in the Presentation window at once.

1] In the Design window, double-click the Box icon at the top of the flowline.
This opens the icon and displays the box graphic in the Presentation window.

2] Return to the Design window and hold down the Shift key while double-clicking the Icon Palette display icon.
You've added the image of the icon palette to the display of the box. You want to see both of these images so you can position the text you're going to create in the interaction icon.

3] Return to the Design window again and hold down Shift while double-clicking the Keypress interaction icon.
The toolbox opens for Keypress, and the images from the Box and Icon Palette icons remain on the screen. Now you're ready to create the text for the question.

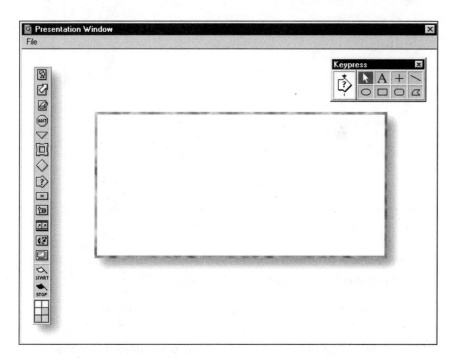

APPLYING TEXT STYLES

In this task you'll use one of the text styles you saved to create a question that asks for a user response. You'll also use a tab setting to indent some of the lines of text.

1] In the Presentation window, click the Text tool in the toolbox. Then click inside the box graphic near the left edge to indicate where you'll enter the text.

To select a style for text, you need an existing **text object**—a selected block of text—or you need to select the Text tool in the toolbox.

2] Choose Text › Apply Styles (Ctrl+Alt+Y) to open the Apply Styles window. Click the Question style to select it .

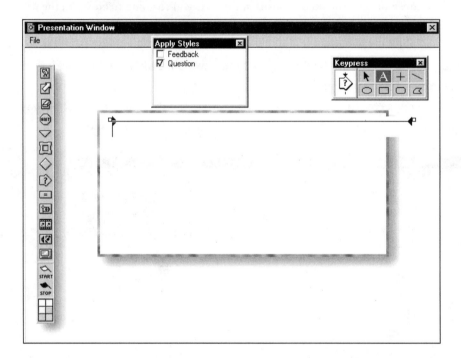

A checkmark appears next to Question in the list of styles. The text you create will be in the font, size, and color you selected for this text style.

Now you'll set a tab so you can indent some of the text in the question.

3] Click just above the paragraph ruler at a spot about one-half inch from the left margin.

The pointer should be barely above the paragraph ruler. When you click, you'll see a triangle above the ruler that indicates the tab setting.

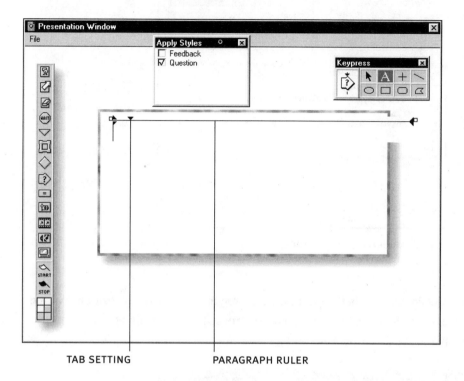

TAB SETTING   PARAGRAPH RULER

4] Choose Text › Alignment › Left (Ctrl+[) to align the text on the left.
The text alignment may already be set to Left.

5] Type the text shown below. Press Enter at the end of each line and press Tab at the start of each of the three lines presenting the choices. Add an extra line space before the last line.
The highlighted icon is used for:

> *A. Erasing objects.*
>
> *B. Moving objects.*
>
> *C. Displaying text and graphics.*

To answer, press A, B, or C on your keyboard.

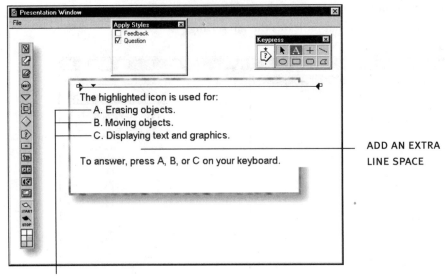

ADD AN EXTRA
LINE SPACE

PRESS TAB BEFORE THESE LINES

6] Click the Pointer tool in the toolbox. Then drag the text object to position it within the box. Use the handles to resize it if necessary so it all fits within the box.

Remember to use the arrow keys for fine adjustments.

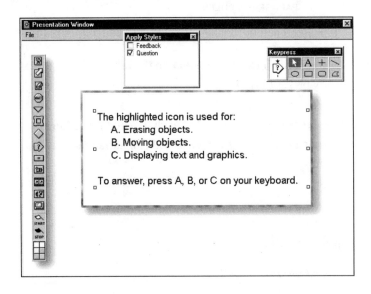

7] Close the Apply Styles window and save your work.

tip *Use anti-aliased text to improve the appearance of large text. Anti-aliasing creates extra pixels of color that fill in around the edges of the letters with a color that's a shade in between the text color and the background color. The effect is to make the edges look smooth instead of jagged. But it works well only for larger text—at least as large as the 14-point size you're using in this task. If you want, you can try it now. Select the text in the Presentation window, and then choose Text > Anti-Aliased.*

CREATING A GRAPHIC WITH THE TOOLBOX

In this task you'll create a rectangle that highlights the display icon in the icon palette image. This is the icon referred to in the first line of the text you just entered.

1] Click the Rectangle tool in the toolbox. Then draw a small rectangle around the display icon in the icon palette image.

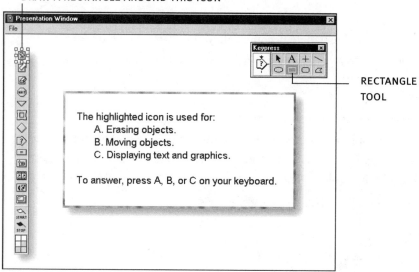

Don't worry about creating and positioning the rectangle perfectly; you'll fix any problems later.

Now you'll select a bright yellow color for the rectangle to make it stand out on the screen.

2] Open the Colors Inspector.

To do this, choose Windows > Inspectors > Colors.

3] Click the Pen color chip and then select the bright yellow shown in the following illustration.

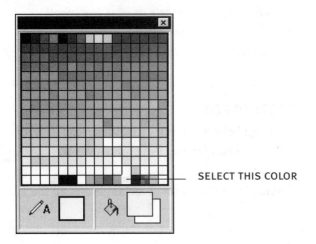

SELECT THIS COLOR

The Pen color chip and rectangle become yellow; however, the border of the rectangle is still not very visible. The solution is to make its line width thicker, using the **Lines Inspector**.

4] Choose Window › Inspectors › Lines to open the Lines Inspector.
The Lines Inspector gives you control over the width of lines and borders on the objects you draw with the tools in the toolbox. The dotted line at the top makes borders on objects invisible, so only the fill color of the objects is displayed. The bottom section lets you attach arrowheads to lines.

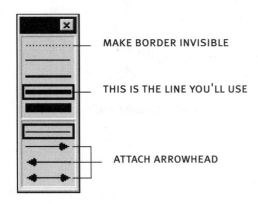

MAKE BORDER INVISIBLE

THIS IS THE LINE YOU'LL USE

ATTACH ARROWHEAD

tip *You can also double-click the Straight Line tool or the Diagonal Line tool in the toolbox to open the Lines Inspector.*

5] Select the fourth line from the top in the Lines Inspector.
This is the second-widest line.

tip *Although the graphics you can produce using the Authorware toolbox don't compare to what an artist can create with a product like Macromedia Fireworks, the toolbox tools can be used to create quite acceptable artwork. In addition, because these graphics are vector based, any graphic you create using the toolbox takes much less disk space and is displayed more quickly on the screen than these other types of graphics. Using the toolbox is especially useful for Web pieces because the graphics it creates can be downloaded more quickly over the Internet.*

6] Close the Lines Inspector and Colors Inspector.
Now that the rectangle is thicker, you'll adjust the position and size.

7] Select the Pointer tool in the toolbox. Then drag the handles on the yellow rectangle to position and resize it to surround the image of the display icon.

THE YELLOW RECTANGLE SHOULD
FIT SNUGLY AROUND THE ICON

8] Save your work.

CREATING A KEYPRESS RESPONSE

Now that you've created a question, you're ready to create the feedback for each possible user response in a **response icon**, an icon you attach to the interaction icon that provides one of the possible responses to user input. You'll create text that gives feedback when users press A, B, or C. In this task you'll create the feedback for an A keypress, one of the incorrect responses.

1] In the Design window, drag a display icon to the right side of the interaction icon.

Authorware opens the Response Type dialog box so you can choose the response type you want to use.

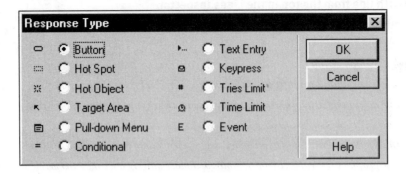

tip   *Authorware opens this dialog box only after you place an icon to the immediate right of the interaction icon. When you set up additional response icons in the same interaction to the right of the first response icon, Authorware assigns them the same type as your first response icon. You can then change that setting if you want. Alternatively, you can place an icon to the immediate right of the interaction icon, select its response type when the Response Type dialog box opens, and then move the icon where you want among the other attached response icons.*

2] Select Keypress and click OK.

3] Double-click the response type symbol above the display icon.

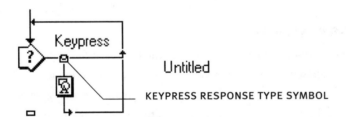

KEYPRESS RESPONSE TYPE SYMBOL

Each response type has its own symbol. The keypress response type symbol looks like a tiny key on the keyboard. When you double-click this symbol, the Response Properties dialog box opens.

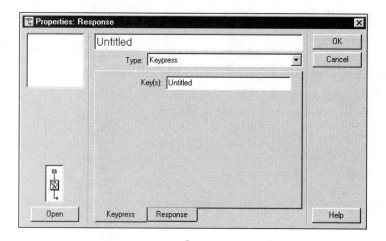

This dialog box contains two kinds of settings. The Keypress tab provides the settings for this response type. The Response tab provides several settings that are shared by all response types.

First you'll specify which keys will be associated with this response.

4] In the Key(s) text entry box on the Keypress tab, select the name Untitled so that it's highlighted. Then type the letter *a*.

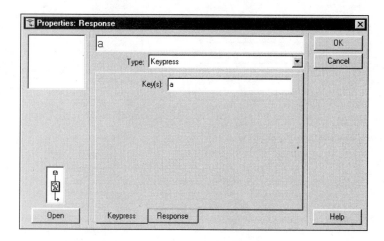

Authorware will now recognize the letter *a* as a match. When the user types *a*, Authorware will branch to the display icon you've attached.

The keypress response type is case-sensitive. That means that, so far, only a lowercase *a* will be recognized as a match. You need to include the uppercase *A* as well.

5] In the Key(s) box, type the | character after the *a*.

The vertical bar (|)—often found as the uppercase variant of the backslash on the keyboard—is considered the "or" bar in Authorware. This character allows you to enter alternative choices that Authorware will accept as a match.

6] Type a capital *A* after the | character.

Be sure not to leave space before or after the |.

Notice that each character you enter in the Key(s) box becomes part of the title for this response at the top of the dialog box.

ICON TITLE

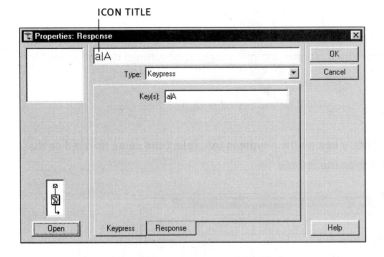

Next you'll select settings to determine what happens after a user types *a* or *A*. You'll select these settings on the Response tab.

7] Click the Response tab.

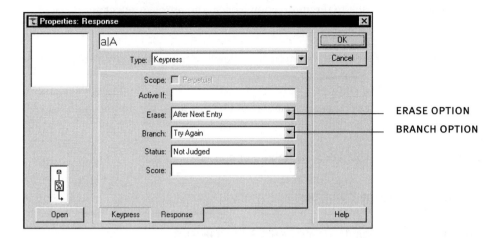

This section of the Response Properties dialog box lets you control what happens after a user's response leads to this response icon.

The four Erase settings control when the content for this response is erased:

After Next Entry: Erases the content for the selected response icon when the user makes another choice.

Before Next Entry: Erases the content immediately after it appears. Usually you need to add a wait icon to keep the display on the screen for a moment or it will simply flash on and then off.

On Exit: Erases the content only when the flow exits the interaction. This option can produce overlapping content if the user chooses several responses before exiting.

Don't Erase: Leaves the content on the screen.

For this project, you'll use the default Erase option, After Next Entry. You want any feedback displayed when a user presses a key to stay on-screen until the user presses another key. The setting you use here does not affect the text and graphics in the interaction icon, and the erase setting you selected earlier for the interaction icon does not affect the text and graphics in the response icon.

The Response tab also provides three Branch options:

Try Again: Loops back to the interaction icon so the user can select another response.

Continue: Continues along the interaction flowline to the right after a response icon is matched to see if any other icons also match.

Exit Interaction: Leaves this interaction and moves on to the next icon on the main flowline.

Again, for this project you'll use the default option, Try Again.

8] Click OK to close the dialog box.

CREATING ADDITIONAL KEYPRESS RESPONSES

In this task you'll set up the responses that are matched when the user presses B or C.

1] In the Design window, drag a display icon to the right of the a|A response.
Now you'll use a shortcut to specify the desired keys that this response should match. You'll type the responses directly on the flowline.

2] Name the new display icon *b|B*.

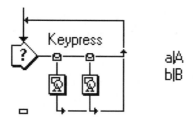

When you attach icons to an interaction icon, the resulting flowline represents the path from the interaction icon, through the attached icons, and—in this case—back around to the interaction icon again because of Try Again branching.

Type the characters just as you did in the Response Properties dialog box for the a|A response, with no spaces. The name you enter for a keypress response becomes the keys that match that response. To see for yourself, double-click the response type symbol for b|B to open the Response Properties dialog box.

3] Drag another display icon to the right of the blB icon and name it *clC*.

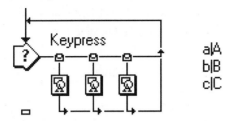

aIA
bIB
cIC

You can see how quickly you can create a string of keypress responses using this shortcut.

Because the response for the C key is the correct answer, you'll set this response icon to branch differently from the two that are for incorrect answers.

4] Open the Response Properties dialog box for clC.

To do this, double-click the response type symbol.

5] On the Response tab, open the Branch menu and select Exit Interaction. Then click OK.

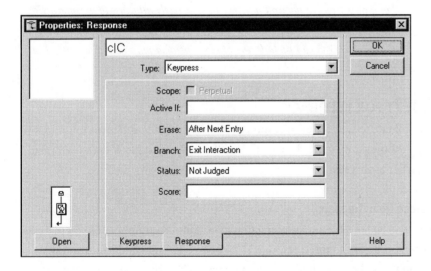

After a user presses *C* on the keyboard and views the feedback you create for the correct response, the user will leave this interaction and move on to the next icon on the main flowline. Remember, however, that users will also need to click a Continue button before exiting because you set up this option for the overall interaction.

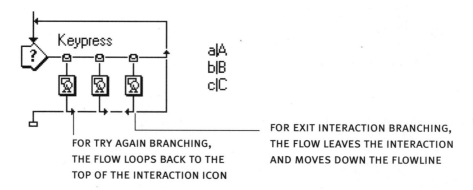

FOR TRY AGAIN BRANCHING, THE FLOW LOOPS BACK TO THE TOP OF THE INTERACTION ICON

FOR EXIT INTERACTION BRANCHING, THE FLOW LEAVES THE INTERACTION AND MOVES DOWN THE FLOWLINE

tip   *You can change branching settings directly in the Design window. Hold down the Control key while clicking the branching symbol to cycle through the branching options.*

6] Save your work.

note   *Not all of the 13 icons in the icon palette can be directly attached to an interaction icon. The icons that you can't attach as response icons are the interaction icon, decision icon, and framework icon. However, you can include any of these inside a map icon that's attached to an interaction icon.*

CREATING TEXT FOR FEEDBACK

In this task you'll create text for each response, so users will see different messages depending on whether they press *A*, *B*, or *C*. You'll use the Feedback text style that you created earlier in this lesson.

1] Run the piece from the start.
When the flow reaches the Keypress interaction icon, Authorware waits for you to press a key that matches one of the three responses. To open each attached icon and fill in the content, you'll simply press the key that matches each of the three responses.

2] Press *A* (or *a*) to match the first response icon.
Authorware stops and opens the a|A display icon.

3] Click the Text tool in the toolbox. Then click somewhere below the left edge of the box graphic to indicate where you'll start typing.

You'll be creating feedback that appears below the box. Don't worry about being precise in positioning the text at this point.

4] Open the Apply Styles window.

To do this, choose Text > Apply Styles.

5] Select the Feedback style.

6] Enter the following text: *Sorry, the erase icon does that.*

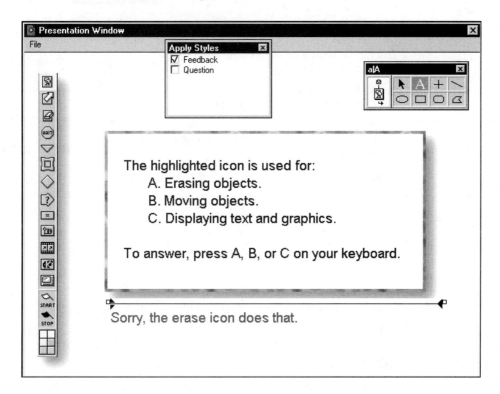

Now you need to make sure the text is transparent so that if it appears over background art, the background will show through.

7] Click the Pointer tool in the toolbox. Then open the Modes Inspector.

To do this, choose Windows > Inspectors > Modes.

8] Select Transparent mode.

If you have been progressing through the lessons continuously from the beginning, Transparent mode will already be selected.

9] Drag and resize the text object so it looks approximately like the following illustration.

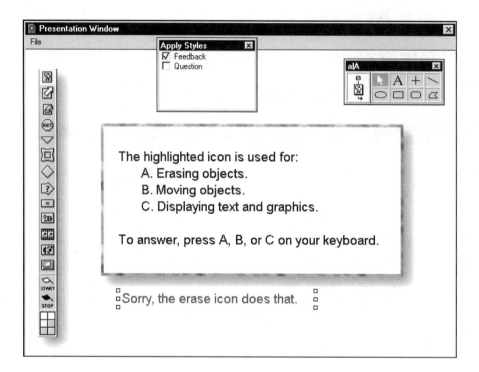

Next you'll create text for the other two responses and make sure it's displayed in the same place as the first feedback.

CREATING ADDITIONAL FEEDBACK

In this task you'll create text for feedback to users who press *B* or *C*. You'll use the Shift-double-click technique to keep text from each response icon on the screen while you create new feedback. Then you'll align each new text element so that all feedback appears in the same place. The result is that users see feedback where they expect, and the piece looks better.

1] In the Design window, hold down Shift while double-clicking the b|B display icon.

The Presentation window opens, and the title in the toolbox reminds you that you're now in the b|B display icon. By using Shift-double-click, you continue to see all previously displayed graphics while you create the new text.

2] In the Presentation window, use the Text tool and the Feedback style to enter a new line of text just below the first feedback text: *Sorry, the motion icon does that.*

Click the Text tool in the toolbox, click the space below the first line of feedback text, and click the Feedback style in the Apply Styles window. Then enter the text.

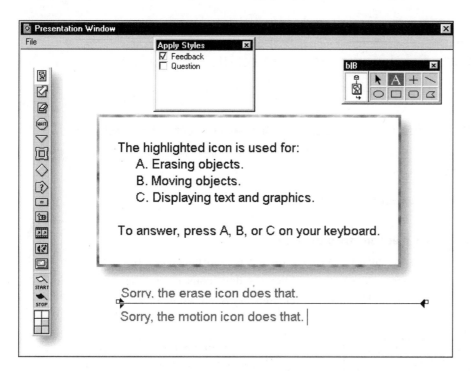

3] Drag the new text object so it overlays the first feedback text you created.

Select the Pointer tool in the toolbox and then drag the text object so the word *Sorry* overlays the *Sorry* in the first line of feedback text. The two *Sorry*s should look like a single word.

TWO LINES OF TEXT OVERLAID

4] In the Design window, hold down Shift while double-clicking the clC display icon.

The content on the screen remains displayed while the clC display icon opens for you to add content.

93

5] Use the Feedback style to create the following text: *That's right! You picked the display icon.*

To do this, click the Text tool, click somewhere below the other feedback text, select the Feedback style in the Apply Styles window, and then enter the text.

Sorry, the material does that.

That's right! You picked the display icon. |

6] Align the new text so it overlays the first two lines of feedback text.

This time there's no word like *Sorry* to overlay. Just do your best and don't worry about being too precise.

Now it's time to test what you've created.

7] Restart the piece and try pressing *A.*

When you press *A*, the flow moves to the a|A response icon and the text in this display icon appears on the screen. Then the flow loops around to the top of the interaction icon again because you selected Try Again branching.

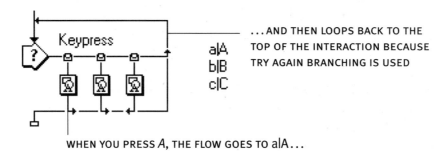

...AND THEN LOOPS BACK TO THE TOP OF THE INTERACTION BECAUSE TRY AGAIN BRANCHING IS USED

WHEN YOU PRESS *A*, THE FLOW GOES TO a|A...

8] Press *B.*

This time the flow moves to the b|B response icon, displaying the text you created for this response. Then the flow loops around to the top of the interaction icon because you selected Try Again branching, and Authorware waits for another keypress.

9] Press C.

Notice that when you press *C*, the Continue button appears, and pressing *A*, *B*, or *C* no longer has any effect. That's because when you match the c|C response icon, the Exit Interaction branching sends the flow out of the interaction. Clicking Continue takes you back to the main flowline.

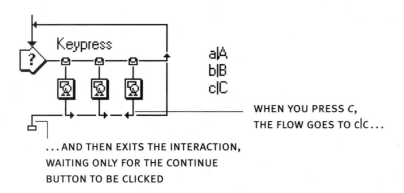

WHEN YOU PRESS *C*,
THE FLOW GOES TO c|c . . .

. . . AND THEN EXITS THE INTERACTION,
WAITING ONLY FOR THE CONTINUE
BUTTON TO BE CLICKED

10] Save your work.

WHAT YOU HAVE LEARNED

In this lesson you have:

- Practiced importing graphics [*page* **66**]
- Used the Define Styles dialog box to define two text styles [*page* **69**]
- Used the Shift-double-click technique to view the contents of several icons at once [*page* **76**]
- Used the Apply Styles window to apply text styles to text [*page* **78**]
- Used the toolbox to create a rectangle [*page* **81**]
- Used the Colors Inspector and Lines Inspector to change the color of a rectangle and thicken its border [*page* **81**]
- Created a keypress interaction using an interaction icon and several response icons [*page* **83**]
- Added text messages to provide feedback to user input [*page* **90**]

interactions

hot spot

LESSON 5

In this lesson you'll use Authorware to create a **hot spot interaction,** in which users click a location on the screen to trigger a response. Hot spots provide one of the most common types of interaction in multimedia productions, and with Authorware they are simple to build. As in Lesson 4, you'll use the icon palette graphic. This time you'll be asking users to identify the tool used for a particular Authorware operation by clicking one of the tools in the icon palette. You'll create feedback for the correct and incorrect answers.

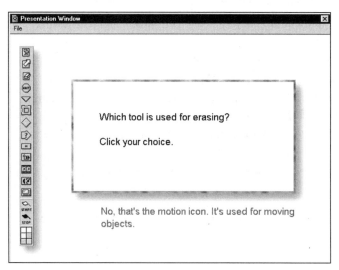

Hot spot interactions— in which users click a location on the screen to trigger a response—are one of the most popular kinds of interactivity in multimedia. In this lesson you will add this type of interactivity to the Authorware game.

Before building a hot spot interaction, you'll prepare your workspace—the Design window—to make your work easier. First you'll group icons from the two previous lessons into two map icons to organize and condense the flowline. Then you'll use a decision icon to create a temporary storage space off the main flowline to hold these two map icons while you work on the new content in this lesson.

If you would like to see the final result of this lesson, open the Final Files folder and play 05_Final.a5p.

WHAT YOU WILL LEARN

In this lesson you will:

- Condense your work into manageable groups on the flowline
- Create a temporary storage location off the flowline to hold content that you're not currently working on
- Create a hot spot interaction, which responds when users click the screen
- Create a catch-all hot spot to respond when users click the area around other hot spots

APPROXIMATE TIME

It should take about 1 hour to complete this lesson.

LESSON FILES

Beginning File
Beginning Files\05_Begin.a5p
Completed Project:
Final Files\05_Final.a5p

USING MAP ICONS TO ORGANIZE THE FLOWLINE

Before you build a hot spot interaction, you need to prepare the Design window for your new work. Your first task will be to create two **map icons** to hold two groups of related icons from the two previous lessons. A map icon's purpose is to contain other icons and thereby break the flowline into manageable segments.

You'll start by selecting the first group of icons with the mouse.

1] Open 05_Begin.a5p in the Beginning Files folder and save it as *05_Game.a5p* in the Game Project folder.

Alternatively, you can use the file you worked on in the previous lesson and save it as *05_Game.a5p*.

2] In the Design window, move the mouse so it is just above and to the left of the second display icon, *Text 1*.

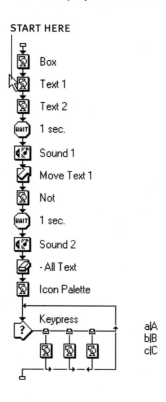

You need to draw a rectangle around the first group of icons you want to place in a map icon.

3] Click and hold down the mouse button to draw a rectangle around all the icons starting with Text 1 and including – All Text.

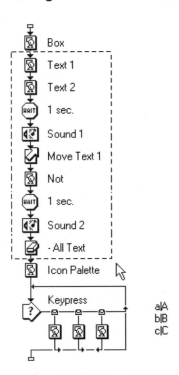

When you release the mouse button, the selected icons are highlighted. This selection method is called **marquee selection**. These icons contain the opening animation.

4] Choose Modify › Group (Ctrl+G).

Now the map icon encompasses the selected icons. The main flowline is much shorter.

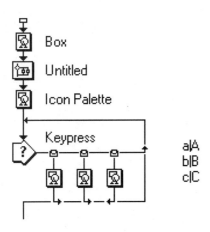

5] Double-click the map icon.

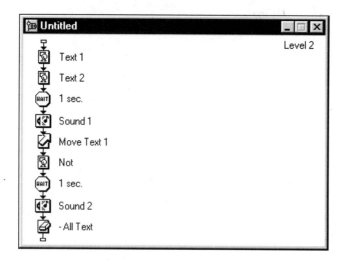

As you can see, the selected icons are stored inside.

Using a map icon to hold a group of related individual icons is the main technique you will use to organize and condense the flowline in Authorware.

6] Click the close box at the upper right to close the map window. Then name the map icon *Opening*.

Now you'll create another map icon containing the keypress interaction from the previous lesson.

7] In the Design window, marquee select all the icons in the keypress interaction.

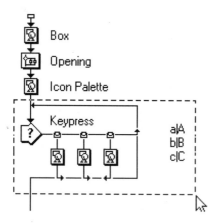

When you release the mouse button, the icons are highlighted.

8] Choose Modify › Group to group the selected icons.

Note that the title of the interaction icon becomes the title of the map icon.

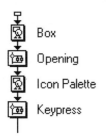

You've just reduced the number of icons on the main flowline from 15 to 4 using two map icons. Keeping the flowline organized like this is essential to successful Authorware development.

STORING CONTENT OFF THE FLOWLINE WITH A DECISION ICON

In this task you'll take one more step in preparing for the main work of this lesson. Your key tool will be the **decision icon**, which is generally used to branch, or select a path, based on some value or expression, such as a user's score on a pretest or the type of computer running the piece. In this case, you'll use a decision icon to temporarily store content off the flowline. To do this, you'll create a decision icon that doesn't branch at all—which might seem puzzling at first, but the logic is simple, as you will see.

You attach icons to a decision icon just as you do to an interaction icon.

1] Drag a decision icon to the flowline just below the Keypress map icon and name it *Temp. Storage*.

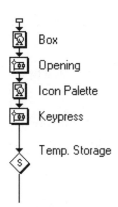

Next you'll set some of the properties of the decision icon.

2] Double-click the Temp. Storage decision icon to open the Decision Icon Properties dialog box.

Decision icons determine which content is displayed to users, but unlike a display or interaction icon, they don't contain content themselves, so when you double-click a decision icon, you go directly to its dialog box.

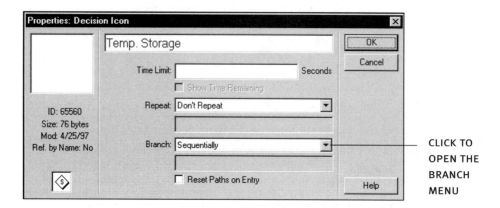

3] Open the Branch menu.

The power of the decision icon lies mainly in the branching options.

Before you attach icons to a decision icon, you can choose branching options that determine which path the flowline will follow. The first icon attached to a decision icon is considered to be path 1, the second icon is path 2, and so on.

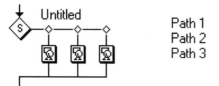

The Branch menu contains four options. The option you choose is represented by a letter on the decision icon.

Sequentially (S on the decision icon): Selects the first path the first time Authorware encounters the decision icon, the second path the second time, and so on.

Randomly to Any Path (R): Selects any path at random.

Randomly to Any Unused Path (U): Selects any path the first time, but doesn't select the same path twice until all paths have been selected.

To Calculated Path (C): Selects a path specified by a value, variable, or expression you enter.

4] Select To Calculated Path.

The box below the Branch box is no longer dimmed; it is now available for you to enter a value or expression.

5] Type *0* as the value for the calculated path.

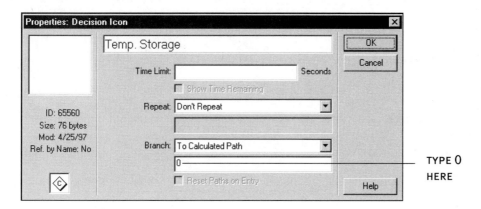

A path set to 0 is actually no path. When you attach icons to this decision icon, Authorware will ignore them as it moves down the flowline.

6] Click OK to close the dialog box.

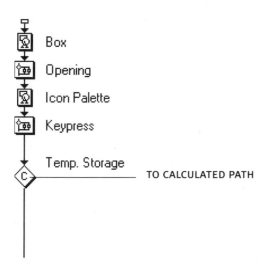

Next you'll attach the two map icons you created earlier to the decision icon, creating paths 1 and 2.

7] Drag the Opening map icon to the right of the Temp. Storage decision icon.

You attach icons to the right of a decision icon, just as you do with interaction icons. When you attach an icon to a decision icon, the resulting flowline structure represents the path from the decision icon, through the attached icon, and back to the flowline below. The symbol above the Opening map icon is the decision path symbol.

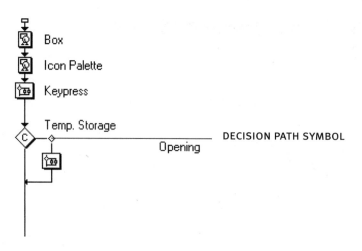

8] Drag the Keypress map icon to the right of the Opening map icon.

As long as the calculated path is set to 0, Authorware will bypass the content in both the map icons you've attached to the Temp. Storage decision icon. Having completed two sections of this piece, you have temporarily set them aside. Yet just by dragging the two map icons back to the main flowline, you can include all the content in the two map icons in the piece again. This is a simple way to manage the content in a piece as it gets larger, and it helps you stay focused on the part that you're working on.

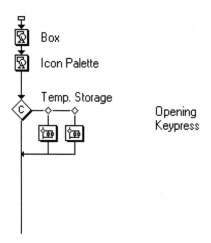

9] Save your work.

10] Run the piece from the start to test your work.

Indeed, all that you see are the contents of the two display icons remaining on the main flowline. This is just what you need to begin work on the hot spot interaction.

SETTING UP A HOT SPOT INTERACTION

In this task you'll drag an interaction icon to the flowline and create the text for a question that will ask the user to click a response on the screen.

1] In the Design window, drag an interaction icon to the flowline below the decision icon. Name it *Hot Spot*.

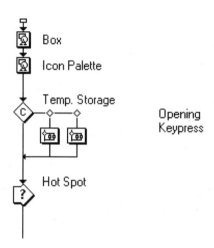

2] Open the Interaction Icon Properties dialog box for the Hot Spot icon.

To do this, choose Modify > Icon > Properties.

3] On the Interaction tab, select Pause Before Exiting and Show Button. Then click OK.

With these settings, Authorware will pause when the branching for one of the responses exits the interaction, and the user will need to click a Continue button to move back to the main flowline. These are the same settings you used for the keypress interaction.

4] In the Presentation window, drag the Continue button to the lower right.

The Continue button will already be at the lower right if Authorware is still open from the previous lesson. The default position of this button is set during each Authorware session.

5] Run the piece from the beginning. When the piece pauses, switch to the Design window and Shift-double-click the Hot Spot interaction icon.

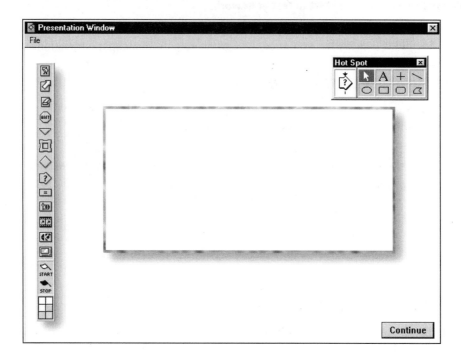

You should see the box graphic, the icon palette graphic, and the toolbox for the Hot Spot interaction icon. Now you can create the text while viewing the contents of the other icons on the flowline.

6] Enter the text below inside the box, using the Question text style, left alignment, and transparent mode. Add a line space between the lines:

Which tool is used for erasing?

<line space>

Click your choice.

To create this text, click the Text tool, click inside the box, and select Question from the Apply Styles window. Then enter and align the text so it looks approximately like the illustration shown here. If the Apply Styles window is not open, choose Text > Apply Styles to open it. To produce left alignment, choose Text > Alignment > Left. To make sure the mode is transparent, open the Modes Inspector by choosing Windows > Inspectors > Modes and then select Transparent.

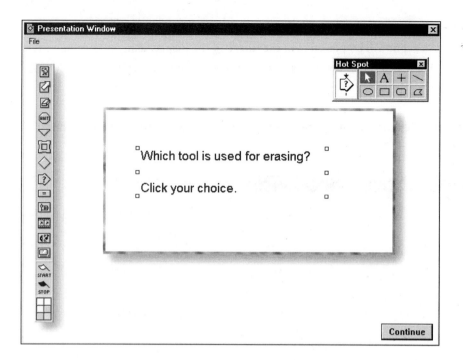

The correct response will be to click the erase icon, but before you set up that response, you'll create hot spots over two incorrect responses.

CREATING A HOT SPOT

A hot spot is an invisible rectangular area that triggers a response when a user clicks it. In this task you'll create a hot spot that will overlay the display icon in the icon palette graphic. When a user clicks that icon as a response to the question, the user will get feedback that says it's the wrong answer.

1] In the Design window, drag a display icon to the right of the Hot Spot interaction icon. In the Response Type dialog box, select Hot Spot and then click OK.

The response type symbol for a hot spot is a small dotted rectangle.

HOT SPOT RESPONSE TYPE SYMBOL

2] Name the icon *Display Icon Choice.*

This first hot spot will be placed over the image of the display icon in the icon palette graphic. When users click the display icon in the icon palette, they'll get the feedback you create.

3] Double-click the hot spot response type symbol to open the Response Properties dialog box.

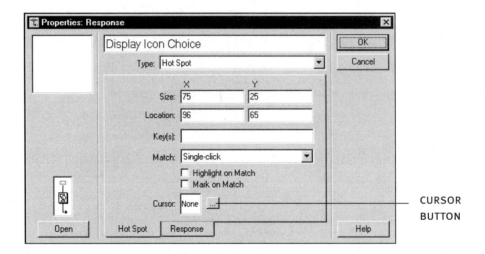

CURSOR
BUTTON

In the Response Properties dialog box, you can set several options for the hot spot. For example, the Size and Location settings on the Hot Spot tab let you specify exact screen coordinates for the size and location of the hot spot, and the Match setting defines the mouse action that will activate a response: Single-click, Double-click, or Cursor in Area (the mouse moving over but not clicking the hot spot).

4] On the Hot Spot tab, select Highlight on Match.

When a user clicks to select this hot spot, Authorware will display the selection in the inverse color to indicate that the user has clicked a hot spot.

Note that the inverse color is the color in the opposite position in the color palette. For example, if the color beneath the hot spot is the dark blue that's five from the left in the top row of the color palette, the inverse will be the bright yellow that's five from the right on the bottom row of the palette.

5] Click the Cursor button to open the Cursors dialog box.

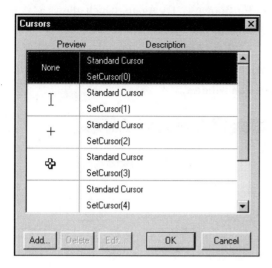

A custom cursor visually indicates that the mouse is over an area that is "hot," or clickable.

6] Select the hand-shaped cursor and click OK.

You'll need to scroll to the bottom of the list.

When you select a custom cursor, its image appears in the Cursor window of the Response Properties dialog box.

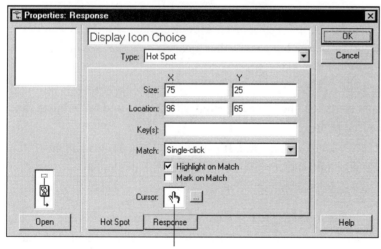

SELECTED CURSOR

109

You'll use the defaults for other settings in this dialog box, including the Branch option on the Response tab. The default for Branch is Try Again, which allows a user to click another choice if the user clicks this response first.

7] Click OK to close the Response Properties dialog box. Then Shift-double-click the interaction icon to open the Presentation window.

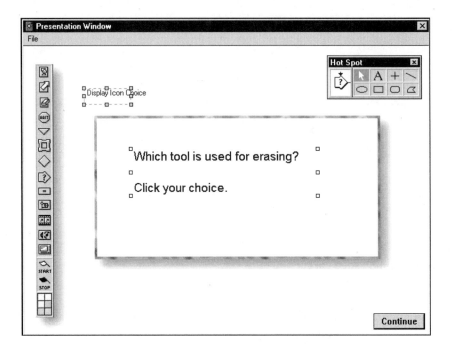

The Display Icon Choice hot spot is displayed with dashed lines and gray handles. You need to move and resize the hot spot so that it covers only the area of the screen that you want.

8] Drag the hot spot so its top and left edge align with the top and left edge of the display icon in the icon palette.
Drag the hot spot by its edge or by its title. If you click other areas inside a hot spot, you might inadvertently select whatever is underneath the hot spot, such as the box graphic.

If both the hot spot and text inside the box have selection handles, first click outside the selected objects so the two objects lose their selection handles. Then click and drag the hot spot.

110

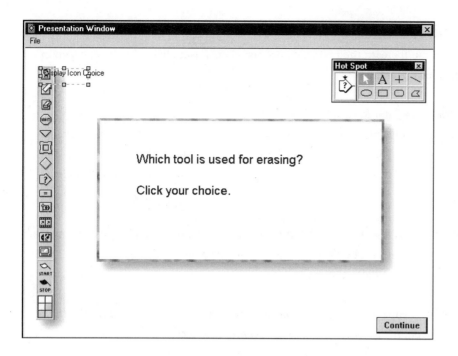

9] Drag the handle in the lower right of the hot spot to resize the rectangle. Make it fit snugly around the image of the display icon.

You'll end up with a very small hot spot, whose handles nearly touch each other.

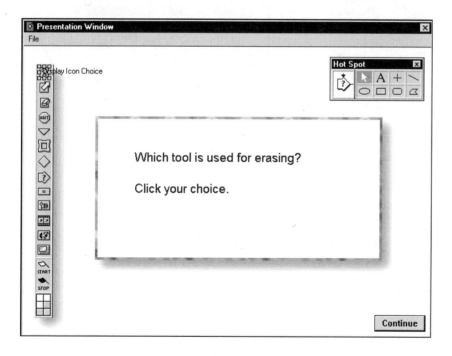

10] Save your work.

CREATING FEEDBACK

In this task you'll create the text that appears when a user clicks the display icon in the icon palette graphic.

1] Run the piece from the start.

The hot spot is invisible when the piece plays, but if you move the cursor over the image of the display icon in the icon palette, the cursor should become a hand. This is because of the custom cursor option you just selected in the Response Properties dialog box.

2] In the Presentation window, click the image of the display icon in the icon palette.

Authorware branches to the Display Icon Choice response icon. Now you'll create the feedback for this incorrect choice.

3] Using the Feedback text style, enter the following text below the box: *No, that's the display icon. It's used for displaying text and graphics.*

When you're done, align the text so it looks approximately like the following illustration.

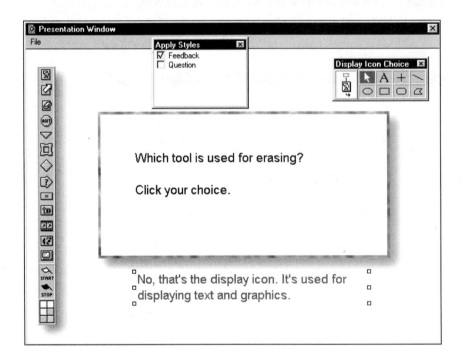

4] Try your hot spot by running the piece and then clicking the display icon.

When you click, notice that the display icon is highlighted. Then the feedback text appears. The flow loops around to allow you to click again because of the Try Again branching you selected.

Next you'll create additional hot spots for other possible responses.

ADDING ANOTHER HOT SPOT

In this task you'll create a hot spot for the motion icon.

1] In the Design window, drag a display icon to the right of the Display Icon Choice icon. Name it *Motion Icon Choice*.

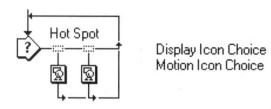

Display Icon Choice
Motion Icon Choice

Authorware automatically assigns this response the same response type and branching as the first one you created: the hot spot response type with Try Again branching.

2] Double-click the response type symbol for the Motion Icon Choice response.

Authorware has also copied the settings for the custom cursor and Highlighting on Match to this response icon. Authorware often saves time for you by making intelligent assumptions about what you want.

3] Click OK to close the dialog box. Then Shift-double-click the interaction icon to open the Presentation window.

Authorware also has copied the size of the first hot spot to the new hot spot. This is exactly what you need, since the motion icon is the same size as the display icon.

4] Move the Motion Icon Choice hot spot to align it over the motion icon image.

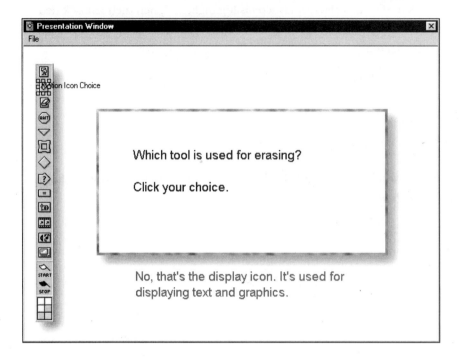

With the hot spot selected—it should have handles around it—use the arrow keys on your keyboard for precise positioning.

Next you'll create the feedback for users who choose the motion icon. This is another incorrect choice.

5] Switch back to the Design window. Then Shift-double-click the Motion Icon Choice icon.

It's always a good idea to view the other graphics and text that will be displayed along with the new content you're about to create so you don't accidentally place the new content on top of existing images.

6] Enter the following text using the Feedback text style and align it over the first response text: *No, that's the motion icon. It's used for moving objects.*

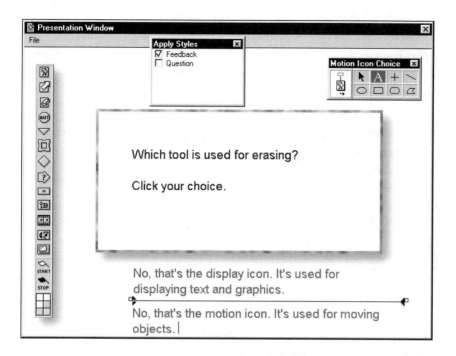

It's easiest to create the text in a clear area below the first response text and then drag it up so that the word *No* in both responses is aligned (it will look like a single word).

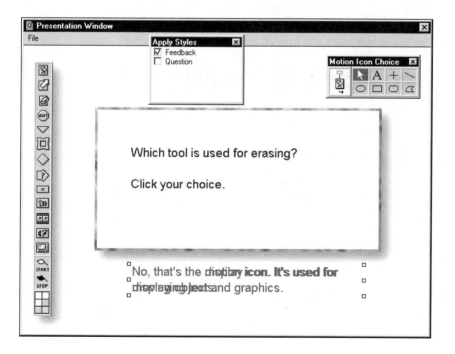

7] Save your work.

ADDING A HOT SPOT FOR THE CORRECT CHOICE

In this task you'll create a third hot spot, this time for the correct choice: the erase icon. You'll set the branching to exit the interaction when this hot spot is selected, and you'll create feedback text to confirm to users that they made the right choice.

1] In the Design window, drag another display icon to the right of the Motion Icon Choice icon. Name it *Erase Icon Choice*.

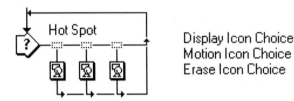

Display Icon Choice
Motion Icon Choice
Erase Icon Choice

2] Open the Response Properties dialog box for the new response.

To do this, double-click the response type symbol for the Erase Icon Choice response icon.

Because this choice is the correct choice, the user doesn't need to stay in the interaction any longer. You'll change the Branch setting to reflect this.

3] On the Response tab, open the Branch menu and select Exit Interaction.

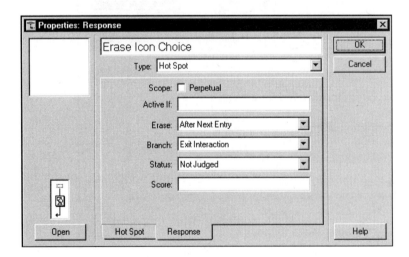

After users click the erase icon—the correct choice—they'll exit the interaction.

4] Click OK to close the dialog box and then Shift-double-click the interaction icon. In the Presentation window, adjust the new hot spot so it's right over the image of the erase icon in the icon palette.

You might find that a few nudges with the arrow keys are all you need.

5] In the Design window, Shift-double-click the Erase Icon Choice icon. In the Presentation window, enter the following text using the Feedback text style:
You're right! You picked the erase icon.

This feedback can be in a different location from the other feedback to emphasize that the user has chosen correctly this time. You might put the line just below the other feedback text, as shown in the following illustration.

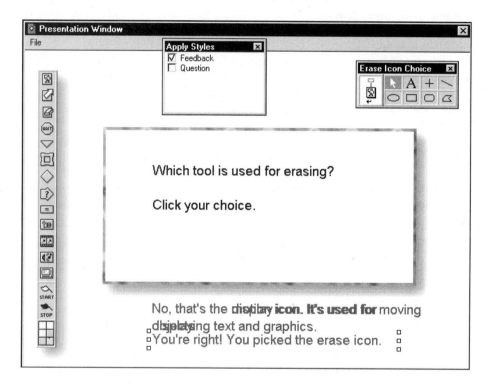

6] Restart the piece and try each choice.

Try clicking the display icon and the motion icon before clicking the erase icon, the correct choice. Once you click the erase icon, the branching you set up for that choice will take you out of the interaction.

7] Save your work.

ADDING A CATCH-ALL HOT SPOT

You could create a separate hot spot for each incorrect choice in the icon palette. In fact, such a series of hot spots, along with feedback that reminds users what each tool is used for, would be a good instructional approach. However, there's another approach you can take when you don't need to give specific feedback for every possible choice. In this task you'll create a hot spot that provides a response for all the other tools that someone might click on the icon palette graphic. This **catch-all hot spot** works because it comes last in the interaction flowline. That is, the catch-all response icon will be on the far right—it will be the last icon that can be matched.

1] In the Design window, drag a display icon to the right of the Erase Icon Choice icon. Name it *Any Other Tool*.

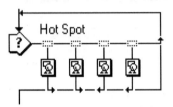

Display Icon Choice
Motion Icon Choice
Erase Icon Choice
Any Other Tool

2] Change the Branch setting for Any Other Tool to Try Again directly on the flowline.

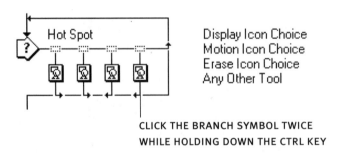

Display Icon Choice
Motion Icon Choice
Erase Icon Choice
Any Other Tool

CLICK THE BRANCH SYMBOL TWICE
WHILE HOLDING DOWN THE CTRL KEY

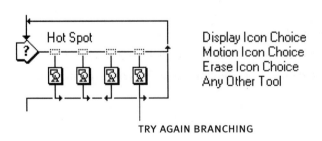

Display Icon Choice
Motion Icon Choice
Erase Icon Choice
Any Other Tool

TRY AGAIN BRANCHING

To do this, hold down the Ctrl key while you click the branch symbol on the flowline two times. Clicking in this way cycles through the Branch options; it takes two clicks to get to Try Again.

The catch-all response will inform users that they've chosen the wrong tool, and the Try Again branching will give them another chance to click the correct choice.

3] Shift-double-click the interaction icon. In the Presentation window, move and resize the Any Other Tool hot spot so it encloses the entire icon palette.
To do this, drag the hot spot so its top and left edges align with the top and left edges of the icon palette graphic. Then drag the lower right handle to expand the hot spot until it surrounds the icon palette.

note *If the Any Other Tool hot spot is not visible in the Presentation window, switch back to the Design window and open the Response Properties dialog box for Any Other Tool. Then click Cancel and open the Presentation window to see the hot spot.*

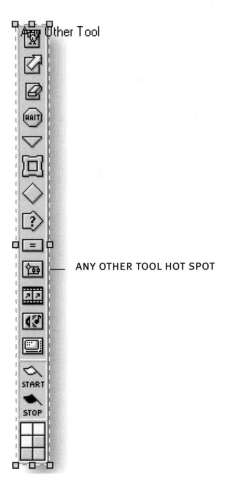

ANY OTHER TOOL HOT SPOT

Notice that this new hot spot encloses all three of the hot spots you created earlier. What's important is that its position in the interaction is on the far right. If users click the Motion Icon Choice hot spot, for example, Authorware will branch to that icon and loop back to the top of the interaction and never reach the Any Other Tool response icon to its right.

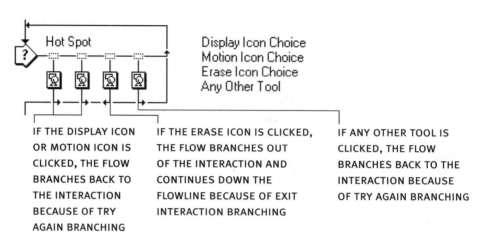

Hot Spot

Display Icon Choice
Motion Icon Choice
Erase Icon Choice
Any Other Tool

IF THE DISPLAY ICON OR MOTION ICON IS CLICKED, THE FLOW BRANCHES BACK TO THE INTERACTION BECAUSE OF TRY AGAIN BRANCHING

IF THE ERASE ICON IS CLICKED, THE FLOW BRANCHES OUT OF THE INTERACTION AND CONTINUES DOWN THE FLOWLINE BECAUSE OF EXIT INTERACTION BRANCHING

IF ANY OTHER TOOL IS CLICKED, THE FLOW BRANCHES BACK TO THE INTERACTION BECAUSE OF TRY AGAIN BRANCHING

4] In the Design window, Shift-double-click the Any Other Tool display icon.

5] In the Presentation window, enter and align the following feedback text using the Feedback text style: *You have the wrong tool. Try again.*

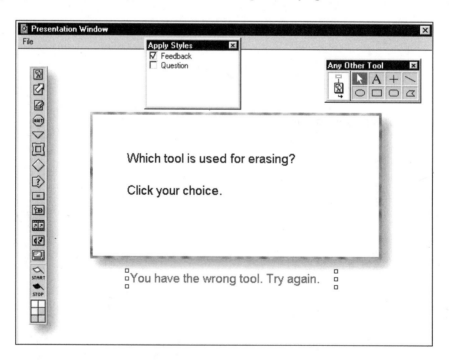

6] Restart the piece and then try clicking each choice.

When you click any incorrect choice, you get another chance because you selected Try Again branching for Display Icon Choice, Motion Icon Choice, and Any Other Tool. When you click the erase icon, you exit the interaction because you selected Exit Interaction branching for Erase Icon Choice. Before exiting, you need to click a Continue button because you selected this option in the interaction icon settings.

7] Save your work.

WHAT YOU HAVE LEARNED

In this lesson you have:

- Used map icons to condense your work into manageable groups on the flowline [*page* **98**]
- Used a decision icon set to a calculated path of 0 to create temporary off-line storage for content [*page* **101**]
- Created a hot spot interaction using an interaction icon and several response icons [*page* **105**]
- Created a catch-all hot spot by attaching an icon at the far right of the interaction flowline [*page* **118**]

interactions

text entry

LESSON 6

In this lesson you'll continue building the Authorware game by using a **text entry interaction** that calls for the user to respond to a question by typing the answer. The text entry response type, however, is useful for much more than games and tests. Whenever you need users to enter information by typing, you'll use a text entry interaction.

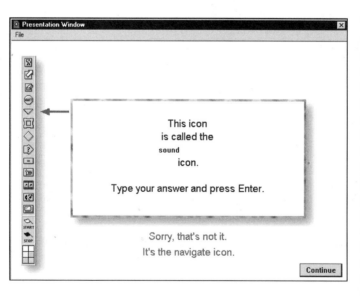

Text entry interactions can be especially engaging because they call for users to type answers or information rather than merely click one of several choices on the screen. Because text entry is so open-ended, it's good to provide some form of safety net if you're looking for a particular response. The Authorware game you'll work on in this lesson shows users the correct answer after three incorrect responses to a question that calls for a text entry.

Authorware gives you considerable flexibility in using text entry interactions. You can look for a specific word or phrase or several variations on a word or phrase, you can ignore additional spaces or capital letters, and you can accept any text a user types by using a wildcard character. In this lesson, the text entry interaction you create will ask the user to type the name of a particular Authorware icon in response to a question. You'll create feedback for the correct response and all other responses. You'll set up the correct response icon to accept either of two variations on the correct answer. You'll also add a **tries limit** response type to the interaction that displays the right answer if the user fails to enter the text you want after three attempts.

If you would like to view the final result of this lesson, open the Final Files folder and play 06_Final.a5p.

WHAT YOU WILL LEARN

In this lesson you will:

- Practice using map icons attached to a decision icon to place content temporarily off the main flowline
- Practice using text styles
- Practice creating a graphic with the toolbox tools
- Create a text entry interaction that responds when users type text that you specify
- Create a catch-all text entry interaction, which responds to any text a user might type
- Create a tries limit that responds after the user tries unsuccessfully three times to type the specified text

APPROXIMATE TIME

It should take about 1 hour to complete this lesson.

LESSON FILES

Beginning File:
Beginning Files\06_Begin.a5p
Completed Project:
Final Files\06_Final.a5p

STORING CONTENT OFF THE MAIN FLOWLINE

You'll begin this lesson by grouping all the icons from the previous lesson into a map icon and then attaching the map icon to the Temp. Storage decision icon you created in Lesson 5. By doing so, you'll place the hot spot interaction off the main flowline while you continue your work on the Authorware game project.

1] Open 06_Begin.a5p and save it as *06_Game.a5p* in the Game Project folder.

Alternatively, you can use the file you worked on in the previous lesson and save it as *06_Game.a5p*.

2] In the Design window, marquee select the Hot Spot interaction icon and its attached icons.

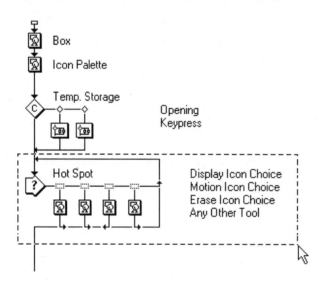

When you release the mouse button, all the selected icons are highlighted.

3] Group the selected icons into a map icon.

To do this, choose Modify > Group.

124

4] Attach the new Hot Spot map icon to the Temp. Storage decision icon by dragging it to the right of the Keypress map icon.

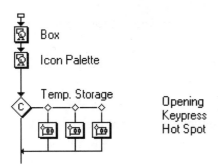

With the content from the previous lessons now temporarily removed from the main flowline, you're ready to begin creating a text entry interaction.

PREPARING A TEXT ENTRY INTERACTION

In this task you'll place an interaction icon on the flowline and create a question inside it.

1] Drag an interaction icon to the flowline below the Temp. Storage decision icon. Name it *Text Entry.*

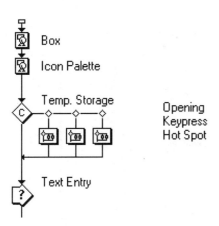

2] Open the Interaction Icon Properties dialog box.

To do this, choose Modify > Icon > Properties.

3] On the Interaction tab, select Pause Before Exiting and Show Button. Then click OK.

These are the same settings you used for other interactions you created in previous lessons. You'll accept the other default settings for now.

4] In the Presentation window, make sure the Continue button is at the lower right.

The Continue button will already be at the lower right if Authorware is still open from the previous lesson.

5] Restart the piece. Then switch to the Design window and Shift-double-click the Text Entry interaction icon.

You should see the box, the icon palette, and the title in the toolbox indicating that you're working in the Text Entry icon.

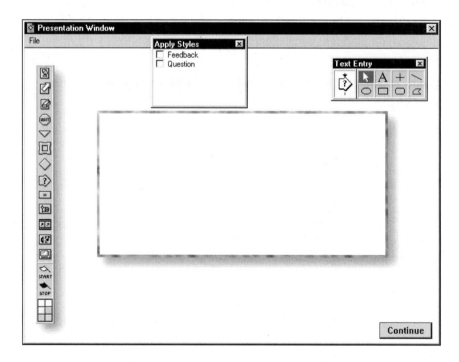

6] Enter the following text in the box using the Question text style and left alignment. Press Enter to insert line spaces at lines 3 and 5.

This icon
is called the
<line space>
icon.
<line space>
Type your answer and press Enter.

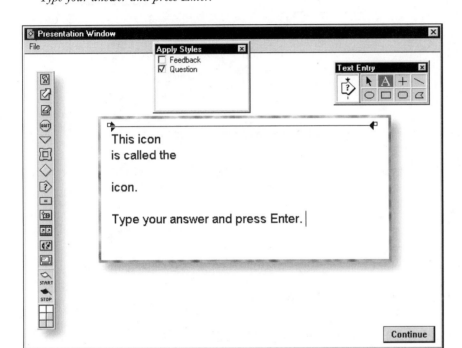

Make sure the text is set to transparent mode. If necessary, choose Windows > Inspectors > Modes and select Transparent.

At the first line space, the user will type the answer. To enhance the appearance of the text, you'll center it.

7] Click the Pointer tool in the toolbox and then choose Text › Alignment › Center (Ctrl+\) to center the text. Move the text so it looks approximately like the following illustration.

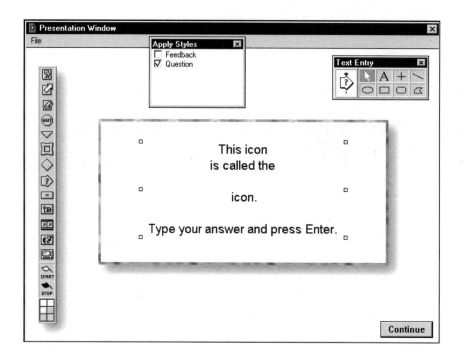

8] Close the Apply Styles window and save your work.

CREATING A GRAPHIC WITH THE TOOLBOX

In this task you'll create an arrow pointing to the icon referred to in the question.

1] Click the Straight Line tool in the toolbox.

This tool draws vertical, horizontal, and 45-degree lines.

STRAIGHT LINE TOOL

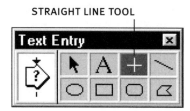

2] Drag the cursor to draw a horizontal line between the icon palette graphic and the edge of the box graphic.

3] Position the line so it's even with the navigate icon in the icon palette graphic.

To do this, click the Pointer tool in the toolbox and then either drag the line or use the up and down arrow keys on the keyboard.

The navigate icon is the triangular icon—the fifth icon from the top.

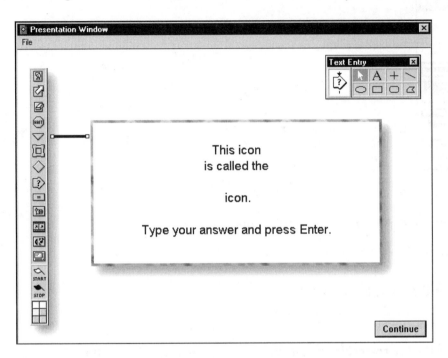

4] Open the Lines Inspector.

To do this, choose Windows > Inspectors > Lines.

5] Make sure the second-thickest line is selected in the Lines Inspector.

It's four down from the top. If you just completed Lesson 5, this setting might already be selected.

6] In the lower section of the Lines Inspector, select an arrowhead so that the line becomes an arrow pointing toward the navigate icon.

Depending on which way you drew the line in a previous step—from left to right or from right to left—either the left or right arrowhead will produce a left-pointing arrow. The right-pointing arrow puts an arrowhead at the end of your line. The left-pointing arrow puts an arrowhead at the beginning of your line.

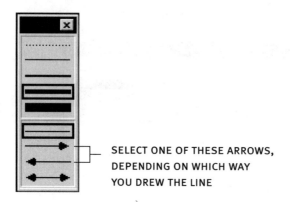

SELECT ONE OF THESE ARROWS,
DEPENDING ON WHICH WAY
YOU DREW THE LINE

The line you created becomes a left-pointing arrow.

Now you'll choose a color for the arrow.

7] Open the Colors Inspector.

To do this, choose Windows > Inspectors > Colors.

8] Click the Pen color chip and then select a bright red from the palette.

The exact color you choose is not important. Just make sure the line is visible against the background.

9] Close the Inspectors.

You've created the question. In the next task you'll set up a response icon for the correct answer.

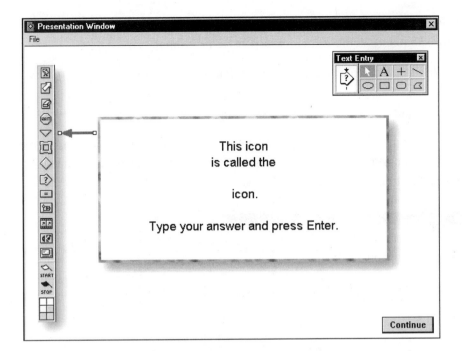

10] **Save your work.**

CREATING A TEXT ENTRY RESPONSE

In this task you'll place a text entry field in the Presentation window and prepare it to accept the desired response.

1] **In the Design window, drag a display icon to the right of the Text Entry interaction icon. In the Response Type dialog box, select Text Entry. Leave the response icon untitled for now.**

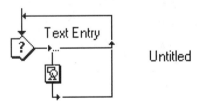

Text entry interactions are somewhat like keypress interactions in the relationship between the title of a response icon and the desired response. When you specify the text entry you want to match this response, that text will become the name of this response icon.

2] Open the Response Properties dialog box for the new icon.

To do this, double-click the text entry response type symbol.

On the Text Entry tab, notice the range of options that Authorware provides for text entry responses. You can be precise or more forgiving about the text that you'll accept as a match.

For example, the default settings ignore capitalization, extra words, extra punctuation, and word order when judging whether to accept as matches text that a user types. You'll accept the default settings.

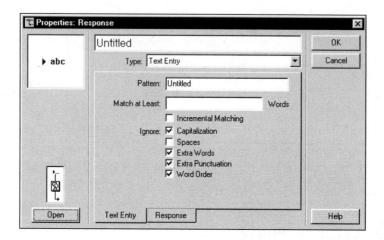

3] In the Pattern box, double-click the word *Untitled* to select it and then type *navigate* over it.

The word *navigate* is the pattern that Authorware will look for. Notice that as you type this word, it also appears in the title box at the top of the dialog box.

tip *If you want to add more text to the icon title to display additional information about it on the flowline, type two hyphens after the title and then type the text. Any text following the two hyphens is considered a comment rather than part of the title.*

ICON TITLE

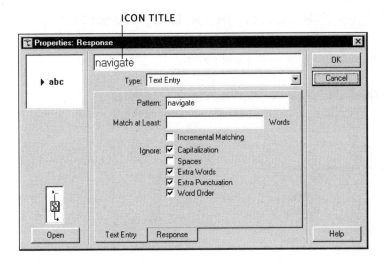

4] Click the Response tab and select Exit Interaction from the Branch menu. Then click OK to close the dialog box.

You're creating the response icon for the correct answer. There's no need for the user to keep trying after getting it right, so the flow should exit the interaction after the correct answer is entered.

Next you'll make sure the size and location of the text entry field are the way you want.

5] Restart the piece.

A black triangle and a blinking text cursor indicate the left edge of the text entry field.

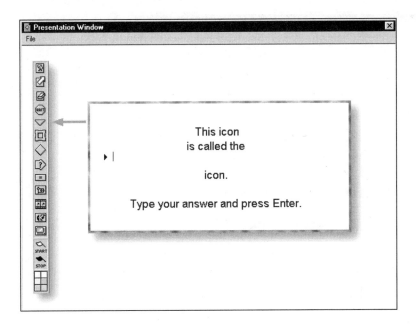

6] Choose Control › Pause (Ctrl+P) to pause the piece (numeric keypad 2).

When you pause the piece, you'll see a gray dotted line showing the border of the text entry field. Now you can adjust its size and position.

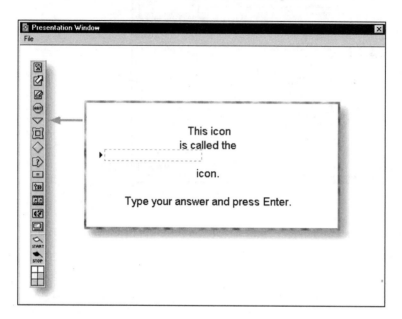

7] Drag the text entry field so it's approximately centered between the second and third lines of text in the question. Drag the handles to make the rectangle about as wide as the second line of text.

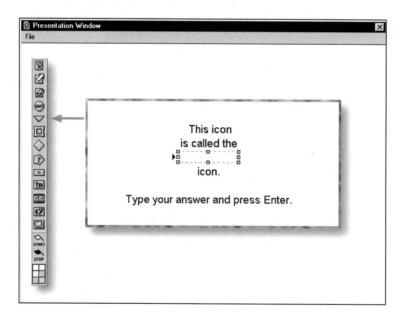

8] Save your work.

Now it's time to test the interaction and create feedback text.

CREATING FEEDBACK FOR THE CORRECT RESPONSE

In this task you'll run your piece and type the correct response. By entering the text you previously set up as the desired pattern, you'll make Authorware branch to the display icon and open the toolbox so you can create feedback.

1] Restart the piece. When the question appears, type *navigate* and press Enter.

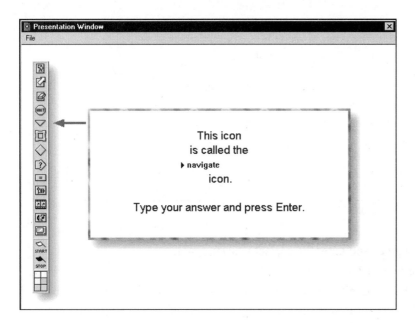

Because you entered the pattern Authorware was looking for, Authorware branches to the response icon for that choice.

tip   *If your text entry response doesn't work as expected, the first place to look is in the Pattern box in the Response Properties dialog box. A minor typing mistake can produce a pattern that's not what you had in mind.*

2] Enter the following text using the Feedback text style: *You're right!*

Place the text below the box as shown in the following illustration.

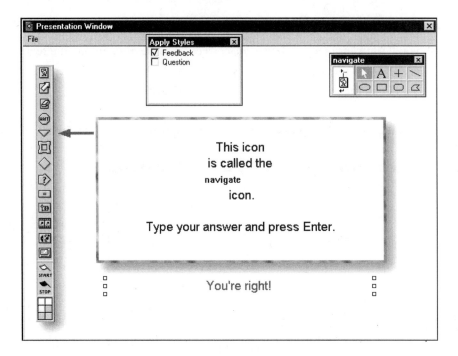

3] Restart the piece and enter the correct answer again.

It works! The feedback is displayed, and the flow exits the interaction because you selected Exit Interaction branching. If you type anything other than the target response, however, Authorware does nothing at this point. In the next step you'll set up another response icon that provides feedback for any other text a user enters.

CREATING A CATCH-ALL TEXT ENTRY RESPONSE

In this task you'll round out the text entry interaction by adding feedback for all the incorrect text entries that a user might type. Creating this catch-all response type is remarkably easy.

For the hot spot interaction in the previous lesson, you created separate hot spots in the Presentation window for every response icon attached to the interaction. A text entry interaction, however, has only one text entry field. You will add another response icon to this interaction, but users will see only a single text entry field in the Presentation window.

1] In the Design window, drag a display icon to the right of the navigate display icon. Don't name it.

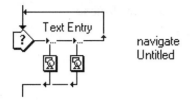

navigate
Untitled

Again, the target response you create will provide the name for the response icon.

2] Open the Response Properties dialog box for the new response icon.

To do this, double-click the text entry response type symbol.

3] On the Text Entry tab, highlight the word *Untitled* in the Pattern box and type an asterisk (*).

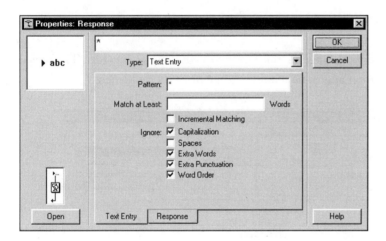

The asterisk does the trick. It's a **wildcard character** that represents any character or string of characters a user might enter in the text entry field.

You want users to have more than one chance to answer correctly, so you need to make sure that they get to try again when they enter the incorrect text.

tip   *To create text entry fields for collecting a user's name or other information that the user types, you use the text entry response type with the asterisk wildcard character. What allows you to save and recall the information later are Authorware's variables and functions. You'll be introduced to variables in Lesson 12.*

4] Click the Response tab. Then select Try Again from the Branch menu.

Now each time a user enters the incorrect response, Authorware will loop back to the question again, so the user can keep trying to get the answer right.

Next you'll create text for the feedback.

5] Click OK to close the dialog box. Then restart the piece. Type *navigate* and press Enter.

The feedback for the correct response is displayed. You're preparing the screen so you can align the text you're about to create.

6] In the Design window, Shift-double-click the * icon.

Now you can see the feedback for the correct response while you create the feedback for incorrect responses.

7] Create and align the following text using the Feedback text style: *Sorry, that's not it.*

Don't worry about perfectly aligning this new text with the previous text. The idea is to have both lines of text appear in about the same place on the screen.

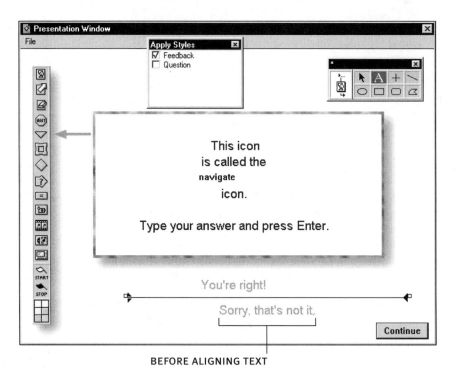

BEFORE ALIGNING TEXT

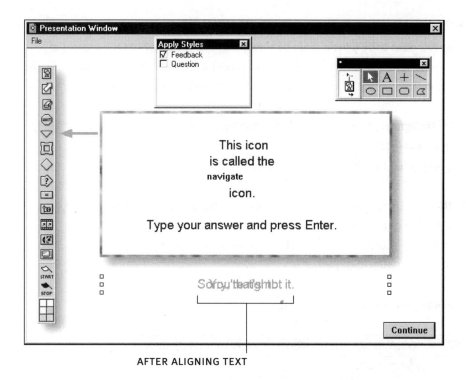

AFTER ALIGNING TEXT

Note that catch-all responses must be to the right of other more specific responses.

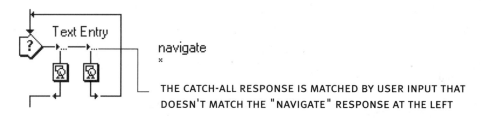

THE CATCH-ALL RESPONSE IS MATCHED BY USER INPUT THAT DOESN'T MATCH THE "NAVIGATE" RESPONSE AT THE LEFT

note *If you were to place a catch-all response at the left, it would defeat the purpose of this interaction. The catch-all response would intercept user input that matched the target response before the flow could reach the target response.*

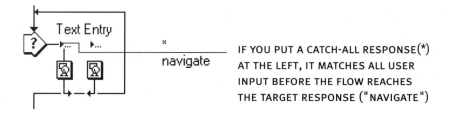

IF YOU PUT A CATCH-ALL RESPONSE(*) AT THE LEFT, IT MATCHES ALL USER INPUT BEFORE THE FLOW REACHES THE TARGET RESPONSE ("NAVIGATE")

8] Save your work.

ACCEPTING MULTIPLE TEXT ENTRY RESPONSES

Suppose you want to be a little more generous in what you accept as the correct response—for example, suppose you want to accept *navigation* as well as *navigate* as the right answer. In this task, you'll create a second pattern that will be considered correct.

1] In the Design window, open the Response Properties dialog box for the response icon named *navigate*.

You're going to add to the text in the Pattern box.

2] On the Text Entry tab, click after the word *navigate* in the Pattern box and type the vertical bar (|) character.

The vertical bar is usually found as the uppercase variant of the backslash on the keyboard. Don't add space before it.

3] Type navigation after the | character.

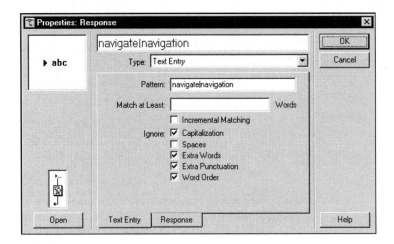

Again, don't add a space.

Recall that the vertical bar means "or"; it tells Authorware to accept either of these entries as the correct response. To continue adding other text that you want to accept as the target response, you could add more vertical bars and more words.

4] Click OK to close the dialog box. Then restart the piece and try entering *navigation* this time.

You should see the congratulatory message.

> **tip**   *You can also use an asterisk in combination with other characters as a way of allowing multiple target responses. For example, if you wanted to accept any word beginning with* navigat *as the correct answer, you'd enter* navigat* *in the Pattern box. Then Authorware would accept as correct responses* navigate, navigation, navigating, *and so on.*

ADDING A TRIES LIMIT RESPONSE

Unlike most other response types, text entry interactions are open ended, providing a nearly infinite number of possible responses. Because of this, text entry interactions can be frustrating for users unless you provide some kind of safety net, or way out. In this task you'll use the **tries limit** response type to display the correct answer after a user makes three unsuccessful attempts.

1] In the Design window, drag a display icon to the right of the * icon, making it the third response icon in the Text Entry interaction. Name it *Three Tries* and then open the Response Properties dialog box.

First you need to change the response type to Tries Limit.

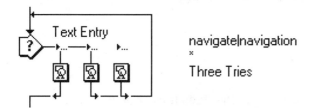

2] Open the Type menu and select Tries Limit.

3] On the Tries Limit tab, enter *3* in the Maximum Tries box.

CLICK TO OPEN THE TYPE MENU

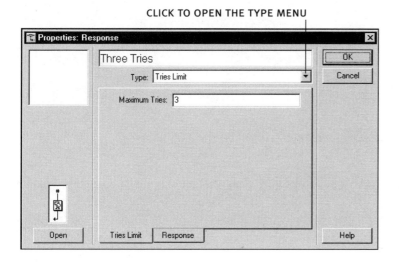

Users will get three attempts at matching the desired response. On their third attempt, the flow will go to the Three Tries response icon.

For branching, you want **Exit Interaction** for this response icon, but you don't have to select it. Authorware selects Exit Interaction branching for a tries limit response type by default.

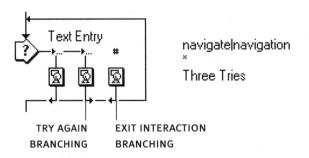

TRY AGAIN   EXIT INTERACTION
BRANCHING   BRANCHING

Exit Interaction means that after the correct answer appears, users won't get another chance to enter it themselves because the flow will exit the interaction and move down the flowline.

4] Click OK to close the dialog box.

5] In the Design window, Shift-double-click the Three Tries display icon.
You'll want the new text to appear below the other feedback text because it will appear on the screen in addition to the feedback for the wrong answer.

6] Enter the following text just below other feedback text, using the Feedback style: *It's the navigate icon.*

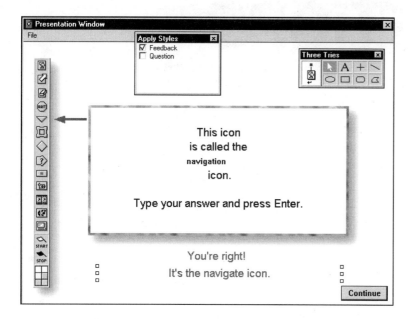

7] Restart the piece and then type three incorrect answers.

After you enter the last incorrect response, Authorware displays the Three Tries feedback and exits the interaction. To satisfy yourself that everything works as it should, you can restart the piece again and try the two correct responses as well.

tip   *If you want to pause the piece to adjust the position of the text, remember the keyboard shortcuts for pausing and proceeding. One keyboard shortcut toggles between Pause and Proceed (Ctrl+P). The other keyboard shortcut uses two different keys on the numeric keypad: 2 to pause and 3 to proceed.*

8] Save your work.

WHAT YOU HAVE LEARNED

In this lesson you have:

- Practiced placing content temporarily off the main flowline [*page* **124**]
- Practiced creating text using text styles [*page* **125**]
- Created an arrow using the toolbox tools, Lines Inspector, and Colors Inspector [*page* **128**]
- Used the text entry response type to create an interaction that responds to user-entered text [*page* **131**]
- Added a catch-all text entry response using the wildcard character [*page* **136**]
- Added a tries limit response to provide feedback after three incorrect answers [*page* **141**]

enhancing interactions

LESSON 7

In this lesson you will learn three ways to make interactions more engaging for users. You'll add a randomly selected sound as feedback when users make a particular choice in an interaction, create a prompt that appears on the screen after a delay, and create a hot spot interaction that displays additional information when users move the cursor over an area without clicking. Although you'll be using these three techniques to enhance the Authorware game project, these techniques are equally useful for a wide range of interactive applications.

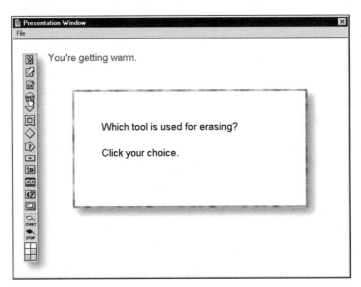

One way to make your Authorware pieces more engaging for users is to add a rollover—a hot spot activated when the user moves the cursor over it without clicking— such as this hint in the Authorware game, which appears when users move the cursor near the correct answer. This is just one of several techniques you can use to add impact to interactions.

If you would like to view the final result of this lesson, open the Final Files folder and play 07_Final.a5p.

A completed version of the Authorware game is included on the CD-ROM that accompanies this book. The game contains different content from the game you're building. To play the game, run Agame.exe. To see how Agame works, open the Agame.a5p file in Authorware.

WHAT YOU WILL LEARN

In this lesson you will:

• Convert a single icon into a map icon to hold additional content
• Create a branching structure that randomly selects content in a piece
• Work with a library, which stores media for easy access and repeated use
• Use the time limit response type to provide feedback to users after a set duration
• Create a rollover—a hot spot that responds when the user moves the cursor over it

APPROXIMATE TIME

It should take about 1½ hours to complete this lesson.

LESSON FILES

Media Files:
Your Files\Game Project\Sounds.a5l
Beginning File:
Beginning Files\07_Begin.a5p
Completed Project:
Final Files\07_Final.a5p

PREPARING THE FLOWLINE

In this lesson you will be working with the hot spot interaction you built in Lesson 5, which is now being held in the Temp. Storage icon. To prepare for the work you'll do, first you'll group the icons from the previous lesson into a map icon. Then you'll move the new map icon to the Temp. Storage icon to keep it off the main flowline. Finally, you will move the Hot Spot map icon back to the main flowline and open it so you can work with it.

1] Open 07_Begin.a5p in the Beginning Files folder and save it as *07_Game.a5p* in the Game Project folder.

Alternatively, you can use the file you worked on in the previous lesson and save it as *07_Game.a5p*.

2] In the Design window, marquee select the icons in the Text Entry interaction.

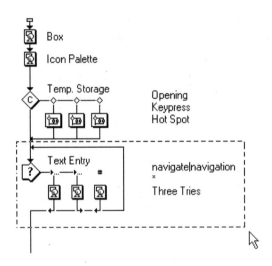

3] Group the icons.

To do this, choose Modify > Group.

4] Drag the new Text Entry map icon to the right end of the map icons attached to the Temp. Storage decision icon.

The Text Entry map icon will be attached at the far right of the map icons.

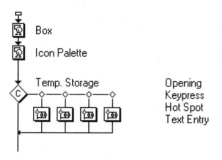

Box
Icon Palette

Temp. Storage

Opening
Keypress
Hot Spot
Text Entry

5] Select the Hot Spot map icon and drag it down to the main flowline.

You're going to be modifying the interaction in this icon, so you want it available on the main flowline.

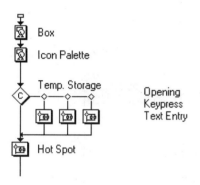

Box
Icon Palette

Temp. Storage

Opening
Keypress
Text Entry

Hot Spot

6] Double-click the Hot Spot map icon to open it.

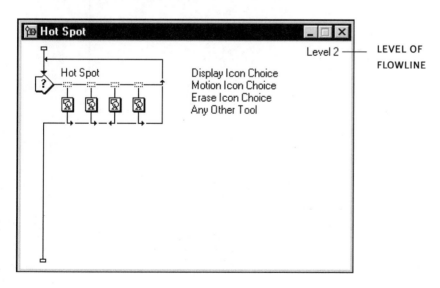

Hot Spot

Hot Spot

Level 2 — LEVEL OF FLOWLINE

Display Icon Choice
Motion Icon Choice
Erase Icon Choice
Any Other Tool

The window for this map icon displays *Level 2* in the upper right corner. Level 1 is the main flowline. Level 2 represents a map icon containing icons grouped on the main flowline. Level 3 would be a map icon nested inside a Level 2 map icon. As you use map icons to structure your pieces, you'll often work two, three, or four levels away from the main flowline.

7] Drag the Hot Spot window to the lower part of the screen so you can see both it and the main flowline at the same time.

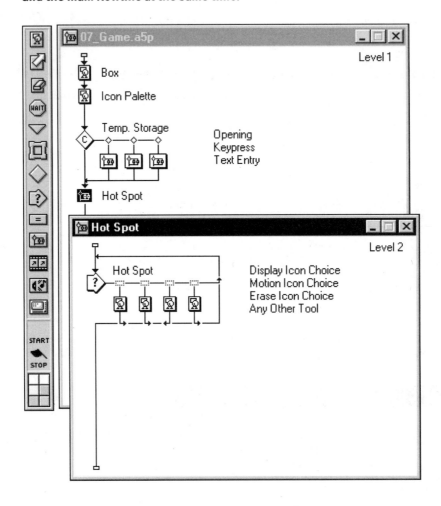

When you work in a map window, you should position it on your screen so you can keep track of the main flowline as you work on a particular segment. This main flowline provides context for the work you're doing within a map window.

Now you're ready to modify the hot spot interaction.

CONVERTING ONE ICON INTO A GROUP

In Lesson 5 you created the Any Other Tool hot spot—enclosing the entire icon palette image—to provide feedback when a user clicked any part of the icon palette not handled by the other hot spots in the interaction. When a user clicks the Any Other Tool hot spot, text is displayed to invite the user to keep trying.

In this lesson you'll add a randomly selected sound to the visual feedback. Adding the structure for randomly selecting a sound will require a whole new structure for the Any Other Tool response icon; it will use a decision icon and several sound icons plus a map icon to contain it.

How do you change a single icon into a group? You could delete the Any Other Tool display icon and start over, but Authorware makes the process easier. You can simply convert a single icon into a map icon by using the Group command.

1] Select the Any Other Tool display icon in the Hot Spot interaction.

2] Choose Modify › Group.

Authorware converts the display icon into a map icon with the same name. You'll often use this technique for cases in which you initially have used a single sound or display icon but later decide to expand to more complex content involving several icons.

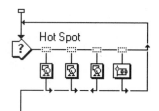

Display Icon Choice
Motion Icon Choice
Erase Icon Choice
Any Other Tool

3] Double-click the Any Other Tool map icon to open it.

Notice that this map icon represents Level 3 of the flowline. Now you can build a more complex flowline structure for this part of your piece.

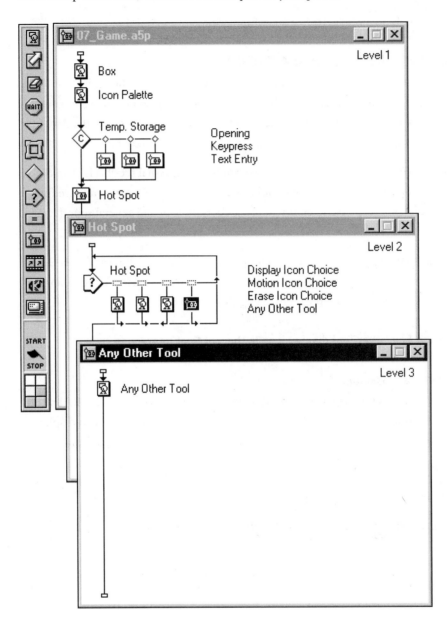

4] Save your work.

SETTING UP RANDOM BRANCHING

In this task you'll place a decision icon for Any Other Tool on the flowline. Then you'll select a random branching option for it.

1] Drag a decision icon to the map icon flowline below the Any Other Tool display icon. Name it *Random Sounds*.

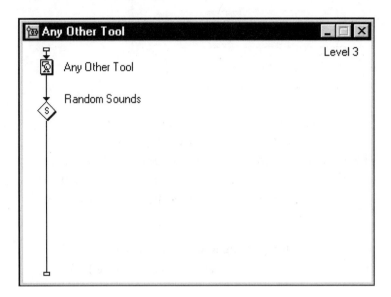

You'll make the branching of this decision icon random, and then you'll attach several sound files.

2] Double-click the decision icon to open the Decision Icon Properties dialog box.
The key to the power of a decision icon are the branching options, which direct the flow of activity in a piece down a path that can be determined in a number of ways. In a previous lesson, you used a decision icon to create temporary storage for content off the main flowline. To do that, you used To Calculated Path branching and specified a path of 0—which prevented the flow from branching to any attached icons. In this case, you'll use a randomly selected path.

3] Select Randomly to Any Path from the Branch menu and then click OK.

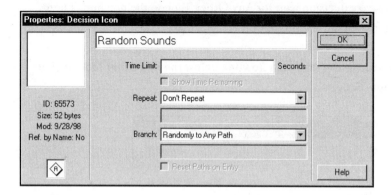

This choice will select a path at random every time the piece reaches the decision icon. After you attach sound icons to the decision icon, each time users select the Any Other Tool hot spot, they'll likely hear a different sound accompanying the text on the screen. This element of unpredictability can make interactivity more interesting to users.

If you chose the other random branching option, Random to Any Unused Path, it would ensure that no path was repeated until all paths had been selected.

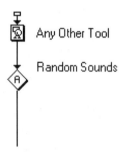

Now you need some sounds to attach to the Random Sounds decision icon.

Libraries provide storage for content that you use repeatedly in a piece. You can use libraries to store the five kinds of icons that contain content—display, interaction, calculation, digital movie, and sound icons. To use library content, you just drag one of the library icons to the flowline. Instead of storing the contents of the icon within the Authorware piece itself each time it's used, Authorware saves a **link** to the library.

Libraries provide many benefits. They help you keep pieces small in size because media content does not have to be duplicated; instead the link to the library is the only information that's added to a file each time you use a library icon. They also enable you to update content quickly. For example, if you're using a logo that's stored in a library and you need to change it every place it appears in a piece, you could just modify the library icon for the logo and every place the logo appears will automatically be updated.

Stored icons in libraries give you ready-made content that you can use in a variety of pieces. In addition, when content is stored in libraries, you can use one piece in different ways simply by changing its libraries. For example, you could replace a library containing English sound and text files with one containing French files with the same names to instantly create a French version of your piece.

In this task you'll open a library containing a ready-made set of sound files that were prepared for this lesson. You'll attach several of these sounds to the Random Sounds decision icon.

1] Choose File › Open › Library.

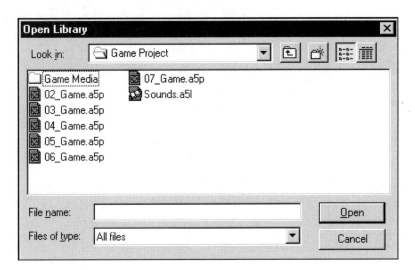

2] Select the file Sounds.a5l in the Game Project folder. Click Open.

These are the sound icons you'll add to your piece.

Notice the row of buttons across the top of the library window. These let you determine how to sort the icons—for example, by the type of icon or the title. The Ascending/Descending button lets you reverse the sort order.

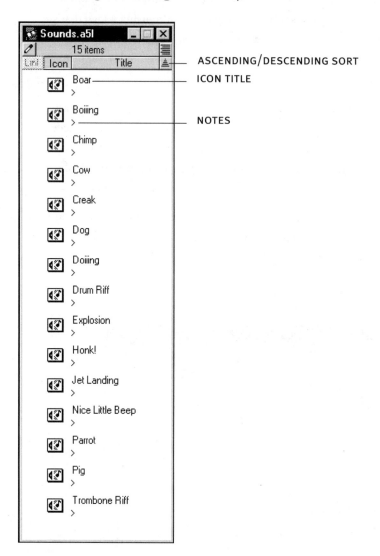

ASCENDING/DESCENDING SORT

ICON TITLE

NOTES

tip *You can use up to 17 libraries within an Authorware piece. For large projects, you need to develop standards for how you use libraries. For example, decide in advance if you'll store sound and graphics in the same library or use different libraries. Establish naming conventions for icons and decide what kind of information you'll enter in the Notes fields.*

3] Choose File › Save All to save the Authorware file and the Sounds library.

CREATING THE BRANCHING STRUCTURE

In this task you'll attach sound icons from the library to the Random Sounds decision icon.

1] Drag the Boiiing icon from the library to the right of the Random Sounds decision icon.

When the sound icon is attached to the decision icon, the decision path symbol appears at the top of the path.

When you click anywhere else in the Design window, you'll notice that the title of the Boiiing icon is displayed in italics. Authorware uses italics to remind you that the icon is linked to a library.

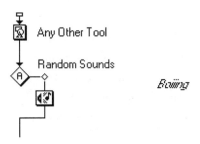

In the next step you'll add more sounds to the Random Sounds decision icon.

2] In the library, select three or four additional sound icons and drag them to the right of the Boiiing icon.

Pick any sounds you want.

When you've selected several more sounds, your Random Sounds branching structure will look similar to the following illustration. Your sound icons will probably be different.

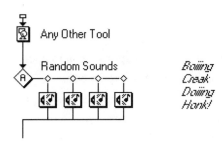

3] Restart the piece and then click any part of the icon palette graphic except the display, motion, or erase icon.

In Lesson 5 you set up individual hot spots for the first three icons in the palette. When you click anywhere else on the icon palette, you should see the text feedback and hear one of the sounds you attached to the Random Sounds decision icon.

4] When you've finished trying out your random sounds, switch to the Design window. Then close the Any Other Tool map icon and save your work.

To close a map window, click the close box or choose File > Close > Window (Ctrl+W).

By closing the Any Other Tool Design window, you're cleaning up your work area in preparation for the next task.

ADDING A TIME LIMIT RESPONSE

In this task you'll use the **time limit** response type to display feedback to users who don't get the right answer after a certain period of time. The time limit response type is somewhat like the tries limit response type, which you used in Lesson 6. However, the tries limit response type is triggered by a certain number of user responses, whereas the time limit response type provides feedback after a specified period of time regardless of whether the user does anything.

1] In the Hot Spot window, drag a display icon to the far right of the Hot Spot interaction. Name it _5 Seconds._

Place this new icon to the right of the Any Other Tool map icon.

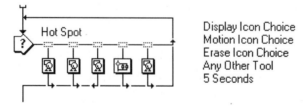

2] Double-click the response type symbol for the 5 Seconds response icon to open the Response Properties dialog box. Select Time Limit from the Type menu.

Remember that Authorware automatically gives a new icon the same response type as the response icon to its left. To change from the hot spot response type to the time limit response type, you have to change the Type setting.

tip *An alternative method of adding a new response icon that doesn't share the same response type as other icons attached to an interaction icon is to first drag the icon to the immediate right of the interaction icon. The Response Type dialog box will open, and you can select the type of response you want. Then drag the response icon to the position you want among the other response icons.*

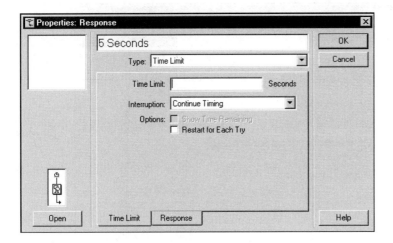

The dialog box presents several settings for controlling a time limit interaction. You'll accept most of the defaults.

3] On the Time Limit tab, type *5* in the Time Limit box.

You can enter whole seconds or fractions of a second, such as 5.3.

4] Click the Response tab and select Try Again from the Branch menu. Then click OK.

Authorware defaults to Exit Interaction branching for a time limit response type. You're choosing Try Again branching because you want users to have another chance to click the correct choice after they see the hint.

5] Shift-double-click the 5 Seconds display icon to open it.

You're going to create one line of text that will appear on the screen after the user has been in the interaction for 5 seconds.

6] Create the following text using the Feedback style and place it above the box as shown in the following illustration. *Hint: It looks like an eraser.*

To do this, click the text tool in the toolbox, click above the box in the Presentation window, and then select the Feedback text style in the Apply Styles window. To open this window, choose Text > Apply Styles.

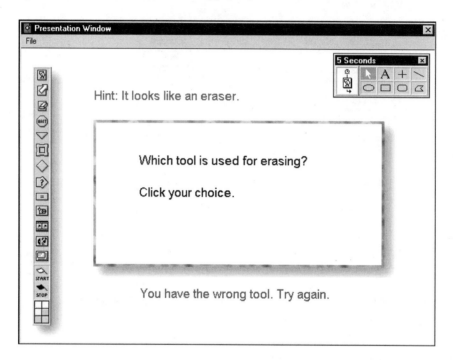

7] Restart the piece and wait for the feedback to appear.

Don't click anything for 5 seconds. After the time limit runs out, the hint text appears.

8] Save your work.

ADDING A ROLLOVER

Rollovers are commonly used in many kinds of interactive productions. Before you click a menu choice, for example, a message might appear that tells you what that menu choice does. What triggers this response is a hot spot that responds to the position of the cursor rather than to clicking.

In this task you'll create a rollover hot spot that is slightly larger than the hot spot that users click for the correct answer. When a user's cursor enters this larger hot spot, text will appear that says, "You're getting warm."

1] In the Hot Spot map window, drag a display icon to the right of the 5 Seconds icon. Name it *Rollover*.

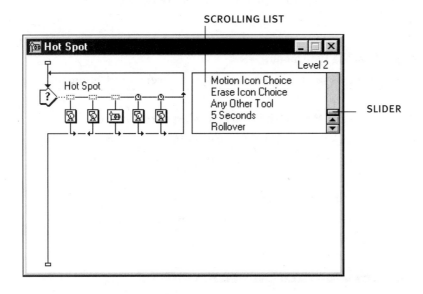

Notice that when you add a sixth icon to the interaction, Authorware displays a scrolling list of the icon titles and truncates the display of the icons to show only five at a time. This is how Authorware makes it possible for you to attach numerous icons to a single interaction without running out of space in the Design window.

To use the scrolling list, you can either drag the slider up and down or click the up and down arrows. The very first icon on the left corresponds to the top icon title in the list. The last icon on the right corresponds to the bottom icon title in the list. However, you see only five icons and their titles at a time.

tip   *If an interaction has so many icons attached that it's hard to locate a specific one, click its title in the list. The icon with that title will be highlighted.*

2] Double-click the response type symbol for Rollover to open the Response Properties dialog box.

You need to change its response type from the time limit type used by the previous icon.

3] Select Hot Spot from the Type menu.

To make this hot spot a rollover, you'll use a setting you haven't used before.

4] On the Hot Spot tab, open the Match menu and select Cursor in Area.

You've used the Single-click setting previously. Cursor in Area tells Authorware to branch to this response icon when the user's cursor moves over the hot spot.

5] Select the hand-shaped custom cursor.

To do this, click the Cursor button and then select the hand-shaped cursor at the bottom of the list.

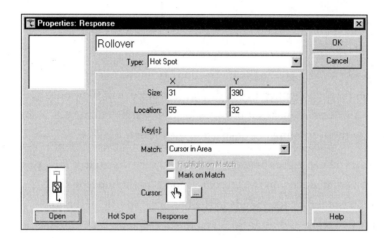

6] Click OK to close the dialog box.

Next you need to resize and position the new hot spot.

7] In the Presentation window, drag and resize the rollover hot spot so it encloses the motion, erase, and wait icons in the icon palette graphic.

To do this, drag the hot spot so its top edge is just above the top of the motion icon in the palette and its left edge is even with the left side of the icon palette. Then drag the handle at the lower right so that its bottom edge is just below the wait icon and its right edge is even with the right edge of the icon palette.

8] Restart the piece. Then move the cursor over the area where you placed the hot spot.
Authorware branches to the response icon for this hot spot and waits for you to create content.

You'll create a line of text that appears when the user moves the cursor over the hot spot.

9] Using the Feedback text style, create the following text near the top of the screen: *You're getting warm*. Then place the text roughly in the same position as shown in the following illustration.

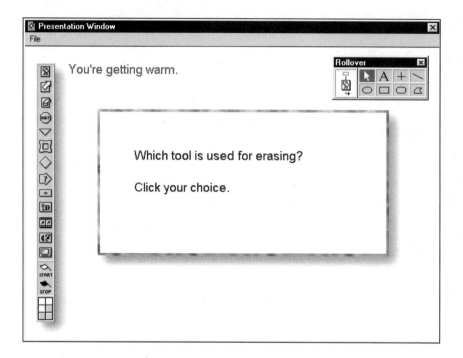

10] Restart the piece again and try the new hot spot again.

When you move your cursor over the part of the icon palette containing the motion, erase, and wait icons, the hint should appear.

There's something missing in this rollover interaction, however. The message doesn't go away when you move the cursor away from the hot spot. In the next task you'll take care of this problem.

11] Save your work.

ADDING A CATCH-ALL ROLLOVER

In this task you'll make the rollover behave the way people expect: The message that appears when a user moves the cursor over a certain area of the screen will disappear when the user moves the cursor away from that area. To make this happen, you'll create another hot spot for Cursor in Area—but this one will cover the entire screen.

1] In the Design window, drag a map icon to the right end of the Hot Spot interaction. Name it *Catch-all*.

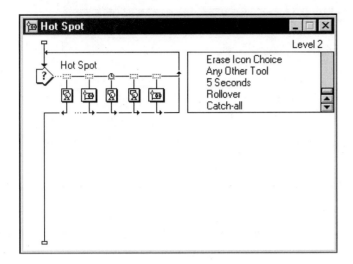

You will not place any content in this map icon. The empty map icon provides a path for the flow when a user's pointer is over any area of the screen except for the other hot spots whose response icons precede Catch-all—that is, are to the left—in the interaction flowline. When a user's pointer moves away from the Rollover hot spot, for example, to other parts of the screen, the position of the pointer will match Catch-all. When that match occurs, the flow proceeds to the Catch-all map icon. Because it's empty, no images or sounds play. Instead, because of its Try Again branching, the Catch-all icon simply sends the flow back to the top of the interaction again—and the user can keep on clicking choices.

2] Open the Response Properties dialog box for the Catch-all map icon.
You'll keep most of the settings copied from the previous hot spot icon. However, you need to change the Cursor setting.

3] On the Hot Spot tab, open the Cursors dialog box. In the list of cursors, select None. Then click OK.
You choose None because this hot spot will encompass the entire window. Anywhere a user moves the cursor will match this response icon. Because it comes at the far right of the other response icons, however, any cursor position that matches one of the other hot spots will branch to its response icon, and the flow will not continue to Catch-all. Because you don't want to indicate that the entire screen is a clickable area, you select None for cursor.

4] Shift-double-click the interaction icon. In the Presentation window, resize and position the Catch-all hot spot to cover the entire window.

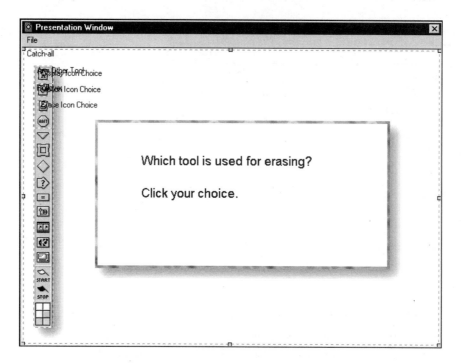

Don't worry about reaching literally to the edges of the screen.

5] Restart the piece. Try moving the cursor over the rollover and then away from it.
When you move away from the rollover this time, the message should disappear.

6] Save your work.
In the last four lessons you've assembled several parts of an interactive game that tests Authorware knowledge. The game project uses the keypress (Lesson 4), hot spot (Lesson 5), and text entry (Lesson 6) response types. In this lesson you expanded on your work in Lesson 5, adding random branching for feedback, a time limit response, and another hot spot that provides additional information when users move the pointer over the hot spot.

tip *You won't usually combine all three of these techniques in one interaction. Just like a piece of music, an effective interactive piece has a cadence and varying levels of intensity that make it engaging to users. Varying the kinds and number of interactive experiences throughout your pieces is part of the art of interactive media.*

ON YOUR OWN

Revise the Authorware game so it plays all the way through. You need to make only minor changes to the structure so you can see the opening animation followed by the interactions you've built. There are two ways to make the necessary changes; choose either approach:

> Drag each of the three map icons attached to the Temp. Storage decision icon back to the main flowline. Optionally, place them in the order you created them: Opening, Keypress, Hot Spot, and Text Entry. You don't need to remove the Temp. Storage decision icon. The flow will simply bypass it.

> Leave the three map icons attached to the Temp. Storage decision icon, but change two settings in the decision icon so the flow passes through each map icon. To do this, change the Branch setting to Sequentially and change the Repeat setting to Until All Paths Used. Optionally, you can drag the Hot Spot map icon from the main flowline back to the decision icon structure between Keypress and Text Entry, so the parts of the game run in the order you created them.

When you've made the changes using either approach, restart the piece. Now you can play each part of the game that you've built over the last six lessons.

WHAT YOU HAVE LEARNED

In this lesson you have:

- Converted a single display icon into a map icon using the Group command [*page* **146**]
- Used a decision icon set to random branching to create a structure that randomly plays one of several sounds [*page* **151**]
- Opened a preexisting library of sounds and used several of them in a random branching structure [*page* **153**]
- Created a time limit response and set its duration [*page* **156**]
- Used a hot spot response type to create a rollover that provides feedback when users move the cursor over it [*page* **158**]

interactions

hot object

LESSON 8

This lesson introduces two important Authorware features. You'll create **hot object interactions,** which permit you to use nonrectangular objects as hot areas on the screen to trigger responses, and you'll use **external media,** which is media stored outside of an Authorware piece. So far in this book, whenever you have used ready-made graphics or sounds, you have imported them into Authorware. (The sounds in the Sounds.a5l library used in Lesson 7 were imported into the library.) The image and sound files have become part of the Authorware piece. There's another way to work with media, however, and for some applications it will prove a better way: Maintain the media files separately from the Authorware file and store only links to the media within the piece.

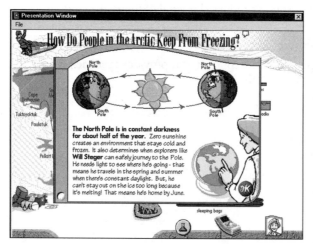

What's the Secret? is a science education CD-ROM based on the Emmy-award-winning PBS television show "Newton's Apple." The CD-ROM product uses Authorware's hot object interactions to present information when users click certain objects on the screen. In this lesson you'll build an abbreviated version of this progam. What's the Secret? was developed by ICONOS inc, Minneapolis (http://www.iconos.com), and is distributed by Imation Corp. Audio design by Intuitive, Minneapolis (http://www.intuaudio.com).

This lesson also introduces a new project, adapted from *What's the Secret?*, which is a children's educational CD-ROM based on the PBS TV science program, Newton's Apple. In the next four lessons, you'll work with an abbreviated version of one portion of this rich multimedia CD-ROM.

You'll start by creating a new file for the new project and creating a library file. Then you'll use the library to store links to several media files to be used in your project. After using one of the linked files as background art, you'll set up a hot object interaction using three images that will trigger responses when they are clicked. In the full product, clicking these objects leads elsewhere in the piece to additional multimedia content. In this lesson, however, you'll use an image and a sound as placeholders for the content of the actual product.

If you would like to see the final result of this lesson, open the Final Files folder and play 08_Final.a5p.

WHAT YOU WILL LEARN
In this lesson you will:
- Incorporate external media files
- Import external graphics and sound files into a library you create
- Practice using Matted mode to make the white background of several graphics disappear
- Create a hot object interaction using nonrectangular images that users can click
- Assemble multimedia content that appears when users click hot objects

APPROXIMATE TIME
It should take about 1 hour to complete this lesson.

LESSON FILES
Media Files:
Your Files\Arctic Project\Arctic Media
Beginning File:
None
Completed Project:
Final Files\08_Final.a5p

INTRODUCING EXTERNAL MEDIA

External media are any graphics, sounds, and movies whose contents are incorporated into a piece but whose files are stored outside the piece. Authorware gives you the choice of storing media inside the Authorware file or using references to externally stored media files. So far in this book you've been importing graphics and sound directly into Authorware, making it part of the piece. In this lesson you'll try another approach. You'll create a library for a series of media elements that will be used in building a hot object interaction. Instead of importing graphics and sound files into the library, however, you'll create links between library icons and media files located on your hard drive.

> **tip** *In an Authorware piece, you can create links to media files at a Web address. These links will work as long as the user has an Internet connection, whether or not your piece is delivered over the Web.*

For users, whether a piece uses internal or external media makes virtually no difference in their experience. For developers, the difference can be significant. When you use external media, a graphic artist can modify a graphic after you've included it in a piece—without ever having to open Authorware. As long as the file name and location stay the same as when you linked the external file to the piece, the revised graphic will appear in place of the old graphic just as if it were contained in the Authorware piece.

External media also means that you can develop applications whose media content can be changed quickly and easily—for example, an interactive catalog of real estate listings. When it's time to substitute one photo of a home for another, your client, the real-estate agent, can do the job without touching Authorware.

One risk in using external media, however, is that doing so makes the media files just as accessible to users as they are to the artists who developed them and the clients who paid for the piece. Partly because of that risk, Authorware provides a third option: Use external media during production because you can continue editing the media files after you've incorporated them into your piece. But when you package the piece for distribution, embed the media inside the Authorware piece, which also can simplify the distribution process. For more information, see Lesson 11, "Distributing a Piece."

STARTING A NEW FILE AND LIBRARY

Libraries offer their own range of benefits, some of them overlapping those for external media. For example, a library allows you to reuse content in the same piece or in multiple pieces without enlarging the size of your Authorware files.

Libraries and external media make a good combination. Libraries let you use the same graphics, text, sound, or video in many places with the same settings, as determined by the options you select in their respective Properties dialog boxes. You can store icons with links to external media in a library and then drag and drop them from the library onto your flowline as many times as you need throughout a piece.

In the following task, you'll get started by creating a new Authorware file and library.

1] Choose File › New › File (Ctrl+N) to create a new Authorware file. Click None in the New File dialog box to close it without using a Knowledge Object. Then close the Knowledge Objects window.

2] Open the File Properties dialog box so you can review and set global properties for your new piece.
To do this, choose Modify > File > Properties.

3] In the text entry box at the top, type *Arctic* as the name of this piece.
You're going to be working on a segment of *What's the Secret?* that deals with the use of dog sleds in the Arctic.

4] On the Playback tab, select Center on Screen. Then click OK.
This setting will keep the 640 × 480 screen centered when it's displayed on monitors with a higher resolution.

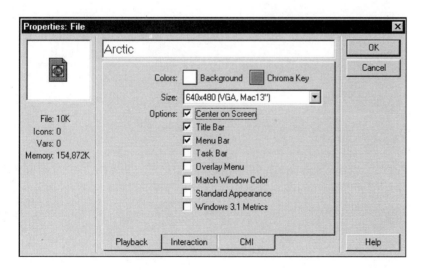

169

5] Save the Authorware file under the name _08_Arctic_.

Authorware automatically adds the .a5p extension to the file name.

6] Choose File › New › Library (Ctrl+Alt+N) to create a new library.

An empty library window appears.

7] Save the library under the name _Objects_.

Authorware automatically assigns the .a5l extension to a library file.

Now that you've set up your new file and library, you're ready to start putting some content into the library.

USING EXTERNAL MEDIA WITH A LIBRARY

In this task you'll link a series of external media files to the library you just created. You'll also learn a bit about the **External Media Browser,** Authorware's tool for keeping your external media organized.

1] Move the library window to the right side of your screen and drag its bottom edge down to the bottom of the screen.

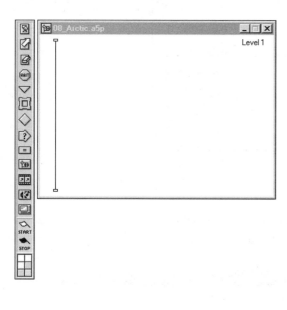

You're making space so you can see all the icons that you'll be adding to the library.

2] Choose File › Import.

The import dialog box opens.

3] Locate the Arctic Media folder and open it.

This folder contains both graphics and sound files.

4] Click the plus sign at the lower right to expand the dialog box.

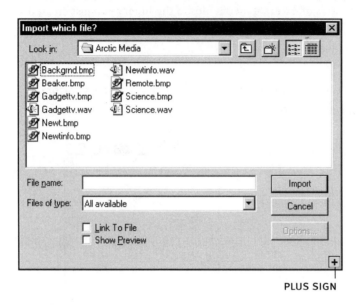

PLUS SIGN

The dialog box expands to include a window that will list the files you select for importing. You want to import all of the files in the list on the left.

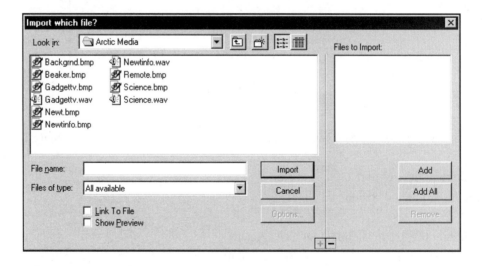

5] Click the Add All button to list all the media files in the Files to Import window.
You're almost ready to bring the media into the piece, but first there's one small step you need to take. You must link the files to the piece instead of importing them into Authorware.

172

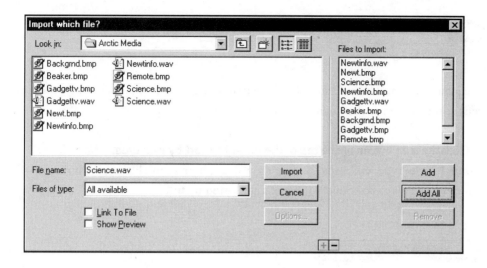

6] Select Link to File. Then click Import.

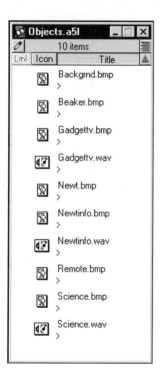

The name of each file in the Arctic Media folder appears as the name of an icon in the library. Authorware creates display icons for the BMP files and sound icons for the WAV files. You can preview the content of each of these media icons and drag them to the flowline, but the actual media is still in its original location in the Arctic Media folder.

tip   *You can use this same procedure to import and link files on the flowline in the Design window.*

The icons are sorted by title. You'll change that in the next step to group the sound icons at the bottom of the library for easier use.

7] Click the Icon button at the top of the library to sort by icon type.

Sorting by icon type will place the sounds at the bottom of the library. Within each icon type—display and sound—the icons are sorted by title.

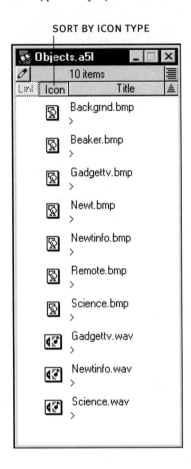

8] Choose File › Save All to save the piece and the library.

USING MATTED MODE

When you import graphics into Authorware, all images start in Opaque mode. In this lesson, however, you need several of the images to be **matted**—which means the white pixels surrounding the images are transparent. In this task you'll change the graphic mode of several images.

1] In the library window, double-click the Beaker.bmp display icon.

The Presentation window opens, displaying the beaker image. The image is not rectangular, yet it's contained in a rectangular background of white pixels. To hide the white pixels, you'll change the mode to Matted.

2] Open the Modes Inspector.

To do this, choose Window > Inspectors > Modes.

 You can also open the Modes Inspector by double-clicking the Pointer tool in the toolbox.

3] Select Matted mode.

The beaker's appearance doesn't change now because the Presentation window is white. When you display the beaker over the background art, however, it will appear without a surrounding white rectangle.

In the next few steps, you'll repeat this process for several other display icons in the library.

4] In the library window, double-click the Gadgettv.bmp display icon to open it.

5] Select Matted mode for Gadgettv.bmp.

6] Open the following display icons one by one and select Matted mode for each:

Newt.bmp

Newtinfo.bmp

Remote.bmp

Science.bmp

Now that you've set up the images the way you need them, you'll explore the External Media Browser.

USING THE EXTERNAL MEDIA BROWSER

The primary tool that Authorware provides for managing external media is the **External Media Browser,** a dialog box that displays file names and locations and lets you specify new locations and file names for linked media. In this task you'll open the External Media Browser and get acquainted with it.

1] Choose Window › External Media Browser (Ctrl+Shift+X).

The External Media Browser opens, displaying a complete list of every external media file in the library.

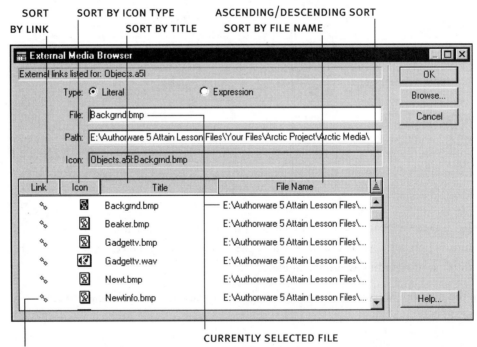

2] In the list of files, select the top file, Backgrnd.bmp. Then select the second file.

The File and Path boxes in the upper part of the dialog box show the name and location of the currently selected file in the list.

The Literal button above the File and Path boxes tells Authorware to show the path and file name for the selected file.

The buttons along the top of the file list allow you to sort the files by link, icon type, title, or file name. If a file is missing at its specified location, the Link column shows a broken link.

3] Click Cancel to close the External Media Browser.

If you use external media in your pieces, you'll use the External Media Browser to keep track of your content and, if necessary, make changes. For example, if your production team moves all the graphics files to a new file server, you need only open the External Media Browser and indicate the new location, and your graphics will remain linked to the Authorware piece.

PREPARING A HOT OBJECT INTERACTION

You've completed the preliminaries by importing the content you need to create a small portion of *What's the Secret?* Now you're ready to assemble the content into a **hot object interaction** in which clicking each of three objects displays a graphic and plays a sound.

One of the key advantages of hot object interactions is that you can use literally any shape as a hot object—you're not limited to rectangles as you are when using hot spots. In this case, you'll use the beaker, Newt, and TV remote control images as the hot objects.

First you need to place display icons on the flowline to contain the background art and each of the objects. When you prepare a hot object interaction, each clickable object must be in its own display icon and must precede the interaction icon on the flowline.

1] Drag the Backgrnd.bmp icon from the library to the flowline in the Design window.

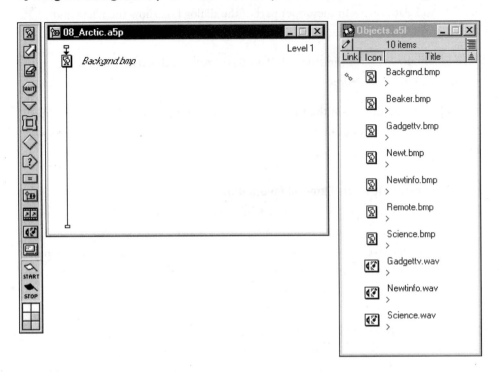

Notice that a link symbol appears beside the Backgrnd.bmp icon in the library. The symbol indicates that this library icon is being used in the piece. When you click elsewhere in the Design window, the name of this icon is displayed in italics to remind you that it's a library icon.

2] Drag the following icons to the flowline below the Backgrnd.bmp icon:

Beaker.bmp

Newt.bmp

Remote.bmp

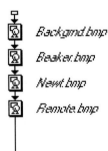

3] Run the piece.

Authorware displays the Backgrnd.bmp artwork and the objects contained in the Beaker.bmp, Newt.bmp, and Remote.bmp display icons.

Imported graphics first appear in the center of the Presentation window or at a point you click in the Presentation window. For that reason you won't see all the objects when you first run the piece; they are stacked on top of one another. Because the Remote.bmp display icon is the last icon on the flowline, it's displayed last and appears in front of the other two images. You need to drag the three objects to their proper locations.

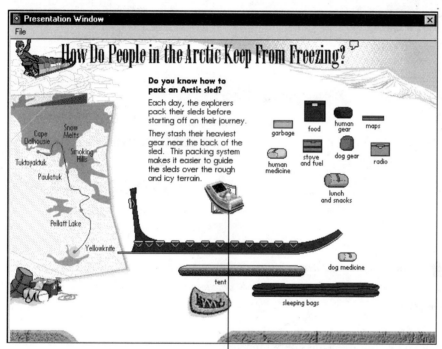

OBJECTS ARE STACKED IN
THE MIDDLE OF THE SCREEN

4] Place each of the objects in approximately the positions shown in the following illustration.

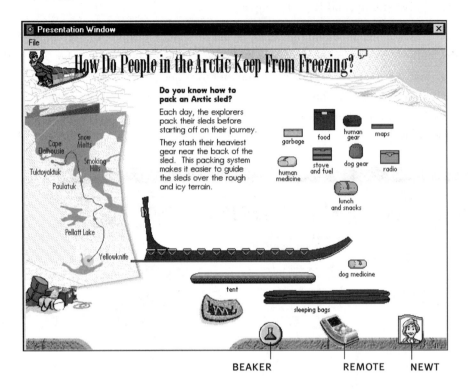

tip *When you author a piece, you can move any object on the screen just by dragging it. Users of the final application, however, won't be able to move the objects (unless you make them movable).*

Now that you've put the icons containing your objects on the flowline, you're ready to create an interaction in which you use them as hot objects.

5] In the Design window, drag an interaction icon to the flowline below the display icons. Name it *Hot Object*.

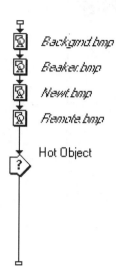

You don't need to open the Interaction Icon Properties dialog box for this icon because you'll use all the default settings. Unlike the interactions you built in previous lessons, there will be no pause and no Continue button when the user exits this interaction.

Next you will attach icons to this interaction to provide a response when the user clicks one of the objects. You'll use map icons because the response will include both sound and display icons.

6] Drag a map icon to the right of the interaction icon, select Hot Object as the response type, and name the icon *Science Try It*.

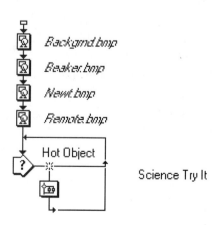

7] Open the Response Properties dialog box for this hot object response type.

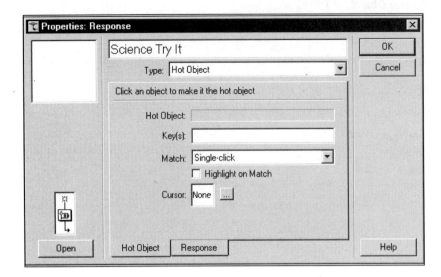

Hot objects have a lot in common with hot spots. You can select Single-click, Double-click, or use Cursor on Object to trigger a response. You can also display a custom cursor over the object and highlight the object when the user selects it. In addition, you can assign a keyboard equivalent as an alternative to using the cursor to select the object.

In this case, you'll change one of the options.

8] Select the hand-shaped custom cursor and then close the Response Properties dialog box.

To select the custom cursor, open the Cursors dialog box by clicking the Cursor button on the Hot Object tab. Then choose the hand-shaped cursor at the bottom of the list and click OK to close the Cursors dialog box.

9] Restart the piece.

When the flow reaches the interaction icon, Authorware stops and opens the Response Properties dialog box for the Science Try It map icon. On the Hot Object tab, the dialog box prompts you to click an object.

PROMPT TO SELECT THE HOT OBJECT

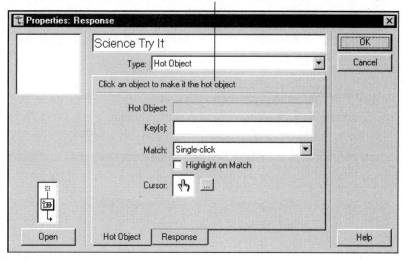

10] In the Presentation window, click the image of the beaker.

You might have to move the dialog box off to the side to see the beaker graphic on the screen.

After you click the object, the object's image appears in the window at the upper left of the dialog box, and the name of the selected object is listed as the hot object.

HOT OBJECT IMAGE   HOT OBJECT ICON TITLE

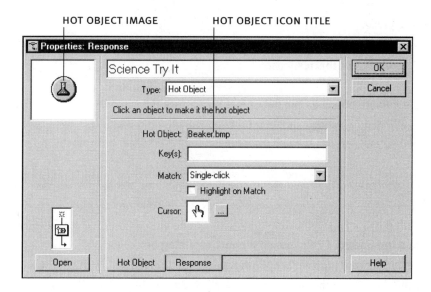

When you create hot object interactions, you can have only one hot object per display icon—that is, all the objects in a display icon are treated as one hot object. If you need to create two hot objects from an image, break the image into two images using a graphics program and then import each image into its own display icon.

11] Click OK to close the Response Properties dialog box.

You've set up the first hot object. Now you'll set up the other two.

12] Attach two more map icons to the interaction and name them *Gadget TV* and *Newt*.

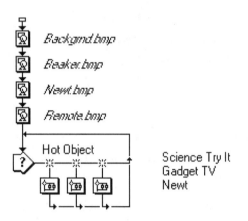

13] Restart the piece.

Authorware opens the Gadget TV Response Properties dialog box and prompts you to select the hot object for this response icon.

14] Select the Remote object as the hot object for Gadget TV.

Notice that the dialog box shows the settings from the previous response icon, which are also correct for this one.

If you're not sure which object goes with which response icon, you can preview the images on the flowline by right-clicking their display icons before you restart the piece.

15] Click OK in the Gadget TV Response Properties dialog box.

As soon as you close the Response Properties dialog box for Gadget TV, Authorware moves along the flowline to the next response icon, Newt, and opens its Response Properties dialog box.

16] Select the image of the boy as the Newt hot object and then click OK.

Newt is the star of *Newton's Apple.*

Now you've set up the paths for each hot object. It's time to add the content that will appear when users click each object.

17] Save your work.

ADDING CONTENT FOR EACH HOT OBJECT

In this task you'll use more media from the library to build an abbreviated version of this section of *What's the Secret?*

1] In the Design window, double-click the Science Try It map icon to open it.

Move the window to the lower part of your screen so you can still see the main flowline as you work in this window.

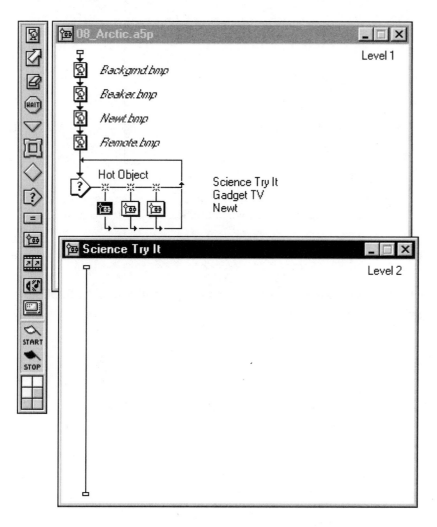

2] Drag the Science.bmp display icon from the library onto the flowline of the Science Try It window.

Science.bmp is an image containing text and graphics that will overlay the screen.

3] Drag the Science.wav sound icon from the library onto the flowline in the Science Try It window, below the Science.bmp display icon.

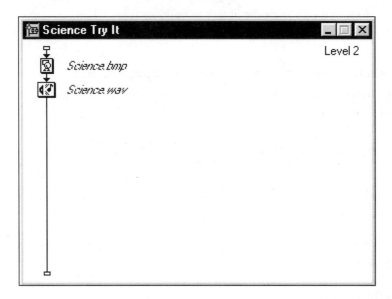

Science.wav is a sound effect that will play when the Science Try It image appears.

4] Close the Science Try It window and then open the Gadget TV window.

5] Drag the Gadgettv.bmp and Gadgettv.wav icons from the library to the flowline of the Gadget TV window.

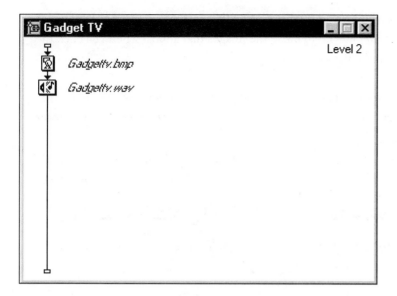

6] Close the Gadget TV window.

7] Open the Newt window and drag the Newtinfo.bmp and Newtinfo.wav. icons from the library to the flowline in the Newt window.

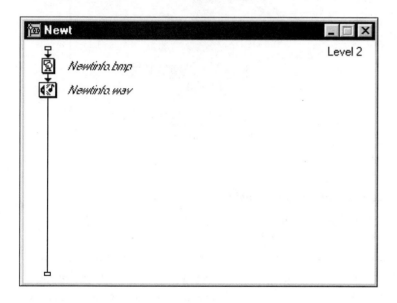

8] Close the Newt window and run the piece. Click each of the three objects.

It works! However, you'll need to move the images that appear when you click the hot objects higher in the Presentation window.

9] Each time you click one of the three hot objects, pause the piece and move the image that appears higher in the Presentation window. Then proceed, click another object, and pause again to adjust the image.

The only image whose placement is critical is Gadget TV. When you pause and then drag it, align the image so it looks as if it's being projected from the Remote image.

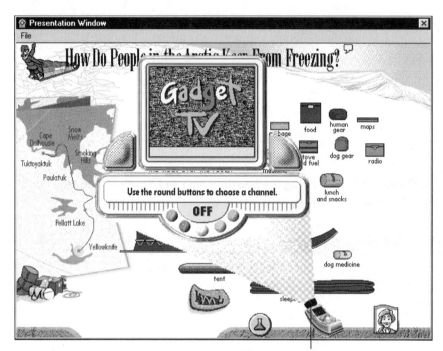

ALIGN THE GADGET TV IMAGE WITH THE REMOTE IMAGE

10] Restart the piece again and click each object.

You've built a simple hot object interaction. When you click any of the three objects, the flow goes to the map icon associated with that object, displaying a graphic and playing a sound. Because each response icon is set to Try Again branching, you can continue choosing any of the three objects as long as you want—you never exit the interaction. The default Erase setting of After Next Entry causes the graphic in each response icon to be erased when you click another object.

11] Save your work.

188

WHAT YOU HAVE LEARNED

In this lesson you have:

- Used external media and the External Media Browser, the main tool for organizing external media [*page* **168**]
- Created a library and imported external graphics and sounds into it [*page* **169**]
- Applied Matted mode to several graphics [*page* **175**]
- Created a hot object interaction using three display icons as the hot objects [*page* **177**]
- Created branching to a graphic and sound for each hot object [*page* **185**]

Target area interactions provide some of the most compelling interactivity you can create with Authorware. The **target area** response type lets you set up interactions in which users drag objects to a target you define. You can have users drag countries to their proper locations on a map or assemble a machine by dragging its parts to fit together. You can even have users determine the order of sections in the piece itself by dragging objects that represent each section into the order they choose.

LESSON 9

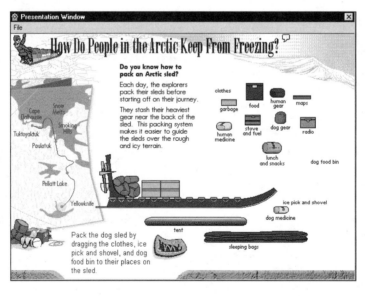

What's the Secret? *challenges users to pack a dog sled by dragging the items needed for an Arctic journey to the sled. In this lesson you'll build a portion of this game using a target area interaction. By setting up objects that users drag to locations you specify, you can build all kinds of interactive games and learning experiences.*

In this lesson you'll create a target area interaction in which users drag three items to their places on a dog sled. It's an abbreviated version of a game in *What's the Secret?* If you would like to see the final result of this lesson, open the Final Files folder and play 09_Final.a5p.

WHAT YOU WILL LEARN

In this lesson you will:

• Practice storing content temporarily off the flowline

• Create an interaction in which users drag objects to locations you define

• Use sounds to provide feedback when each object in an interaction reaches its target location

• Enhance an interaction by returning each object to its starting location if users fail to reach the target location

• Prevent users from accidentally dragging objects off the screen

APPROXIMATE TIME

It should take about 1 hour to complete this lesson.

LESSON FILES

Media Files:

Your Files\Arctic Project\Sleditem.a5l

Beginning File:

Beginning Files\09_Begin.a5p

Completed Projects:

Final Files\09_Final.a5p

STORING CONTENT OFF THE FLOWLINE

Because you won't need the content from Lesson 8 for this lesson, you'll create a temporary storage area with a decision icon to hold the icons from that lesson off the main flowline. The only icon you will exclude from this group is Backgrnd.bmp, the background art, which you will continue to use in this lesson.

1] Open 09_Begin.a5p in the Beginning Files folder and save it as *09_Arctic.a5p* in the Arctic Project folder.

Alternatively, you can use the file you worked on in the previous lesson and save it as *09_Arctic.a5p*.

2] In the Design window, marquee select all the icons from the previous lesson except Backgrnd.bmp.

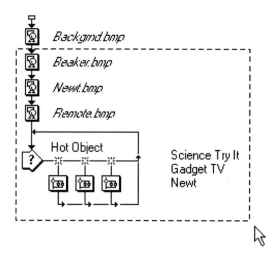

3] Group the icons into a new map icon and name it *Hot Objects*.

To group the icons, choose Modify > Group.

192

4] Drag a decision icon below the map icon and name it *Temp. Storage*.

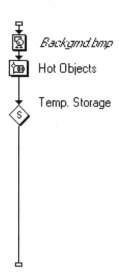

You'll be using this decision icon to temporarily hold the Hot Objects content while you work on this lesson.

5] Double-click the decision icon to open the Decision Icon Properties dialog box. Select To Calculated Path from the Branch menu.

6] Type *0* in the text entry field below the Branch box. Then click OK.

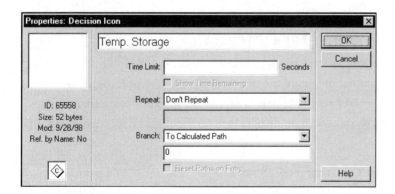

Specifying 0 as the path tells Authorware to bypass any content you attach to this decision icon.

7] Move the Hot Objects map icon to the right of the Temp. Storage decision icon.

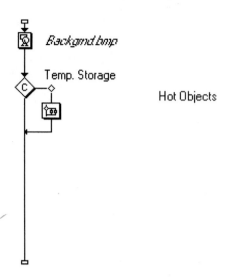

The Hot Objects map icon becomes a decision path for the Temp. Storage decision icon.

8] Restart the piece.

Now you see only the background art. With the content from the previous lesson stored off the flowline, you're ready to start the project for this lesson.

9] Save your work.

PREPARING FOR A TARGET AREA INTERACTION

In the previous lesson you started developing a hot object interaction by creating objects in display icons that preceded the interaction icon. The procedure for working with the target area response type is somewhat similar. Before creating the interaction, you must place a separate display icon on the flowline for each item that you want users to drag.

In this task you'll open a library of media for this lesson. Then you'll drag three display icons from the library onto the flowline to prepare for the target area interaction. These display icons contain images of an ice pick and a shovel, clothes, and a dog food bin. Users will be asked to drag these items when they pack the dog sled.

1] Open the Sleditem.a5l library.

To do this, choose File > Open > Library. In the Open Library dialog box, select Sleditem.a5l in the Arctic Project folder and then click Open.

READ-WRITE STATUS

This is the second library you're using with this piece; you used another library in Lesson 8. Using multiple libraries is common, and Authorware allows up to 17 libraries to be linked to one piece.

tip *Several authors can share a library that's stored on a network. To allow this, Authorware requires you to make the library read-only by clicking the Read/Write Status button at the upper left. When a library is read-only, the status button has a diagonal line through it. That way, one author won't unintentionally change content that other authors are using.*

2] Drag the Eager Dogs sound icon from the Sleditem library to the flowline below the Temp. Storage decision icon.

This is the sound of dogs getting ready to start an Arctic journey. It will play as users enter the interaction.

3] Drag the Dog Food Bin display icon from the Sleditem library to the bottom of the flowline.

This is one of three objects that users will place on the dog sled.

4] Drag the Ice Pick and Shovel and Clothes display icons to the bottom of the flowline.

The three display icons contain the three items that users will be asked to drag to the dog sled.

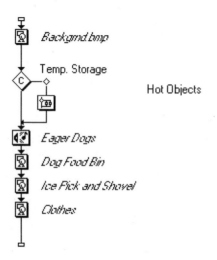

Hot Objects

5] Restart the piece.

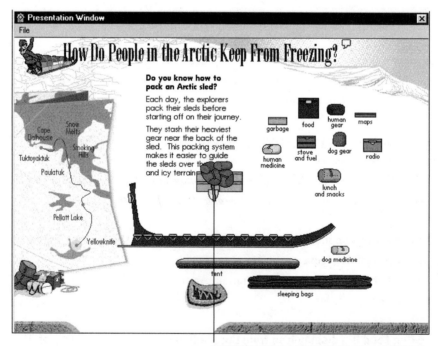

THREE OBJECTS ON TOP OF ONE ANOTHER

As Authorware moves down the flowline, the Eager Dogs sound icon plays as the three objects appear in the center of the screen.

When you import a graphic into Authorware, the image first appears centered in the Presentation window. You need to move the objects to their starting positions among the other sled items on the right side of the screen.

6] Pause the piece. Then drag each object to the right side of the screen among the other sled items. Leave space below each object for a line of text that will describe it.
When you select an object, gray handles appear around it.

Precise positioning is not important. Just make sure there's room for text below each object.

7] Save your work.

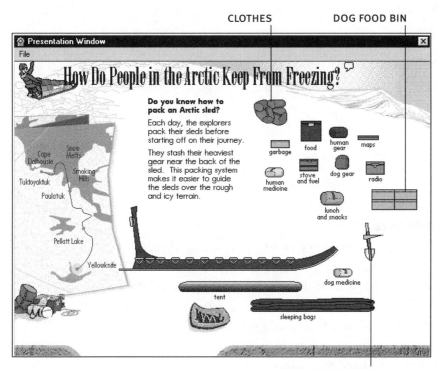

CLOTHES   DOG FOOD BIN

ICE PICK AND SHOVEL

CREATING TEXT FOR THE INTERACTION

In this task you'll set up an interaction icon with text that prompts users to drag the items and provides labels for each item.

1] Drag an interaction icon to the flowline below the three display icons. Name it *Target Area*.

2] Restart the piece.

The three objects should now appear where you placed them on the screen.

3] In the Design window, Shift-double-click the Target Area interaction icon.

The Presentation window opens, and the toolbox for the Target Area icon appears. Now you'll create text that labels each of the three objects.

4] Select the Text tool and then select Arial as the font.

To do this, click the Text tool in the toolbox and then choose Text > Font > Arial.

198

Next you'll select a point size.

5] Choose Text › Size › Other.

You need to specify a 7-point size, which is smaller than the smallest size on the Size menu.

6] In the Font Size dialog box, highlight the number displayed for Font Size. Type 7 and click OK.

You're going to create text to label each of the three sled items.

7] Open the Colors Inspector and make sure black is selected as the Pen color.

To do this, choose Window > Inspectors > Colors. In the Colors Inspector, click the Pen color chip. If the black square at the upper left is not selected, click it.

SELECT THIS COLOR

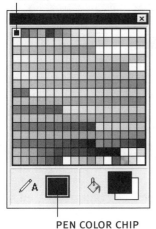

PEN COLOR CHIP

8] Open the Modes Inspector and select Transparent mode.

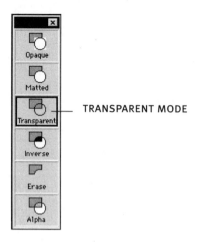

TRANSPARENT MODE

You are using Transparent mode so that if the text overlaps any background art, the background will show through.

9] Click any clear area of the window and then type this text: *clothes*

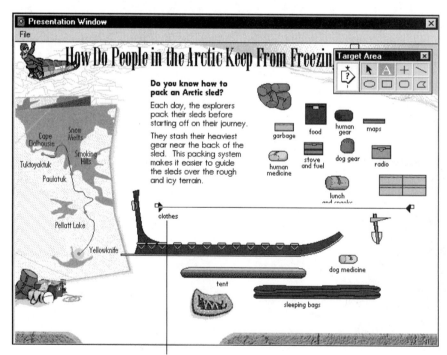

CREATE THIS TEXT

It doesn't matter where you create the text. You'll move it in a moment.

You need to create three separate text objects so you can label each display object you added to the piece.

10] Click the Pointer tool, click the Text tool again, and then click another location on the screen to create this text: _ice pick and shovel_

You need to select the Pointer tool before clicking the Text tool so you can click elsewhere and create a separate text object.

11] Click the Pointer tool again, and then click the Text tool. Then click somewhere else on the screen. Create this text: _dog food bin_

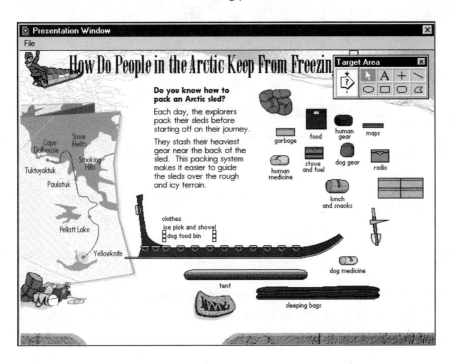

You've created three text objects. Now you need to move them to their correct positions.

12] Click the Pointer tool and then drag to position each text object just below the item it describes.

Don't worry about being precise. Your screen should look similar to the following illustration.

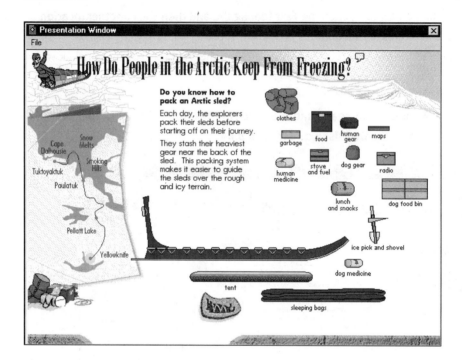

Next you'll create text that prompts users to pack the sled.

13] Add the following text in the same font as before but using 10-point type:
Pack the dog sled by dragging the clothes, ice pick and shovel, and dog food bin to their places on the sled.

14] Move the instruction text approximately to the location shown here.

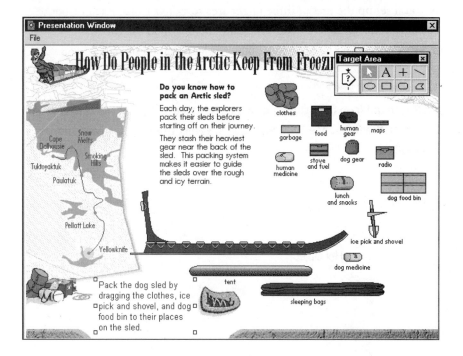

The text should stand out more. To accomplish that, you'll make it a bright blue.

15] Use the Colors Inspector to select a bright blue for the text.

In the Colors Inspector, click the Pen color chip and then click a bright blue.

You've set up the interaction artwork. Now you're ready to make each of the three items an object that users can drag.

16] Save your work.

CREATING A TARGET AREA RESPONSE

In this task you'll set up the first of three target area response icons. Each response icon will be a different sound icon. You will make the dog food bin the first target object and then indicate the target area by placing the dog food bin where you want users to drag it.

1] Drag the Bin sound icon from the Sleditem library to the right of the Target Area interaction icon. In the Response Type dialog box, select the Target Area response type and click OK.

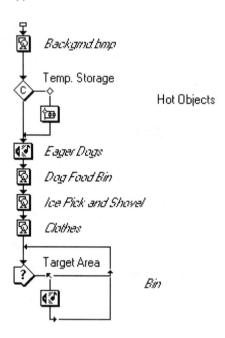

2] Restart the piece.

When the flow of activity reaches the Bin response icon, the Response Properties dialog box opens for this response. On the Target Area tab, the dialog box prompts you to click the object you want to associate with Bin. Authorware is prompting you to create a target object for dragging in the same way it prompted you to select a hot object in the previous lesson.

204

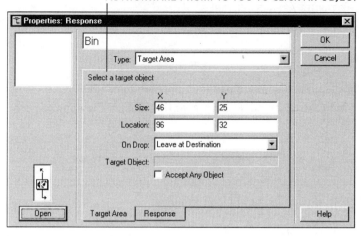

3] Click the dog food bin in the Presentation window.

You might need to move the dialog box off to the side to get a clear view of the Presentation window. When you click the dog food bin, the message in the dialog box changes, and the Bin target area jumps to the object you clicked so that it's centered over the object. Notice that a target area looks somewhat like a hot spot. The X in the middle indicates its center point.

 CENTER OF TARGET AREA

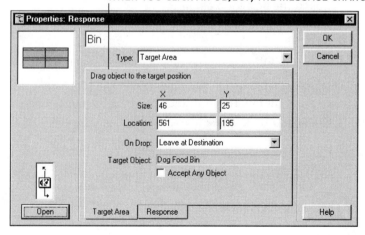

THE TARGET AREA IS CENTERED
OVER THE OBJECT YOU CLICKED

4] Drag the dog food bin to the dog sled. Place it near the back, in the approximate position shown here.

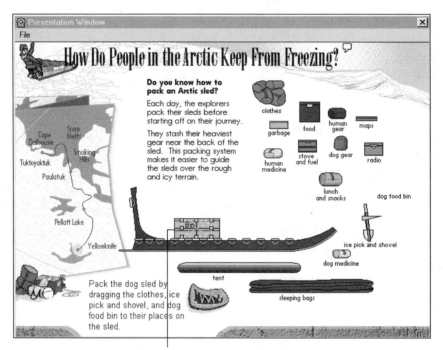

DRAG THE DOG FOOD BIN HERE

Don't drag the target area itself. Carefully select a portion of the dog food bin that's not within the target area and then drag it where you want it; the target area will follow when you release the mouse button. If you accidentally drag the target area, choose Edit > Undo (Ctrl+Z) to put it back where it was.

The target area defines the location that will be considered a match when the user drags the object. If the user drags the object so that its center is within the target area, Authorware will consider it to have matched the target area and will branch to the Bin response icon.

In the next step you'll set an option that will pull the object's center to the center of the target area when the user releases the mouse button.

5] In the Response Properties dialog box, open the On Drop menu on the Target Area tab. Select Snap to Center.

This setting will move the dog food bin to the exact center of the target area when the user gets the center of the object within the target area and releases the mouse button.

If you selected Leave at Destination, the object would stay wherever it was dragged within the target area.

If you selected Put Back, the object would return to its original location on the screen if it was dragged within the target area.

You'll accept the other default settings.

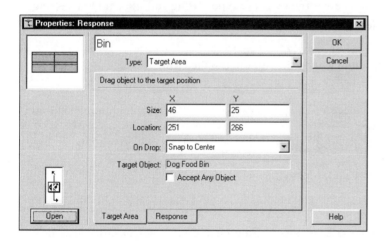

6] Click OK to close the dialog box.

7] Restart the piece and drag the dog food bin to the place you selected.

When you release the mouse button, you should hear the clank of the bin hitting the sled.

When the flow reaches the Target Area interaction icon, Authorware waits for the user to drag an object to a target area. When you move the object more than halfway into the Bin target area, Authorware considers your response a match and directs the flow to the Bin response icon. The result is that you hear the sound contained in the Bin sound icon.

8] Save your work.

CREATING ADDITIONAL TARGET AREA RESPONSES

In this task you will attach two more sound icons as the response icons for this interaction. Then you'll select the clothes and the ice pick and shovel as movable objects and define the target area for each.

1] Drag the Pick sound icon from the library to the right of the Bin icon.

The Pick response icon receives the response type setting and the On Drop setting of the Bin icon to its left, so you don't need to change its settings.

2] Drag the Clothing sound icon to the right of the Pick icon.

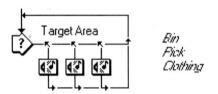

Now you're ready to associate an object with each of these two icons. Because the two response icons are not yet associated with objects, Authorware will open the Response Properties dialog box for each one when the flow reaches the interaction.

208

3] Restart the piece. When the Response Properties dialog box for the Pick icon opens, click the ice pick and shovel in the Presentation window.

The Pick target area is centered on the object you click.

ice pick and shovel

4] Drag the ice pick and shovel to a position on the back of the sled.

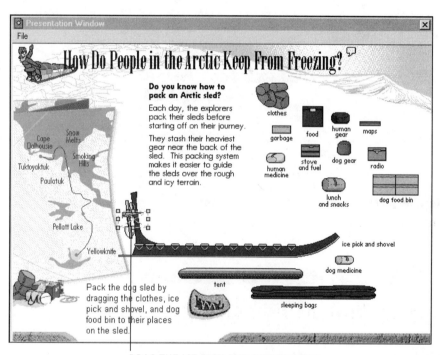

DRAG THE ICE PICK AND SHOVEL HERE

When you release the mouse button, the target area moves to the position you chose.

5] Click OK to close the dialog box.

The flow of activity moves along the interaction flowline to the next response icon that has no object associated with it. The Response Properties dialog box for the Clothing icon opens.

6] In the Presentation window, click the Clothes object to associate it with this response icon. Drag the clothes to a position near the back of the sled. Then click OK to close the dialog box.

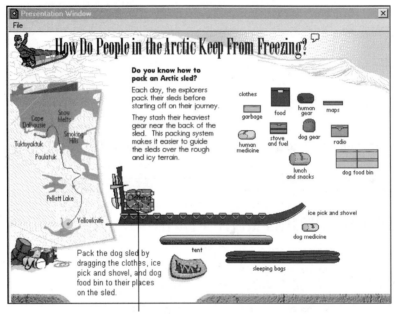

DRAG THE CLOTHES HERE

7] Restart the piece and drag each item to its spot.

You should hear the sound associated with each item as you drag it to its target area and release the mouse button.

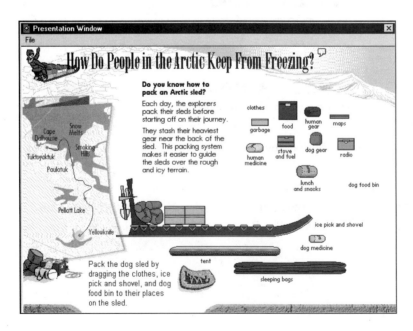

The interaction works but it's not yet complete, as you'll see in the next step.

8] Restart the piece again. This time drag one of the objects toward—but not all the way to—its target area and then release the mouse button.

The object stays where you leave it. You haven't set up Authorware to handle this situation.

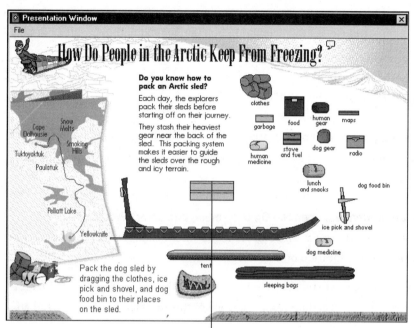

THE OBJECT STAYS WHERE YOU LEAVE IT

To complete this target area interaction, Authorware needs to move the object back to its starting point if the user fails to reach the target. In the next task, you'll take care of this.

ADDING A CATCH-ALL TARGET AREA

In previous lessons you created catch-all responses for hot spots, hot objects, and text entry interactions. By now you probably understand the principle: You place a response icon at the far right of the interaction flowline to respond to all the user input that doesn't match the preceding responses.

In this task you'll create a catch-all target area that will return an object to its starting position if the user leaves it outside its target area.

1] Drag a map icon to the right of the Clothing response icon. Name it *Put Back*.

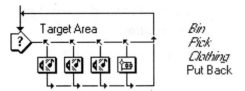

This map icon will contain no content of its own. Its purpose is simply to "catch" all the user input other than that which matches the target areas and then move whichever of the three objects is selected back to its starting position.

2] Open the Response Properties dialog box for the Put Back icon.

You need to change two settings to make this new target area return objects to their original positions.

3] On the Target Area tab, open the On Drop menu and select Put Back.

This setting does what it says: An object dragged into this target area will be returned to its starting location on the screen.

Before moving to the next step, notice the prompt in this dialog box, "Select target object." For the three preceding response icons in this interaction, you selected an object—but not this time.

4] Select Accept Any Object.

Rather than associating one object with this target area, you're associating all three of the objects with this interaction. When you select this check box, the phrase "Select target object" disappears.

212

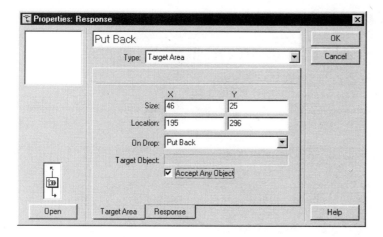

5] Click OK.

6] In the Presentation window, find the Put Back target area. Resize it to include the entire screen.

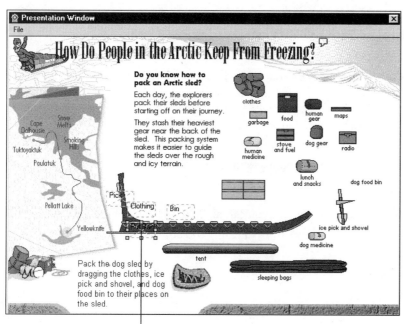

PUT BACK TARGET AREA BEFORE RESIZING

213

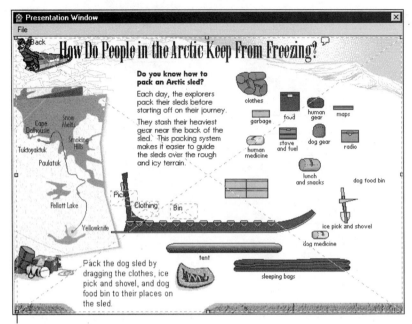

PUT BACK TARGET AREA AFTER RESIZING TO COVER THE ENTIRE SCREEN

7] Restart the piece. Drag an object halfway to its target area.

When you release the mouse, the object floats back to its starting point because of the Put Back target area you just created.

If you drag an object within its target area, the response for that area is matched first because the flow of the interaction reaches the three specific target areas before it reaches the Put Back target area. If you drag an object anywhere else on the screen, however, the position at which you leave the object falls within the Put Back target area, and Authorware selects the Put Back response.

There's still one more enhancement you can make to this target area interaction. In the next task you'll prevent users from dragging the objects off the screen.

8] Save your work.

LIMITING THE DRAG AREA

You may have noticed one problem with this interaction: Users can drag the objects off the screen entirely and so lose them from the game.

In this task you'll limit the area to which the three objects can be dragged.

1] In the Design window, select the Dog Food Bin display icon and open its Display Icon Properties dialog box.

To open the dialog box, choose Modify > Icon > Properties.

2] Click the Layout tab.

The settings in this section of the dialog box give you a wide range of control over an object's position and movement in the Presentation window.

3] Open the Movable menu and select On Screen.

This setting limits the range of motion to the area within the Presentation window.

4] Click OK.

5] Select the Ice Pick and Shovel display icon. Open its Display Icon Properties dialog box. On the Layout tab, select On Screen from the Movable menu. Then click OK.

6] Repeat the same procedure as in step 5 for the Clothes display icon.

7] Restart the piece and try dragging the three objects off the screen.

Authorware won't let you do it. You've now eliminated the possibility of users accidentally dragging one of the objects off the screen.

8] Save your work.

In this lesson you've created an interaction in which users drag objects to target areas on the screen. When a user moves an object into a target area you've defined, the associated response icon is matched and the flow moves to that icon. In this lesson, the flow moved to a different sound icon for each target area, playing a sound associated with each item being packed on a dog sled.

ON YOUR OWN

Experiment with changing the dimensions of the target areas in this lesson. By making a target area larger, you make it easier for users to succeed. By making a target area smaller, you force users to be more precise. You need to keep the center of the target area where you want the center of the object to be, however. If you enlarge a target area by dragging one edge outward, you should click the target object while the Response Properties dialog box for the target area is open. This will readjust the target area to the position of the object. This is especially important when using irregularly shaped objects.

WHAT YOU HAVE LEARNED

In this lesson you have:

- Used a decision icon and a calculated path of 0 to hold content off the flowline [*page* **192**]

- Used a target area interaction to set up objects that users drag to locations you designate [*page* **194**]

- Used sound icons to play sound as feedback when each object reaches its target area [*page* **204**]

- Used a catch-all target area to put back each object when users fail to reach the target [*page* **211**]

- Used the Movable setting in the Response Properties dialog box to prevent users from dragging objects off the screen [*page* **215**]

pull-down menus

perpetual

LESSON 10

Pull-down menus are useful when you want to offer users options or additional information without taking up space on the screen. Pull-down menus are especially useful when they provide their options or information throughout an entire section or entire piece rather than just during one section. For this reason, pull-down menus in Authorware are usually created as perpetual interactions. A **perpetual** interaction is activated by Authorware and then bypassed on the flowline. It remains active and available to users from anywhere on the flowline.

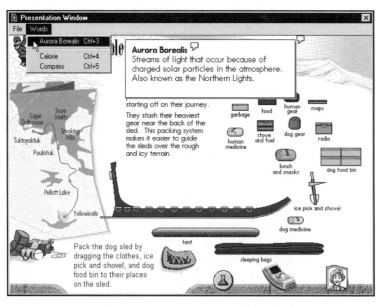

In **What's the Secret?** *users have access to definitions for Arctic terms on a pull-down menu while they're enjoying other interactive activities in the game. In this lesson you'll build an abbreviated version of this pull-down menu.*

In this lesson you continue working on the Arctic project. The pull-down menu you create will provide definitions for three Arctic-related terms. After completing the pull-down menu, you'll make it perpetual. Then users will have access to the definitions while they're in the target area interaction you created in the previous lesson. If you would like to see the final result of this lesson, open the Final Files folder and play 10_Final.a5p.

WHAT YOU WILL LEARN

In this lesson you will:

- Practice storing content temporarily off the flowline
- Create a pull-down menu that displays a graphic and plays a sound for each menu item
- Enhance a menu by adding a separator bar between menu items and optional keys users can press to select items
- Make a pull-down menu accessible to users throughout a piece

APPROXIMATE TIME

It should take about 1 hour to complete this lesson.

LESSON FILES

Media Files:
Your Files\Arctic Project\Words.a5l

Beginning File:
Beginning Files\10_Begin.a5p

Completed Project:
Final Files\10_Final.a5p

MOVING CONTENT OFF THE FLOWLINE

In this task you'll prepare for the main work of this lesson by moving your work from Lesson 9 to the temporary storage area you created in that lesson.

1] Open 10_Begin.a5p in the Beginning Files folder and save it as *10_Arctic.a5p* in the Arctic Project folder.

Alternatively, you can use the file you worked on in the previous lesson and save it as *10_Arctic.a5p*.

2] In the Design window, marquee select the icons used for the target area interaction. Include the sound icon and three display icons preceding the interaction icon on the flowline.

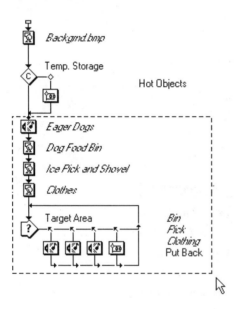

3] Group the icons into a map icon and name it *Target Area*.

To group the icons, choose Modify > Group.

4] Drag the Target Area map icon to the right of the Hot Objects map icon.

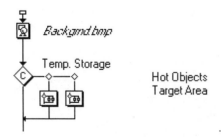

You now have the work from two lessons stored off the main flowline. You're ready to start building a pull-down menu.

SETTING UP A PULL-DOWN MENU

In this task you'll open a library containing graphics and sound media. The media will be used to create a pull-down menu that presents definitions of Arctic-related terms accompanied by the pronunciation of each term. Then you'll set up an interaction icon and the first response icon in the pull-down menu interaction.

1] Open the Words.a5l library.

To do this, choose File > Open > Library. Locate the Words.a5l file in the Arctic Project folder and click Open.

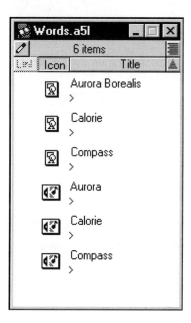

This library contains graphics and sounds that will appear when users select a term from the pull-down menu you'll create. Each graphic contains the definition of a term. Each sound icon contains the recording of a voice pronouncing one of the terms. When a definition appears on the screen, the voice will pronounce the word.

2] Drag an interaction icon to the flowline and name it *Words*.

The title you choose for this interaction icon is very important. This title will become the title of the menu that appears at the top of the screen.

3] Drag a map icon to the right of the Words interaction icon. In the Response Type dialog box, select Pull-Down Menu as the response type and click OK. Name this icon *Aurora Borealis*.

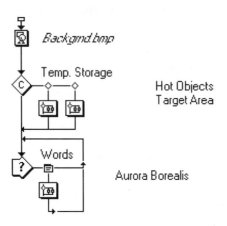

The title of the response icon for a pull-down menu becomes the title of the menu item. In this case, the first definition you will provide on the menu will be for *Aurora Borealis*.

4] Double-click the response type symbol to open the Response Properties dialog box for Aurora Borealis.

You're going to change the Erase setting.

5] On the Response tab, open the Erase menu.

You've used After Next Entry as the Erase setting for most of the interactions you've created so far in this book. The After Next Entry setting erases the contents of the response icon only when the user makes a different selection. Users generally want to use a pull-down menu in a different way, however. Usually, they want to view the contents of a pull-down menu and then resume viewing what they originally were watching on the screen instead of making another selection from the same menu. To enable this, you need a different Erase setting.

6] Select Before Next Entry from the Erase menu.

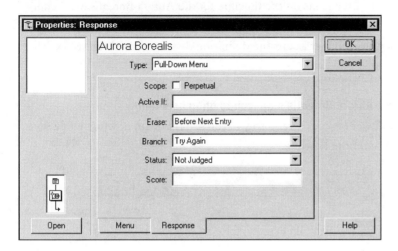

The Before Next Entry setting displays the contents of the response icon and then erases the contents before the user makes another choice. This setting means that any content will be displayed and then erased as the flow loops around within the interaction. This action could cause the definition to flash on and off very quickly, so you don't have a chance to read it. To prevent that, you'll add a wait icon to the flowline in the next task.

7] Click OK to close the dialog box.

You've set up a response icon for the first entry on your pull-down menu, Aurora Borealis. Next you'll create the content that appears when a user selects this menu item.

8] Choose File › Save All to save the piece and library.

ADDING CONTENT FOR A MENU ITEM

In this task you'll put three icons on the flowline for the Aurora Borealis map icon: a display icon containing the definition, a sound icon containing the pronunciation of the term, and a wait icon that keeps the definition displayed until the user clicks the screen.

1] Double-click the Aurora Borealis map icon to open its window.

Move the window lower on your screen so you can see the main flowline while you work on this segment of the flowline.

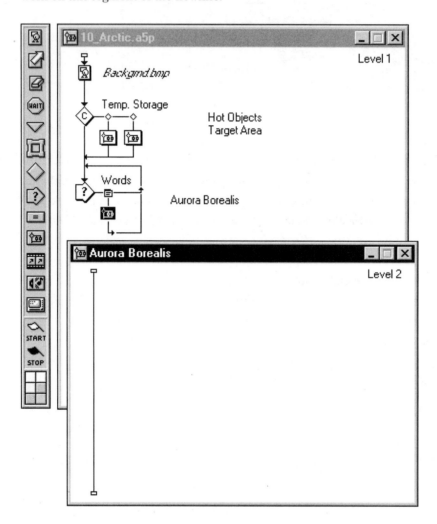

2] Drag the Aurora Borealis display icon from the library to the flowline in the Aurora Borealis window.

This icon contains text that defines Aurora Borealis.

3] Drag the Aurora sound icon to the flowline below the display icon.

This sound icon contains the sound of a voice pronouncing the term. The Concurrency setting is Wait Until Done, which will play the sound completely before the flow continues down the flowline.

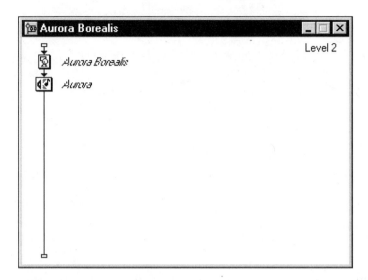

Now you'll try out what you've done so far.

4] Restart the piece. Then select Aurora Borealis from the Words pull-down menu.

When you select Aurora Borealis on the menu, Authorware branches to the Aurora Borealis response icon; the Aurora Borealis display icon displays the definition and the Aurora sound icon—set to Wait Until Done—plays the sound of a voice pronouncing the word. As soon as the sound completes, the text is erased and the flow loops back to the top of the Words interaction icon. The Erase setting you selected for this response icon—Before Next Entry—causes the text to be erased as soon as the two media elements have been presented.

If the sound icon was the only media element, this setup would work. However, you need to keep the text on the screen until the user is done reading it. You'll use a wait icon to do that.

5] In the Design window, drag a wait icon from the icon palette to the flowline below Aurora. Name it *Wait for Click*.

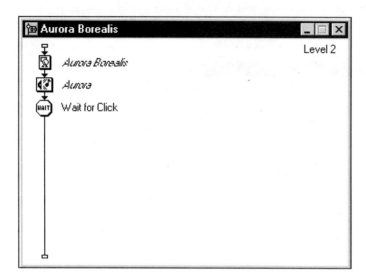

This wait icon will work in conjunction with the Erase setting for this response icon. The Before Next Entry setting by itself removes the definition as soon as the sound finishes. The wait icon will keep the text on the screen until the user is ready to erase it.

6] Double-click the wait icon to open the Wait Icon Properties dialog box.

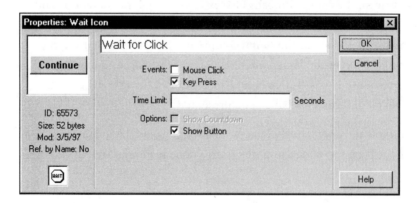

Previously you used the wait icon to pause the piece for a duration you set and to stop the flow until the user clicked a Continue button. In this case, you want to stop the flow but not display a Continue button. You'll allow the user to move on by clicking anywhere on the screen or by pressing any key on the keyboard.

7] Select the Mouse Click box.

Now the user will be able to click anywhere on the screen to continue the flow of the piece; the definition will be erased and the flow will loop around to wait for another selection from the user. Keep the Key Press option checked as well so that the user can also press any key to continue.

8] Click the Show Button box to remove the checkmark and prevent the Continue button from being displayed.

A Continue button would be intrusive and unnecessary for a pull-down menu. The user can either click the mouse or press any key to erase the definition.

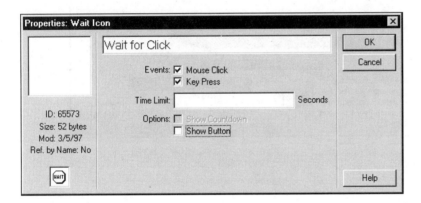

9] Click OK. Then close the Aurora Borealis map window.

In a moment you'll add two more definitions to the pull-down menu—but first, check out what you've done so far.

10] Restart the piece and open the Words pull-down menu.

The Words menu appears as the flow reaches the Words interaction icon. When you select Aurora Borealis on the menu, Authorware branches to the Aurora Borealis response icon; the text appears, the sound plays, and the wait icon stops the flow before the term is erased.

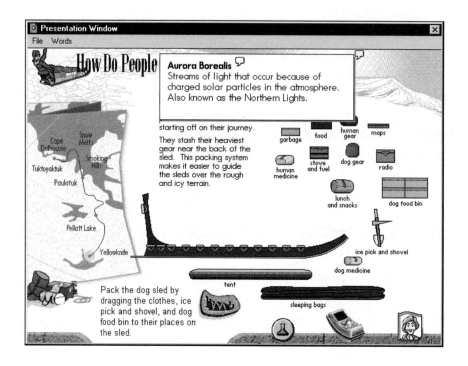

When you press a key or click anywhere on the screen, the flow moves on.

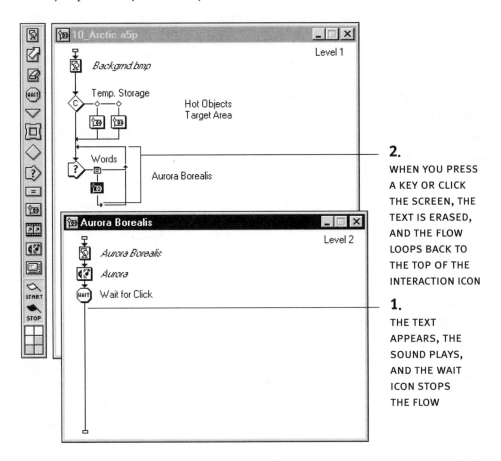

2.

WHEN YOU PRESS
A KEY OR CLICK
THE SCREEN, THE
TEXT IS ERASED,
AND THE FLOW
LOOPS BACK TO
THE TOP OF THE
INTERACTION ICON

1.

THE TEXT
APPEARS, THE
SOUND PLAYS,
AND THE WAIT
ICON STOPS
THE FLOW

11] **Save your work.**

ADDING TWO MORE MENU ITEMS

Now you'll create two more menu items—for Calorie and Compass—by adding two map icons to the pull-down menu interaction. Then you'll place a display, sound, and wait icon inside each map icon just as you did for Aurora Borealis.

1] In the Design window, drag a map icon to the right of Aurora Borealis and name it *Calorie*.

Because this map icon receives the settings of the first response icon in the interaction, you don't need to make any changes to its response properties.

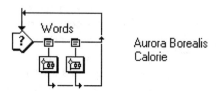

2] Open the Calorie map icon.

You'll drag three icons to the flowline in this window.

3] Drag the Calorie display icon and Calorie sound icon from the library to the Calorie flowline.

You're using the same image and sound sequence you used for the Aurora Borealis response icon.

4] Drag a wait icon from the icon palette. Name it *Wait for Click*.

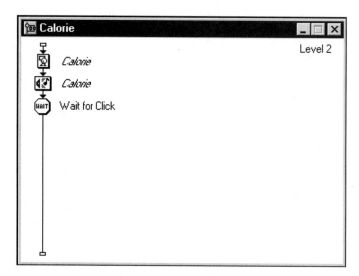

You'll need to adjust the wait icon settings so that a mouse click will move the piece past the wait icon.

5] Double-click the wait icon to open it. Then select the Mouse Click box and click the Show Button box to remove the checkmark.

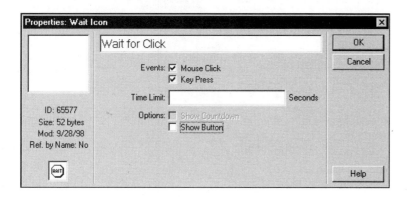

tip *An alternative to reentering the settings that you used in the wait icon for Aurora Borealis is simply to copy that wait icon and paste it into the Calorie window. You can then also paste it into the Compass window.*

6] Click OK. Then close the Calorie window.
Now you're ready to set up the Compass icon in the same way you set up Aurora Borealis and Calorie.

7] Drag a map icon to the right of the Calorie icon. Name it *Compass*.

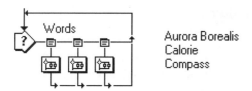

8] Open the Compass window. Drag the Compass display icon and Compass sound icon from the library to the Compass window.

9] Drag a wait icon to the Compass flowline below the sound icon and name it
Wait for Click.

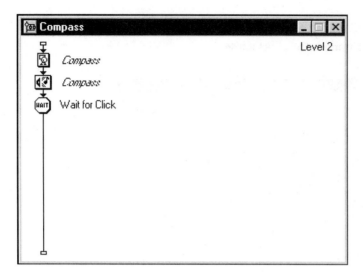

You'll set the same options as you used for the previous two definitions.

10] Open the Wait Icon Properties dialog box. Click the Show Button box to remove the check mark. Select the Mouse Click box.

Alternatively, you can copy and paste the wait icon you used for Aurora Borealis and Calorie.

11] Click OK and then close the Compass window. Restart the piece and select the menu items.

Each time you select an item on the pull-down menu, Authorware directs the flow to one of the three response icons. When you select Compass, for example, Authorware branches to the Compass map icon, where it displays the compass definition, plays the voice saying, "Compass," and then stops at the wait icon. When you click the screen anywhere or press any key on your keyboard, Authorware erases the definition and loops around within the interaction, waiting for your next selection.

12] Save your work.

In the next task you'll enhance the pull-down menu with a device that helps organize the menu items.

ADDING A SEPARATOR BAR

Pull-down menus often separate groups of related items with a horizontal bar. Authorware makes it easy to create these **separator bars** using a specially named response icon. In this task, you will group the list of terms alphabetically by adding a separator bar between Aurora Borealis and Calorie.

1] Drag a map icon to the interaction flowline between Aurora Borealis and Calorie.

The key to creating a separator bar is the name you give the response icon.

2] Name the icon *(-*.

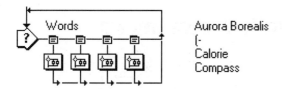

You use a left parenthesis followed by a hyphen to create a separator bar on a pull-down menu instead of a menu item that users can select.

3] Restart the piece and open your menu.

A horizontal bar appears between Aurora Borealis and Calorie.

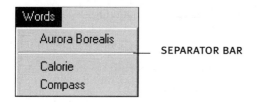

SEPARATOR BAR

There's something else you can do to make pull-down menus easier to use. In the next task you'll add **optional shortcut keys** so users can select a menu item using the keyboard.

ADDING OPTIONAL SHORTCUT KEYS

You can make a pull-down menu easier to use by adding an optional shortcut key for each menu item. Authorware will remind users of the shortcut keys by displaying them beside each menu item.

In this task you'll create an optional shortcut key for each menu item.

1] In the Design window, double-click the response type symbol for Aurora Borealis.
You'll enter the shortcut key in the Key(s) box.

2] On the Menu tab, type 3 in the Key(s) box.

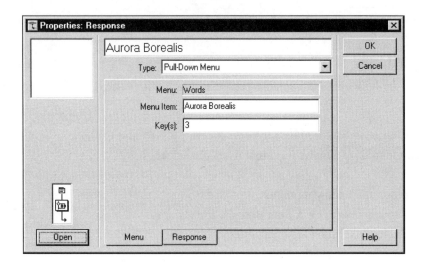

Authorware automatically creates a combination of the Ctrl key with the key you specify. In this case, the shortcut key combination will be Ctrl+3.

tip *If you want to use the Alt key with the specified key, type Alt3 in the Key(s) box.*

3] Click OK to close the dialog box. Open the Response Properties dialog box for Calorie.

4] In the Key(s) box, type 4. Then click OK.

5] Open the Response Properties dialog box for Compass. In the Key(s) box, enter 5. Then click OK.

6] Restart the piece. Open the Words menu.

The shortcut keys are listed after the menu choices.

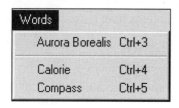

7] Close the menu, and then try a shortcut key combination.

Remember to press Control along with 3, 4, or 5. Each definition is displayed just as before. You now have two ways to choose each of your menu options.

8] Save your work.

You've completed the pull-down menu. Now you're ready to make it perpetual.

CREATING A PERPETUAL INTERACTION

Perpetual interactions are interactions that you make available throughout an entire piece or a section you designate. Perpetual interactions are commonly used to provide information or options that you want to make available continuously—such as the ability for a user to return to a main menu screen or exit a piece.

When Authorware comes to an interaction icon on the flowline, it usually waits for a user response before continuing down the flowline. Authorware treats perpetual interactions differently. When it reaches a perpetual interaction, Authorware activates the interaction and continues down the flowline. Although the flow has passed the interaction icon for the perpetual interaction, the interaction remains active on the flowline, awaiting a response from the user.

In this task you'll move the Target Area interaction from Lesson 9 back to the main flowline. Then you'll transform the pull-down menu into a perpetual interaction. When you've completed this project, users will be able to view the definitions for Arctic terms while they're packing the dog sled.

1] In the Design window, drag the Target Area map icon from the Temp. Storage area to just below the Words interaction icon.

After you move the Target Area map icon to its new location, you won't see the flowline extending from the Words interaction icon because the flow doesn't yet go past that interaction. This is because all of the response icons in the Words interaction are set to Try Again branching—there's no way to exit the interaction. When you change the Words interaction into a perpetual interaction, however, the flowline will pass through it to Target Area.

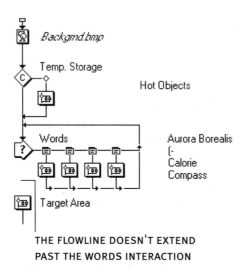

Backgrnd.bmp

Temp. Storage

Hot Objects

Words

Aurora Borealis
(-
Calorie
Compass

Target Area

THE FLOWLINE DOESN'T EXTEND
PAST THE WORDS INTERACTION

2] In the Design window, open the Response Properties dialog box for Aurora Borealis.
You'll change two settings.

3] On the Response tab, select Perpetual for the Scope option.
To make the entire pull-down menu perpetual, you have to make each item on the menu perpetual. Otherwise, rather than continuing down the flowline, the flow will stop at any nonperpetual menu items attached to the interaction icon.

You will select the same Perpetual check box for each of the other response icons in the Words interaction.

4] Open the Branch menu.
When you select Perpetual for the Scope option, an additional branching option becomes available: Return. Use the Return option when you want to go back to the place on the flowline where the user responded to the perpetual interaction. In this case, Return means that after a user views one of the definitions and clicks the screen, Authorware will return to the Target Area interaction.

236

5] Select Return from the Branch menu and click OK.

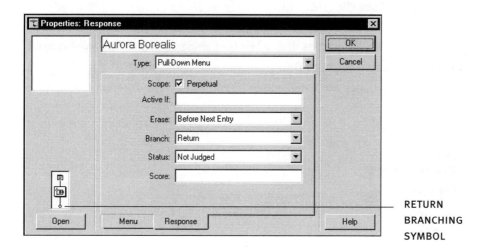

RETURN
BRANCHING
SYMBOL

Notice the symbol for Return branching on the flowline and in the Response Properties dialog box.

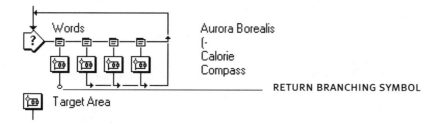

RETURN BRANCHING SYMBOL

In this task you changed the first menu item on the Words pull-down menu into a perpetual interaction. To complete the process—to make the entire menu perpetual—you must apply the same settings to each response icon in the Words interaction.

CREATING ADDITIONAL PERPETUAL RESPONSES

You'll apply the settings you used for Aurora Borealis to the other items on the pull-down menu.

1] Open the Response Properties dialog box for the (- icon. For Scope, check the Perpetual box. For Branch, select Return. Click OK.

In applying the settings to make this menu perpetual, you treat the separator bar just as you do other menu items.

237

2] Open the Response Properties dialog box for Calorie. Select Perpetual scope and Return branching. Then click OK.

3] Open the Response Properties dialog box for Compass. Select Perpetual scope and Return branching. Then click OK.

When you close the dialog box for Compass, the flowline has a different look from before.

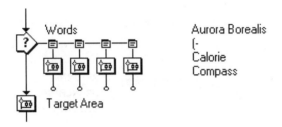

Now the flowline runs through the Words interaction icon to the Target Area interaction icon. The Words pull-down menu doesn't stop the flow like a normal interaction, yet it will be available to users after the flow passes it.

Now it's time to see how your perpetual pull-down menu works.

4] Restart the piece. Drag one object to the sled. Then open the menu to see a definition.

When you select an item on the menu, the flow jumps from the Target Area interaction to the Words interaction on the flowline. Then, as soon as you click the screen or press a key and erase a definition, Authorware jumps back to the Target Area interaction.

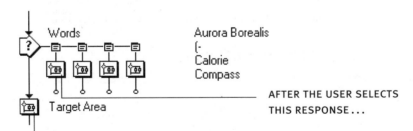

AFTER THE USER SELECTS THIS RESPONSE . . .

. . .THE FLOW OF THE PIECE RETURNS TO THE PLACE ON THE FLOWLINE WHERE THE USER ENGAGED THE PERPETUAL INTERACTION

238

5] Save your work.

In this lesson you created a pull-down menu and added a separator bar and keyboard shortcuts to make it easier to use. Then you changed the pull-down menu into a perpetual interaction so users can have access to it from anywhere in the piece. You'll find many uses for perpetual pull-down menus and other types of perpetual interactions in your projects.

ON YOUR OWN

Change the Hot Objects interaction into a perpetual interaction. Start by dragging the Hot Objects map icon back to the main flowline above the Words interaction. Then apply the same two settings for each of the three hot objects as you used for each pull-down menu item: Perpetual scope and Return branching. Optionally, delete the now-unused Temp. Storage decision icon.

To complete the process of making the three hot objects perpetual, two more steps are needed so the image displayed when a user clicks any of the objects is erased when the user is done viewing the image. For each of the three response icons, you need to change the Erase setting to Before Next Entry and add a wait icon set up with Mouse Click and Key Press selected, but not Show Button. Then users can click the screen or press a key to remove the image that appears for the Science Try It, Gadget TV, and Newt objects.

When you're done, the pull-down menus and three icons should all be accessible while users are using the Target Area interaction.

WHAT YOU HAVE LEARNED

In this lesson you:

- Used a decision icon and a calculated path of 0 to store content off the flowline [*page* **220**]
- Used the pull-down menu response type to create a menu [*page* **221**]
- Added a separator bar to a menu by using (- to name a menu item [*page* **233**]
- Added an optional shortcut key for each menu item [*page* **234**]
- Used the Perpetual scope and Return branching options to convert a pull-down menu into a perpetual interaction [*page* **235**]

a piece

distributing

LESSON 11

All the skills you use in developing an Authorware piece generally have one goal: to create an interactive experience that you share with an audience. With Authorware, how you share your work is up to you: Copy it onto floppy disks, burn it onto a CD-ROM, or **stream** it over an intranet or the Internet. The important point is that if you know in advance how your piece will be distributed, you can make better decisions about designing and assembling the piece.

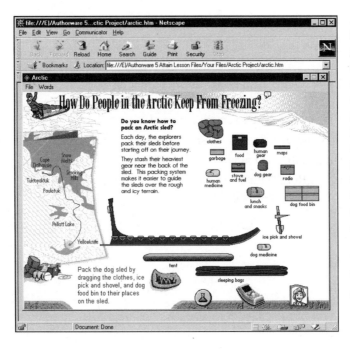

Authorware pieces, such as the Arctic piece, can be packaged into applications that run on Windows or Macintosh computers or over the Internet. When you package an Authorware piece, it runs independently of Authorware. When you prepare a piece for the Internet, it runs in a Web browser equipped with Authorware Web Player. An Authorware piece on the Web can be viewed within a Web page or as a separate window on top of the Web page, as shown here.

For example, suppose you're producing a training course for the Internet—a streaming piece that users download in segments and run in a Web browser with Authorware Web Player. How could you make the most of this delivery medium?

Use compressed audio formats for sounds that download faster. The Voxware (VOX) format is ideal for voice narration. Shockwave Audio (SWA) is good for music.

Use compressed image formats such as GIF, JPEG, and PNG to include more graphics with less of a performance penalty.

Play off the strengths of the Web by incorporating such capabilities as downloading documents from a Web site, uploading information to a Web server, and launching a Web browser.

Use Knowledge Stream, a new feature in Authorware 5 Attain, to dramatically improve performance over standard 28.8 kbps modem connections. Knowledge Stream pre-downloads segments of an Authorware piece that are likely to be needed—before they're needed—based on other users' downloading patterns.

In this lesson you'll try out two ways of preparing an Authorware piece for distribution. First you'll **package** the Arctic piece from Lesson 10 into an application that a user can install from a CD-ROM or floppy disks and can run without Authorware being installed on the user's computer. Then you'll take the same piece and prepare it for Internet delivery using Authorware **Web Packager,** a separate application provided to Authorware users at no charge.

To view the final results of this lesson, first go to the Final Files folder and double-click Arctic.exe to run the packaged piece that you'll create. Next open a Web browser equipped with Authorware **Web Player** and open the Arctic.htm file, which contains HTML code that launches the Internet version of the Arctic piece.

WHAT YOU WILL LEARN

In this lesson you will:

• Produce a version of a piece that can be distributed to users and played without Authorware

• Produce a version of a piece that can be delivered over the Internet

• Run the Internet version of the piece in a Web browser

APPROXIMATE TIME

It should take about 30 minutes to complete this lesson.

LESSON FILES

Media Files:

None

Beginning Files:

Beginning Files\11_Begin.a5p

Completed Project:

Final Files\Arctic.exe

Final Files\Arctic.aam and *Arct0001.aas–Arct0010.aas*

PACKAGING A PIECE

When you package a piece for distribution, you produce a file or a set of files that runs without Authorware. At its simplest, a packaged piece can be a single file incorporating all the content in a piece, including libraries, as well as the Authorware **runtime**—a play-only version of Authorware that takes the place of the regular Authorware application in running the piece. At the other extreme, your application can consist of numerous files that might include:

A number of packaged Authorware files

A separate Authorware runtime file

Library files used in the piece

External media files used in the piece (see Lesson 8 for more information about using external media)

Drivers for any media that require them, such as QuickTime movies

Xtras—extensions to Authorware—required for screen transitions, graphics, sounds, and any extra features you include that require these add-ons

Fonts used in the piece that might not be available on the user's computer

Virtually all Authorware pieces require a number of Xtras to play back various kinds of media. To run your piece, users must have these Xtras in an Xtras folder within the folder that contains the piece. The best way to handle the correct copying of all necessary files to the user's hard drive is to use an installation program, a separate program that copies all necessary files to the proper locations on the hard drive in preparation for running the piece. Authorware does not include an installation program. For more information on Xtras and other files needed when you distribute an Authorware piece, see "Determining Which Files You Need to Distribute" in Authorware's online help.

In this task you'll package the Arctic piece as a stand-alone application.

1] Open 11_Begin.a5p in the Beginning Files folder and save it as *11_Arctic.a5p* in the Arctic Project folder.

Alternatively, you can use the file you worked on in the previous lesson and save it as *11_Arctic.a5p*.

2] Choose File › Package to open the Package dialog box.

You can select from a variety of packaging options. The first group of options, presented in a drop-down list, affects the runtime.

Without Runtime: Use this option when you will include the runtime separately or if users already have a copy of the runtime on their computers. When your project consists of several Authorware files, you should either package the runtime separately or package it with only the first file that users run, such as a log-on routine or welcome menu. Additional files can use the same runtime as the opening piece, saving disk space.

Authorware provides these additional options:

For Windows 3.1: This option provides a 16-bit runtime that's needed if any of your users are running Windows 3.1. Users with Windows 95, Windows 98, and Windows NT will also be able to run the piece.

For Windows 95, 98 and NT: This option provides a 32-bit runtime that can be used only in Windows 95, Windows 98, and Windows NT 3.5.1 or later. If you know all users will have one of these 32-bit operating systems installed, this option makes sense because it provides faster performance than the 16-bit runtime.

3] From the Package File menu, select For Windows 95, 98 and NT.
The packaged piece will include the 32-bit runtime.

The Package dialog box lists several other options:

Resolve Broken Links at Runtime: Use this option to have Authorware relink broken links to libraries before the piece runs. Broken links can occur when Authorware can't locate the library linked to a piece or if you change the link

244

name of a library icon (which is different from the title of the library icon). Generally, if you carefully check your work during production and include libraries in the same folder with the packaged piece, you can avoid this option and thereby save time for users. Selecting this option causes a delay at the beginning of the piece as Authorware checks for broken links.

Package All Libraries Internally: Use this option when you want to include libraries along with your piece in a single packaged file. This procedure makes sense for simple pieces. If you use one library with several Authorware files, however, you will save disk space by packaging the library externally so it can be shared.

Package External Media Internally: Use this option to convert linked external media to embedded media in the distributed piece. Embedded media makes an Authorware file larger while eliminating external media files. Digital movies, however, cannot be embedded.

Use Default Names When Packaging: Use this option if want to use the name of your Authorware file as the name of the packaged piece.

tip   *Select Package External Media Internally when you package for the Web. The piece will generally run more efficiently over the Internet, especially if you're using Knowledge Stream.*

4] Select Package All Libraries Internally.

This option will combine the Arctic file and the libraries used with Arctic into a single packaged file.

5] Select Package External Media Internally.

This option eliminates the need to distribute the external media files with the Arctic piece.

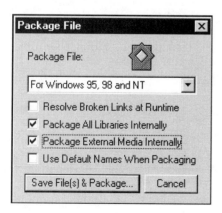

6] Click Save File(s) & Package.

The Package File As dialog box opens. The file name of your piece appears in the File Name box with the extension *.exe*. You'll change the file name and select a new location for saving the file.

7] Locate the Arctic Project folder.

The Arctic Project folder includes an Xtras subfolder that contains the Xtra files needed for this piece.

note *Each time you distribute one of your pieces, you'll need to either package the piece to include the runtime—as you're doing in this task—or include the runtime in the same folder as your piece. You'll also need to copy all necessary Xtras into a subfolder of the folder used for your piece. This subfolder must be named* Xtras.

8] Rename the file *Arctic.exe*.

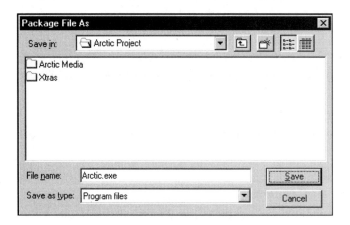

9] Click Save. Then close Authorware.

The packaged piece is ready to run.

10] On your computer, locate the Arctic Project folder within the Your Files folder.

11] Double-click Arctic.exe.

The piece runs just as it did while you were authoring. Now, however, the piece uses the Authorware runtime instead of Authorware, and you can't edit the piece in any way.

12] When you're done viewing the Arctic piece, close it.

To do this, click the close box at the upper right or choose File > Quit.

In the next task, you'll package the piece again in preparation for converting it into a streaming piece.

PREPARING A PIECE FOR WEB PACKAGING

In this task you'll package the Arctic piece a second time, but with one different setting required for Internet delivery. You'll package the piece without a runtime. Authorware Web Packager, which converts your Authorware piece into segments for streaming, requires this setting. In a user's Web browser, Authorware Web Player takes the place of the runtime in playing back the piece.

1] Open Authorware, and then open the file 11_Arctic.a5p.

This is the same file that you packaged in the previous task.

2] Choose File › Package to open the Package dialog box.

3] From the Package File menu, select Without Runtime.

Web Packager requires a packaged piece without the runtime.

4] Make sure that Package All Libraries Internally and Package External Media Internally are selected.

As in the previous task, you'll include the libraries and embed all media in the packaged piece.

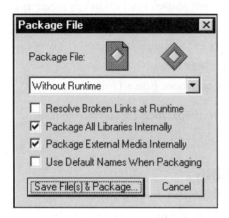

5] Click Save File(s) & Package.

Notice that the packaged piece has a different extension without the runtime: a5r. The Package File As dialog box opens.

6] Locate the Arctic Project folder.

7] Rename the file *Arctic.a5r*.

8] Click Save. Then close Authorware.

You're ready to use Web Packager to convert the packaged piece into the streaming format, ready for Web delivery.

OBTAINING WEB PLAYER AND THE BROWSER SOFTWARE

When you develop a piece for Internet distribution, you can use virtually all the features of Authorware. You can include all kinds of media and interactivity. You have the option of embedding your piece in a Web page or having it float above the browser. You can even have your piece retrieve information from the Web and jump to other Web pages.

What makes all of this possible is Macromedia's streaming technology. This technology involves two components: Web Packager is an application that segments an Authorware piece for efficient downloading and creates a map file to provide instructions for the downloading. Authorware Web Player works within a user's browser to manage the downloading of the segments and run the piece.

248

Web Packager was installed on your computer when you installed Authorware. Web Player is available from Macromedia's Web site. For more information about Web server configuration, authoring tips and tricks, and troubleshooting, see "Streaming, Intranets, and the Web" in Authorware online help.

1] If you don't already have a Web browser that supports Authorware Web Player, install the necessary browser now.

A Web browser is software used to navigate and view information on the World Wide Web. Netscape Navigator (versions 3 and up) and Microsoft Internet Explorer (versions 3 and up) are two popular Web browsers that support Authorware Web Player. Both are available at no charge for downloading from the Web. To download Netscape Navigator, go to *http://www.netscape.com*. To download Internet Explorer, go to *http://www.microsoft.com*.

Once you have installed a browser application, you can proceed to the next step.

2] If your browser is not yet equipped with Authorware Web Player, install Web Player now.

To download and install Web Player, follow the instructions on the Authorware Attain Web Player page (*http://www.macromedia.com/software/authorware/productinfo/webplayer*). Once your browser is equipped with Web Player, you're ready for the next task.

PREPARING A PIECE WITH WEB PACKAGER

Authorware Web Packager is the application that segments packaged Authorware pieces, converting them into the form needed for playing back in a Web browser with Authorware Web Player.

In the previous task you completed the first step in preparing a piece for distribution over the Internet: packaging the piece without the runtime. In this task you'll segment the piece and generate a map file using Web Packager, a separate application that Macromedia provides at no charge to Authorware developers.

In a browser, Authorware Web Player serves as the runtime for the streaming piece. Because a streaming piece is delivered one segment at a time, it's possible to deliver sizable Authorware pieces over intranets and the Internet.

To help you try out your streaming piece, the Final Files and Arctic Project folders contain an HTML document—a file prepared using the hypertext markup language, the language used to create Web pages. This HTML document includes commands that embed and launch the streaming piece from a Web page. All you need to do is prepare the piece with Web Packager and test it using your browser.

1] Start Authorware 5 Web Packager.

You can start Web Packager from the Windows Start menu (Programs > Macromedia Authorware 5 > Authorware 5 Web Packager) or locate it in the Authorware 5 folder on your hard drive and then double-click Authorware 5 Web Packager.

The Select File to Package for Web dialog box opens.

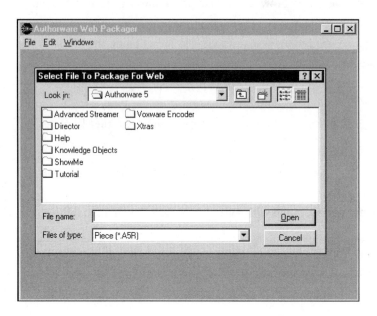

2] Locate the Arctic.a5r file you packaged in the previous task.

The file should be in the Arctic Project folder.

3] Click Open.

The Select Destination Map File dialog box opens.

4] Specify the Arctic Project folder as the destination folder for the map file that Web Packager will create.

250

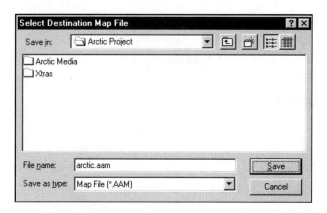

The destination you specify for the map file will also be used for the segments that Web Packager produces.

tip *When you produce your own Web-packaged pieces, first create an empty folder on your hard drive to hold the segments and map file that Web Packager produces. After preparing the piece, you will need to transfer the segment files and map file to a Web server. By using a folder that contains only these files, you make it easier to upload them to the server.*

5] Click Save.

The Segment Settings dialog box opens. In this dialog box you specify a prefix for the segment names and a size for the segments. A suggested prefix and segment size are displayed.

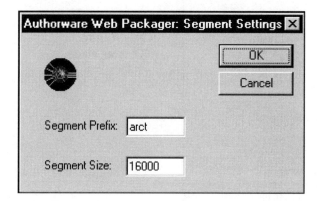

You can enter a prefix of up to four characters. Each segment will be named with your prefix and a four-digit number. In this case, you'll accept the suggested prefix, *arct*.

For the segment size, you can enter a value from 4,000 to 500,000 bytes. The suggested segment size, 16,000 bytes, is a good choice for many pieces; it provides a balance between the duration and frequency of downloading delays. Smaller segments produce more frequent, but shorter, delays for downloading. Larger segments produce fewer, but longer, delays.

The value you enter as the segment size is a guide that Web Packager uses rather than a limit or average size. Web Packager will segment the piece according to the internal structure of the piece. For example, a single graphic will usually not be broken into two segments. Instead, Web Packager is likely to create one large segment that includes the entire graphic, even if that segment is much larger than the segment size you specified.

tip *Experiment with segment sizes. There's no rule about what works best for all pieces under all circumstances.*

For this piece, you'll accept Web Packager's suggestion for the segment size.

6] Accept the suggested prefix and segment size and click OK.

Web Packager segments the piece, producing several segment files (with the *.aas* extension) and one map file (with the *.aam* extension). Then Web Packager displays the map file, Artic.aam.

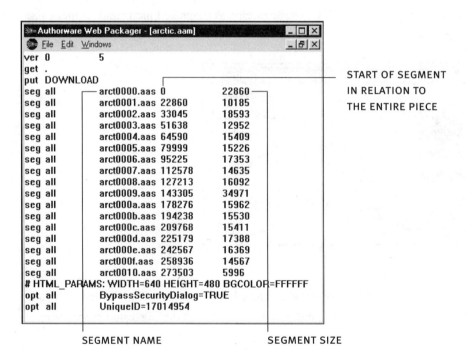

SEGMENT NAME   SEGMENT SIZE

START OF SEGMENT IN RELATION TO THE ENTIRE PIECE

The map file provides information that the Web server will need to download the segments to users.

This map file lists the names and sizes of the segments, among other information. If your streaming piece uses certain kinds of external media or performs actions on the user's hard drive, you may need to make changes to the map file. You can use Web Packager or any text editor to make those changes. For a detailed explanation of the changes you can make to the map file, see "Streaming, Intranets, and the Web" in Authorware online help.

For this sample piece, you won't make changes to the map file.

7] Close Web Packager.

The segmented Authorware file is ready to be embedded in a Web page.

If you were going to deliver the Arctic piece over the Internet, the next step would be to copy all the segment and map files to a Web server. In many cases, a Web administrator would probably perform this task.

EMBEDDING A STREAMING AUTHORWARE PIECE IN A WEB PAGE

In this task you'll use the HTML file provided for this lesson to embed the Arctic piece in a Web page.

1] Using a text editor such as Notepad, open the Arctic.htm file in the Arctic Project folder or the Final Files folder and review the contents.

```
<HTML>
<EMBED SRC="arctic.aam" WINDOW=ONTOP>
</HTML>
```

The text you see is in HTML. This simple file includes the minimum information needed to embed a streaming Authorware piece. The expression *WINDOW=ONTOP* will display the piece in a separate window that floats above the Web page. If you were planning to display the piece within a page, you would use *WINDOW=INPLACE* instead. In most situations, you'll use more complex HTML than this example to embed your Authorware Web pieces. For more information, see "Using EMBED to add a web-packaged piece to a web page" and "Using the AW Web Player control for ActiveX" in online help.

When you embed a piece in a Web page instead of in a separate window, you can make it blend with the page by using a screen size considerably smaller than 640 × 480, which provides space around the piece for other visual elements on the page, and by eliminating the title bar and menu bar so the piece looks less like a separate application and more like part of the page.

2] Close the text editor.

3] Drag the Arctic.htm file from the Arctic Project folder to a browser with Web Player installed.

This should open the file in the browser. If it does not, open the file by using the browser's File > Open command. (In some versions of Netscape Navigator, the command is File > Open File in Browser.)

The Arctic piece will begin playing in the browser.

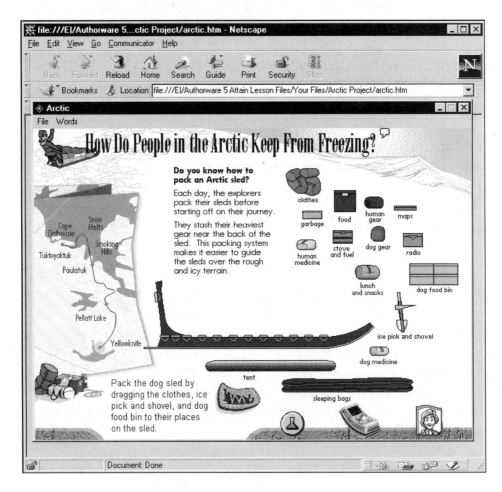

4] Try out each section of the piece. Try dragging the sled items and clicking the beaker, remote control, and Newt. Then use the pull-down menu to hear and read definitions for the terms.

You've just created a streaming Authorware piece. The piece runs segment by segment, each downloading as it's needed by the browser. (Of course, you're not really viewing the piece over the Internet because it's stored on your hard drive. To see how it would really play, you would have to put the Authorware map files and segment files on a Web server.)

tip   *Although you can include virtually all elements of multimedia in streaming Authorware pieces, how well your multimedia piece plays depends on the user's connection speed, the volume of network traffic, and the performance of the Web server. In general, when you create for the Web, you need to streamline your pieces by using the smallest possible file sizes for graphics, sounds, and movies. The good news is that interactions and animations in Authorware take up little space and therefore download quickly.*

WHAT YOU HAVE LEARNED

In this lesson you have:

• Packaged a piece so it can run on a user's computer without Authorware [*page* **243**]

• Used Authorware Web Packager to segment a piece and create a map file so the streaming piece can run over the Internet [*page* **249**]

• Opened and ran a streaming piece in a Web browser using Authorware Web Player [*page* **253**]

variables

introducing

LESSON 12

You can accomplish a lot in Authorware without doing any programming. To build even more powerful interactive applications, however, you must do something very different from dragging icons to the flowline. You need to carefully type phrases in a new language, the language of Authorware **variables** and **functions**.

Variables extend the power of Authorware in numerous ways. In this lesson you'll get acquainted with what variables can do by building a text entry interaction that uses a variable to store and then display the user's name on the screen.

Variables are containers for information. A variable represents a value that Authorware stores and can use in many ways. This value can change—that is, it can *vary*. Functions are "doers," performing tasks in Authorware such as quitting the Authorware piece, jumping to another piece, and creating text files on a user's hard drive to store information. You will often use variables and functions together. Functions are beyond the scope of this book, but in this lesson and the next you will start to become familiar with the remarkable power of variables.

Authorware provides more than 220 **system variables**. These variables keep track of all kinds of activities while a piece is running—including the time of day, the computer and operating system being used, and where a user clicks on the screen. For example, the *EntryText* system variable can store users' names when they log on to a training course, *SessionTime* can keep track of how long a person has been viewing a piece, and *MatchedIconTitle* and *MatchedEver* can provide customized information to users based on choices they make throughout a piece.

In most cases, Authorware assigns—and changes—the values of system variables. For example, *EntryText* contains the most recent text that a user has entered into a text entry field. At one point *EntryText* might contain the value "Sandra" because a user named Sandra just typed her name in a text entry field used to log on to a training course. At another point, *EntryText* might hold the value "navigate" because Sandra just typed her response to a question asking her to name the Authorware icon that's used for navigation.

In addition to system variables, you will also use **custom variables**. You name custom variables and assign their values yourself. For example, you might create a variable called *Score* and assign a value of *1* to *Score* when a user picks the correct answer in a quiz.

In this lesson, you'll begin using variables in a simple exercise. You will create a text entry interaction that uses the *EntryText* variable to capture what a user types. Then you'll **embed** the value of *EntryText* in a display icon so that what the user types is displayed on the screen in another part of the piece. If you would like to see the final result of this lesson, open the Final Files folder and play 12_Final.a5p.

WHAT YOU WILL LEARN

In this lesson you will:

- Explore the Variables window
- Examine several examples of variables
- Create an interaction that uses an Authorware variable to store information and then display it to users

APPROXIMATE TIME

It should take about 30 minutes to complete this lesson.

LESSON FILES

Media Files:

None

Starting Files:

None

Completed Project:

Final Files\12_Final.a5p

SETTING UP A TEXT ENTRY INTERACTION

To prepare for displaying a variable on the screen, you'll create a text entry interaction that accepts any typed input from users. This interaction will simply ask users to type their names.

You'll start by creating a new file for this lesson.

1] Choose File › New › File (Ctrl+N) to create a new Authorware file. Click None in the New File dialog box to close it without using a Knowledge Object. Then close the Knowledge Objects window.

2] Drag an interaction icon to the flowline and name it *Sign In*.

 Sign In

You'll create a text entry interaction with a single response icon.

3] Double-click the Sign In icon to open it. In the Presentation window, create the following text using 18 point Arial: *Please type your name and press Enter.*

To select the font, choose Text > Font > Arial. To select the point size, choose Text > Size > 18.

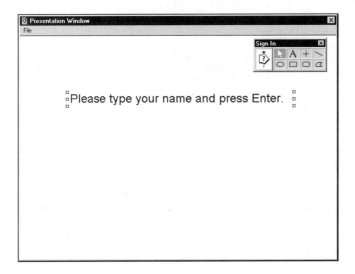

4] In the Design window, drag a display icon to the right of the interaction icon, select Text Entry as the response type, and name the icon *.

In a text entry interaction, using an asterisk for the title of a response icon designates * as the text pattern that will be accepted as a match. The asterisk is a **wildcard** character that indicates that any text a user enters will be accepted. For this interaction, you don't want a particular response from the user. You just want the user's name so you can store it and then display it in a different part of the screen.

5] Double-click the response type symbol to open the Response Properties dialog box. On the Response tab, select Exit Interaction from the Branch menu.
The purpose of this interaction is to capture the user's name. After that occurs, you want Authorware to exit the interaction and move down the flowline.

6] For Erase, select Don't Erase. Then click OK.

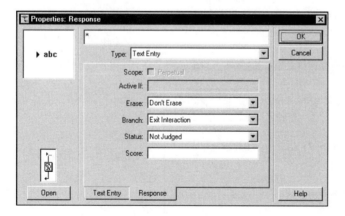

The display icon for this response will display the user's name along with a welcome message. You want this text to stay on the screen after the user exits the interaction.

7] Restart the piece and then pause it. In the Presentation window, align the text and the text entry field so they look approximately like the following illustration.

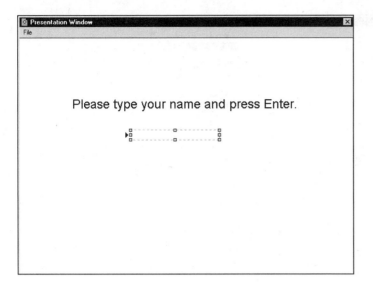

You might need to double-click either object to drag it.

8] Save this file under the name *12_Signin.a5p*.

The text entry interaction is ready. Now you can create the feedback that appears after the user presses Enter.

CREATING TEXT IN THE RESPONSE ICON

In this task you'll start to create the text in the response icon that appears after the user types a name and presses Enter. When you complete the next three tasks, this text will include *EntryText* as an embedded variable. When users run the piece, they won't see the variable name, *EntryText*. Instead, they'll see the current value of that variable—which will be whatever text they typed in the text entry field in the interaction.

1] In the Design window, Shift-double-click the * display icon to open it so you can add content.

You should see the text you created in the previous task, the text entry field, and the toolbox title reminding you that you're in the * display icon.

2] Using the font and size you used for the interaction, create the text *Welcome*, and press Enter to start a second line.

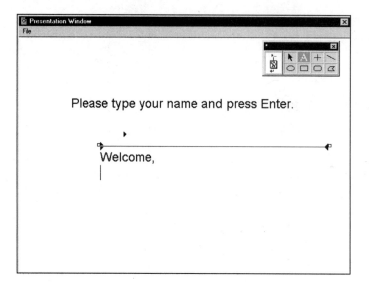

In the second line you'll embed the *EntryText* variable, which will display the most recent text that the user entered. Before embedding this variable, you'll get acquainted with the Authorware tool for organizing, describing, and tracking the values of variables in a piece: the Variables window.

USING THE VARIABLES WINDOW

In this task you'll open and examine the Variables window, which lists and describes all variables.

1] Choose Window › Variables (Ctrl+Shift+V).

The Variables window opens.

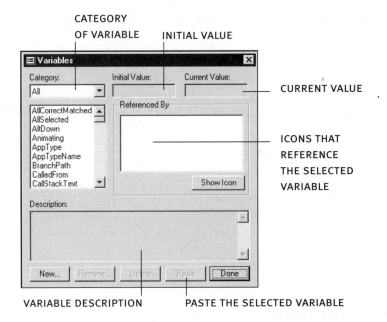

CATEGORY OF VARIABLE
INITIAL VALUE
CURRENT VALUE
ICONS THAT REFERENCE THE SELECTED VARIABLE
VARIABLE DESCRIPTION
PASTE THE SELECTED VARIABLE

The Variables window lists all system variables and any custom variables you've created in a piece. Use this window to determine the initial value and current value for variables you're using. In the Referenced By window, you can locate every icon in the piece that uses the variable you select in the list.

tip *Until you're confident of the correct spelling and usage of a variable, use this window to paste variables into icons wherever you need them.*

2] Open the Category menu.

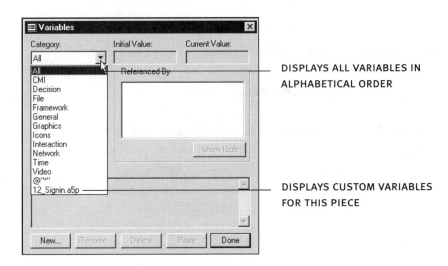

DISPLAYS ALL VARIABLES IN ALPHABETICAL ORDER

DISPLAYS CUSTOM VARIABLES FOR THIS PIECE

Authorware contains more than 220 system variables, organized in 11 categories.

tip   *Get to know the variables according to their categories and start with the categories that appear to be most relevant to your current projects. For example, if you're using decision icons and interaction icons in a piece, look for variables in the Decision and Interaction categories that might be useful. Experiment to see how you might use them in your projects. While looking up a variable you need in a given category, you may well find another variable in the same category that would also be useful.*

Along with the 11 categories, an additional category, All, displays the entire list of variables in alphabetic order. If you know the name of a variable but are unsure of the category, use the All option to find the variable you want.

Custom variables you've created in the current file appear under the file name of the piece at the end of the list of categories.

You can also create custom **icon variables**, which are specific to an individual icon. The @"*" listing would display any custom variables you had created for the * icon. For more information, see Authorware online help.

In a moment you'll locate *EntryText* in the list and paste it into the display, but first you'll examine examples of variables.

Earlier you learned that Authorware provides system variables and that you can create your own custom variables. Both system and custom variables can be one of several types. In this lesson you'll learn about three types. **Logical variables** contain one of only two values: true or false. **Numeric variables** contain a number and can have arithmetic operations performed on them. **Character variables** contain a text string. For more information about types of variables, see Authorware online help.

Before using *EntryText*, which is a character variable in the Interaction category, you'll look at two examples of other variables that are useful in interactions.

3] Select Interaction from the Category menu.

4] Locate the *MatchedEver* variable in the list of Interaction variables.

tip   *Click the list of variables and start typing the name of the variable you want. Authorware will locate the first variable in the list that contains the characters you type.*

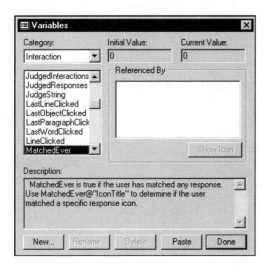

MatchedEver is a logical variable—it's either true or false. *MatchedEver@"IconTitle"* is true if the user has previously matched the response icon you specify in *IconTitle*. For example, in Lesson 5, in which you created a hot spot interaction, *MatchedEver@"Display Icon Choice"* is true when the user clicks the hot spot over the display icon in the image of the icon palette. You can use this variable to provide feedback to users based on choices they made in an interaction, even after they've exited the interaction.

5] Locate the *CorrectChoicesMatched* variable.

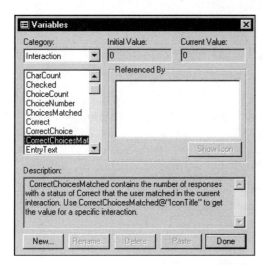

CorrectChoicesMatched is a numeric variable that tracks user choices in an interaction. In the Response Properties dialog box for a response icon, you can select a status of Correct Choice for any given response icon in an interaction. This variable keeps track of the number of correct choices a user makes. In Lesson 13 you'll use this variable to help determine the feedback that users receive when they complete an interaction.

Now you'll locate the variable you'll use in this task.

EMBEDDING A VARIABLE IN A DISPLAY

In this task you'll locate *EntryText* and paste it into the display. Then you'll try out the interaction you've created.

1] Locate EntryText in the Interaction category.

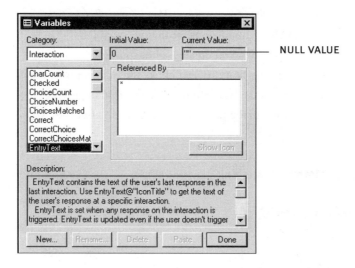

This is a character variable. *EntryText* contains the text most recently entered by the user in a text entry interaction.

Notice that the current value of *EntryText* is *""*. For a character variable, two adjacent quotation marks are used to indicate the absence of a value, also called a **null** value. The variable has a null value because no text has been entered in the text entry interaction.

2] Click Paste to paste *EntryText* into the display.

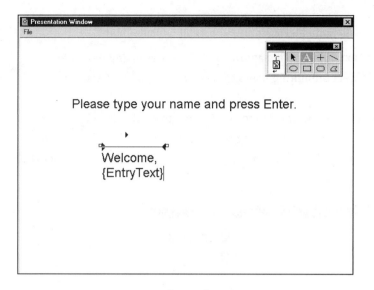

Authorware pastes the variable name where the text cursor is placed. Notice that *EntryText* appears between curly brackets. Authorware provides curly brackets whenever you paste a variable into a display. When you enter a variable into a text object by typing it, you need to type the curly brackets yourself.

3] Click Done to close the Variables window.

tip *If you use variables frequently, you can keep this window open and move it to one side.*

4] Click the Pointer tool in the toolbox.

ENTRYTEXT HAS NO VALUE

The name of the variable and the curly brackets disappear. What you now see is the current value of the variable. In this case, no value is specified because no text has been entered into the text entry field. To embed a variable in a display icon, you need to use the Text tool. When you select the Pointer tool, you'll see the current value instead of the variable name. The value of the variable is what you want users to see.

To make the Welcome text look better on the screen, you'll make two adjustments.

5] Drag the Welcome text object so it's approximately centered and nearly as wide as the first text object prompting users to sign in. Then select Center for text alignment.

These modifications improve the appearance of the text that's displayed after the user signs in. Because you can't tell how long someone's name will be, it's a good idea to make the text object almost as wide as the first line of text in the interaction, as in the following illustration.

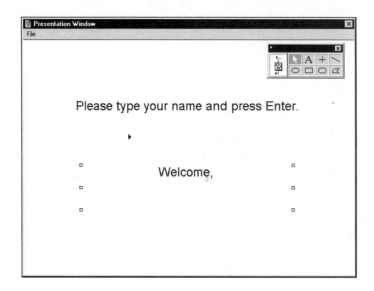

6] Restart the piece and type your name.

Please type your name and press Enter.

▶ Arthur Wear

7] Press Enter.

You should see the name appear after "Welcome," on the screen.

Welcome,
Arthur Wear

8] Save your work.

You've just used a system variable, *EntryText*, to store text that users enter, and you've embedded that variable in a display icon to display the text on the screen. This is just the beginning of what you can do with variables.

ON YOUR OWN

Try embedding other system variables in the display along with *EntryText*. Here are some you might try embedding:

MachineName: The name of the machine running the piece

ScreenDepth: The color setting that you're using

TimeInInteraction: The amount of time you spent in the interaction

FullDate: The current day and date

ClickSeconds: The number of seconds since you last pressed the mouse button

StartTime: The time you began working on the file

WHAT YOU HAVE LEARNED

In this lesson you have:

- Explored the basics of using Authorware variables [*page* **259**]
- Explored the Variables window, Authorware's main tool for organizing, describing, and tracking variables in pieces [*page* **262**]
- Viewed examples of logical, numeric, and character variables [*page* **264**]
- Used the EntryText system variable with a text entry interaction to store and then display a user's name [*page* **266**]

using variables for branching

LESSON 13

In the last lesson you began learning about Authorware variables by using *EntryText*. In this lesson you'll use two more system variables, *WrongChoicesMatched* and *RightChoicesMatched*. You'll use these two numeric variables in a multiple-choice interaction to determine which of two feedback messages to provide to users. What makes the interaction more complex than other interactions you've developed in

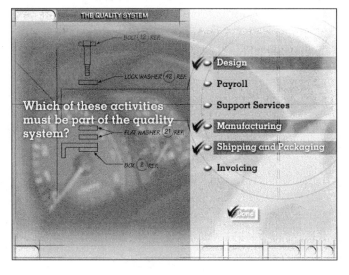

Starting the QS-9000 Process *uses text, graphics, digital movies, and various interactive activities. In this lesson you'll build a small portion of this piece that asks users to identify three activities in a corporation that help set quality standards. Starting the QS-9000 Process is a product of Reality Interactive, Inc., Minneapolis (http://www.realtools.com).*

this book is that it contains a total of six responses. Three are correct choices, and three are incorrect. If a user picks all three correct answers and none of the incorrect answers, an audio message will confirm that the user made the right choices. If the user makes any other combination of choices—including no choice—a different audio message will be played.

In this lesson you'll work on a new project, an interactive learning piece based on *Starting the QS-9000 Process*, an interactive CD-ROM product developed by Reality Interactive. *Starting the QS-9000 Process* teaches the principles of assessing and fostering quality in a corporate environment. (QS-9000 is a set of quality requirements, based on the ISO 9000 international quality standard, for suppliers to the Big Three automakers.) If you would like to see the final result of this lesson, open the Final Files folder and play 13_Final.a5p.

WHAT YOU WILL LEARN

In this lesson you will:

- Use an Authorware feature that permits a piece to display graphics using a specific range of colors
- Create a complex hot spot interaction in which users must choose three correct responses
- Use variables to track users' responses in an interaction and provide feedback based on the results

APPROXIMATE TIME

It should take about 1½ hours to complete this lesson.

LESSON FILES

Media Files:

Your Files\Quality Project\Question.a5l

Your Files\Quality Project\Quality Media

Beginning File:

None

Completed Project:

Final Files\13_Final.a5p

STARTING A NEW PROJECT

For the project you create in this lesson, you'll start a new file and open an existing library of media content. After setting file properties, you'll import a custom palette that will permit the proper display of the images in this piece.

1] Start a new file.

To do this, choose File > New > File. An empty Design window appears on the screen.

2] Open the Question.a5l library.

To do this, choose File > Open > Library. Locate the Question.a5l library in the Quality Project folder and click Open.

This library contains display and sound icons that you'll use in this project.

3] Open the File Properties dialog box.

To do this, choose Modify > File > Properties.

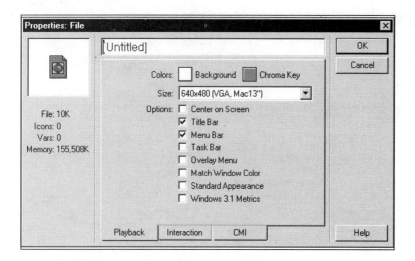

Develop the habit of setting file properties at the start of each new project. In this case you will change four settings.

4] Select the [Untitled] text in the text entry box and type *Quality* as the title of the piece.

5] On the Playback tab, select the Center on Screen option.
You'll use the default resolution of 640 × 480. If a user's screen has a higher resolution, you want the piece to be displayed in the center of the screen.

6] Click the Title Bar and Menu Bar boxes to remove the checkmarks.
This piece will not have a title bar or menu bar.

> **tip** *If you select Menu Bar in the File Properties dialog box, the piece you distribute will have both a menu bar and title bar, even if you don't select Title Bar.*

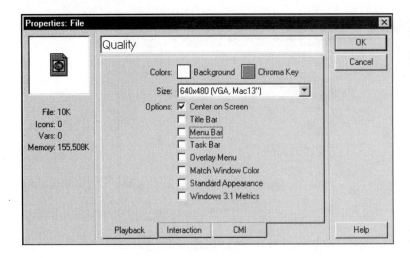

7] Click OK to close the dialog box.

You need to make one more global change before beginning production. In the next task you'll create a custom palette that allows Authorware to display the range of colors used in the artwork created for this piece.

LOADING A CUSTOM PALETTE

A **color palette** provides the range of colors that are available for displaying all visual elements—text, graphics, and movies. The standard Authorware 256-color palette provides a broad range of colors, but this may not suit the needs of a particular project. For example, your first project in this book used a custom palette that included several colors needed to display the shadow behind the box, the icon palette, and the word *NOT*. A piece about oceans may require a palette that includes additional shades of blue and green.

There's a trade-off, however, to adding colors. If you add 15 additional shades of blue and green, you have to remove 15 other colors from a 256-color palette. (If you know that your users' computers are capable of displaying 16-bit or 24-bit color—64,000 colors or 16 million colors, respectively, you don't have to worry about palettes. However, for most of your projects you'll have to plan for the 256-color limitation.)

The Quality piece uses graphics and movies that include additional shades of red and brown. To provide for this, you'll use a custom palette.

1] Choose Modify › File › Palette.

The Palette dialog box opens. Use this dialog box to view the current palette and to load a custom palette.

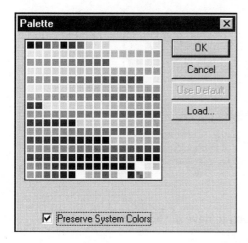

2] Click the Load button.

The Load Palette dialog box opens.

There's more than one way to load a custom palette into Authorware. You can import a palette file, a special kind of file created in some graphics programs—or you can load one of the images in your piece that includes all the colors you need. Authorware will then create a custom palette using the colors in this image.

When you import or create a custom palette, you have the option of preserving system colors. This is generally a good idea. Preserving system colors ensures that the palette will retain the 20 colors commonly used for such Windows interface elements as buttons and dialog boxes.

3] Locate the Quality Media folder inside the Quality Project folder.

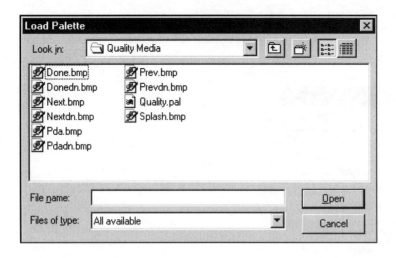

4] **Select the Quality.pal file. Then click Open to have Authorware import the palette file.**

5] **Click OK to complete the loading of the custom palette.**

You've loaded a custom palette that will ensure the proper display of the color images in this piece.

6] **Choose File > Save All to save the file and library. Locate the Quality Project folder. Name the file *13_Quality.a5p*.**

Now you can begin building the interaction for this lesson.

CREATING A HOT SPOT INTERACTION

This interaction will ask users to respond to a question. Six responses will be provided, only three of which are correct.

In this task you'll set up an interaction icon and create the first response for the interaction. The feedback for each response will be a graphic that highlights the user's choice on the screen.

1] **Drag the Quality Background display icon from the library to the flowline.**

This image is the background for the interaction you're going to create. To see what it looks like, open the display icon.

2] Double-click the Quality Background display icon.

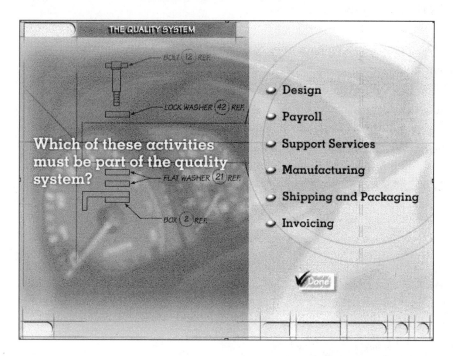

In response to the question presented on this screen, a user will be able to choose up to six responses, only three of which are correct. Each time a user clicks a response, a graphic highlighting that response will appear on the screen. When the user clicks Done, feedback will be returned on the user's choices.

3] Switch to the Design window. Then drag an interaction icon from the icon palette to the flowline below the Quality Background display icon. Name it *Quality Question*.

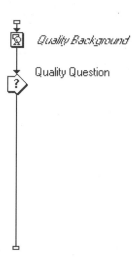

USING VARIABLES FOR BRANCHING

In this interaction, the user will be asked to choose the correct responses from six choices by clicking hot spots over the choices.

4] Open the Interaction Icon Properties dialog box for the Quality Question interaction icon.

To do this, select the icon and choose Modify > Icon > Properties. You're going to add a pause before the user exits the interaction.

5] On the Interaction tab, select Pause Before Exiting. Then click OK.

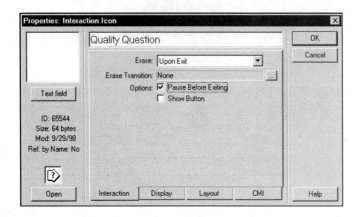

Pause Before Exiting will keep the feedback from being erased before the user is ready to exit.

6] Drag the Design display icon from the library to the right of the interaction icon. Select Hot Spot as the response type.

This display icon contains a highlighted image of the word *Design* that will appear when a user clicks Design in response to the question.

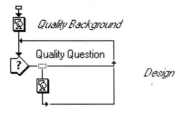

You won't have to align the artwork for each of the responses in the Presentation window. Each graphic has been prepared so it appears in the correct location on the screen.

278

7] Double-click the response type symbol for Design to open its Response Properties dialog box.

You'll set two options for this response icon.

8] On the Hot Spot tab, select the hand-shaped custom cursor.

To do this, open the Cursors dialog box and select the hand-shaped cursor at the bottom of the list.

9] Click the Response tab.

In the interactions you created for previous lessons, you usually accepted the default Erase setting, After Next Entry. This setting works well when you want to provide different feedback for each response. For this interaction, however, users will be making multiple selections. You want a visual reminder of each selection—in this case, the highlighted word *Design*—to remain on the screen so users can see all the choices they've made. To make this happen, you need to change the Erase setting.

10] From the Erase menu, select On Exit.

This setting ensures that the highlighted image of the word *Design* will stay visible until a user makes all the choices, clicks Done to receive feedback, and leaves the interaction.

Next you'll change another setting on the Response tab to allow Authorware to track whether a user picks a correct or incorrect choice.

11] From the Status menu, select Correct Response. Then click OK.

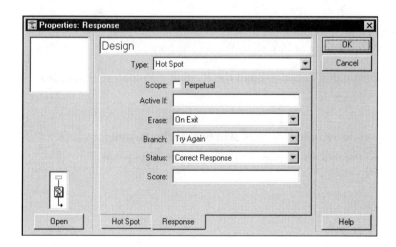

In previous lessons, you accepted the default setting of Not Judged for this option. By defining a response icon as a Correct Response or Wrong Response now, you involve Authorware in tracking a user's correct and incorrect choices in the interaction. This tracking will make it possible to provide two different feedback messages based on users' choices.

In the Design window, the Design icon title now has a plus sign beside it. The plus sign marks this response icon as a correct response.

INDICATES A CORRECT RESPONSE

12] Save your work.

Now you're ready to set up the hot spots for the other five choices in this interaction.

CREATING ADDITIONAL HOT SPOTS

You will add five more hot spots that let users select the other choices on the screen. In addition to Design, the other two correct responses are Manufacturing and Shipping and Packaging. The remaining three choices will be incorrect responses.

1] Drag the Payroll display icon from the library to the right of the Design response icon.

Authorware copies the settings of the first response icon to this one. In this case, you need to change the Status setting of Payroll to Wrong Response.

To change this setting, you don't need to open the Response Properties dialog box. Authorware provides a shortcut.

2] Press the Ctrl key while you click the plus sign next to the Payroll icon title.

This changes the plus sign to a minus sign, indicating Wrong Response.

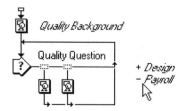

3] Double-click the response type symbol for Payroll.

Notice that on the Response tab, Status is now set to Wrong Response.

4] Click Cancel to close the dialog box.

You can Ctrl-click next to the response icon title to cycle through the three Status settings: Correct Response (+), Wrong Response (-), and Not Judged (empty).

5] Drag the Support Services display icon from the library to the right of Payroll.

This is another incorrect choice. Because Support Services copies the settings of the previous icon, you can leave the settings unchanged.

6] Drag the Manufacturing icon to the right of Support Services.

This is a correct choice, so you need to change its Status setting.

7] Ctrl-click the minus sign. Then Ctrl-click again to display a plus sign.

The first click changes the setting to Not Judged, and the second click changes it to Correct Response.

8] Drag the Shipping and Packaging display icon to the right of Manufacturing.

This choice is correct, so you can leave the settings unchanged.

9] Drag the Invoicing display icon to the right of Shipping and Packaging.

Because Invoicing is the sixth response icon in this interaction, the Design window changes to a scrolling list.

You need to change the Status setting for this choice.

10] Ctrl-click the plus sign to change it to a minus sign.

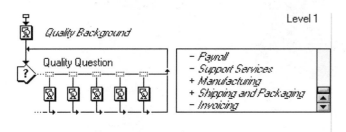

You've set up three responses that are correct and three that are incorrect. The three correct responses are Design, Manufacturing, and Shipping and Packaging. The three incorrect responses are Payroll, Support Services, and Invoicing.

In a moment you'll complete the interaction by creating the hot spot over the word *Done* so users can click it when they're ready to receive feedback. First you'll switch to the Presentation window to align the six hot spots you've created.

ALIGNING HOT SPOTS

When you created the hot spots, Authorware used a default size and placed each one on the screen at a default distance from the preceding hot spot. In this task you'll change the size and location of the hot spots so they overlay the choices that users will click on the screen.

1] Restart the piece and then pause it.

The hot spots are visible where Authorware placed them.

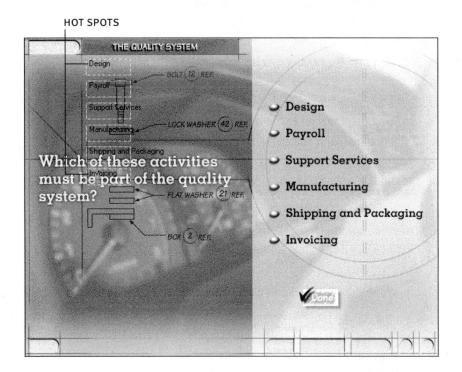

2] Align each hot spot over the choice that the user will see on the screen.

When you're done, your screen should look like the following illustration.

If you're using a screen resolution of 640 × 480 on your computer, you may need to turn off the Authorware toolbar before you can align the hot spots. To do this, choose View > Toolbar (Ctrl+Shift+T).

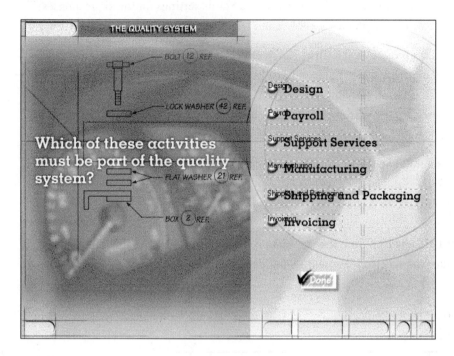

tip *If you accidentally move the background while attempting to drag a hot spot, choose Edit > Undo (Ctrl+Z) to restore the background to its original position.*

You've set up the interaction so users can select up to six responses and see their choices highlighted on the screen. Authorware will track each user choice as a correct or an incorrect response.

3] Save your work.

In the next task you'll embed two variables in a display icon to see how Authorware keeps track of the correct and incorrect choices.

EMBEDDING VARIABLES

In Lesson 12 you embedded the *EntryText* variable, which displays the most recent text that a user has entered in a text entry interaction. In this task you'll embed two new variables, *CorrectChoicesMatched* and *WrongChoicesMatched,* to display the results of a user's choice in response to the question on the screen. Because you selected Correct Response and Wrong Response as the Status settings for the six responses, Authorware will track which are correct and which are not.

In a real-world project, embedding variables is often done as part of debugging a project. By embedding a variable, you make visible some of the operations that Authorware performs "under the hood." Seeing how the value of a certain variable changes while a piece is running can often help you figure out what changes you need to make to resolve a problem.

In this case, the embedded variables will make it easier to understand the rest of this lesson. When you're all done with the lesson, you can remove the embedded variables just as you would do if you were using them to help debug an actual project.

1] Drag a display icon from the icon palette to the flowline just below the Quality Background display icon. Name it *Embedded Variables*.

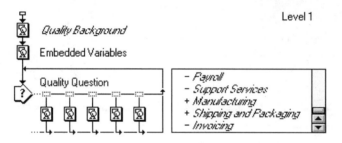

You'll embed the *CorrectChoicesMatched* and *WrongChoicesMatched* variables in this display icon so you can keep track of how their values change when different choices are selected in the interaction.

2] Double-click the new display icon to open it.
You'll create a rectangle as a background for the text that includes the embedded variables.

3] Use the Rectangle tool in the toolbox to create a small rectangle at the lower left of the screen. Use the Colors Inspector to fill the rectangle with any light color you want.

Your rectangle should approximately match the one in the following illustration. The rectangle's dimensions are not important because it's just the background against which you'll create text—and you'll remove the rectangle at the end of the project.

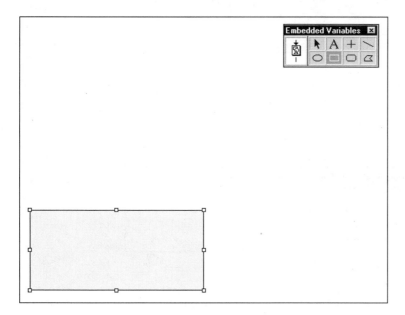

4] Use the Text tool to create the following text inside the rectangle, using a font and size you select:

The number of correct choices is {CorrectChoicesMatched}

Type the variable name inside curly brackets and with no spaces. When you run the piece, the sentence will appear on the screen as "The number of correct choices is" followed by a number indicating the number of correct choices the user has clicked up to that point.

285

5] Use the Text tool to create this text in a second line:

The number of wrong choices is {WrongChoicesMatched}

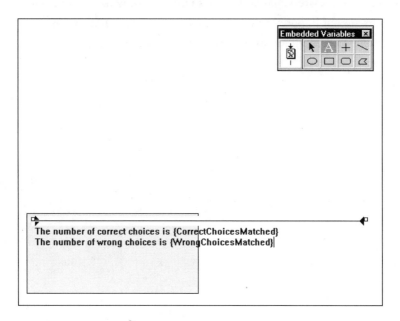

When you run the piece, Authorware will display the number of correct and incorrect choices a user has selected in these embedded variables.

6] Use the Pointer tool to align the text within the rectangle. Use the Modes tool to make the text transparent.

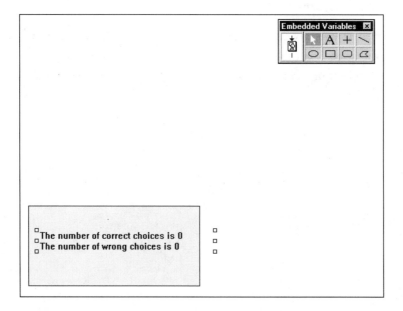

As soon as you select the Pointer tool, notice that numbers appear in place of the variable names. In this case, the numbers are *0* because at this point no correct or incorrect choices have been selected.

One more step is needed to accurately display the current value of each variable.

7] Open the Display Icon Properties dialog box for this display icon.
To do this, choose Modify > Icon > Properties.

8] On the Display tab, select Update Displayed Variables.

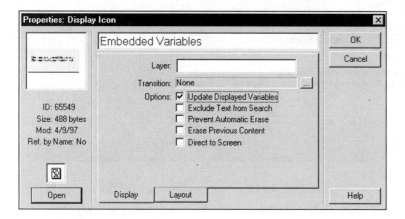

Now Authorware will display the value of each variable as soon as the value changes.

9] Click OK to close the dialog box. Then restart the piece.
When the question appears on the screen, the value shown for each variable is 0.
Now see what happens when you select answers.

10] Click any one of the answers. Then click another.

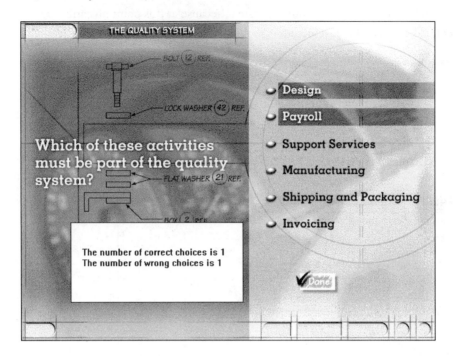

Notice how the value for a variable changes each time you click an answer. This occurs because each time you click a choice, Authorware updates its count of the number of correct and incorrect choices you've made. The embedded variables simply make Authorware's information-tracking visible to you.

11] Save your work.

Now that you've seen how Authorware tracks the choices a user makes, you'll use this information in the next task to determine which of two hot spots is active. This will be the way you determine which of two feedback messages users receive.

USING VARIABLES TO ACTIVATE HOT SPOTS

This interaction will provide users with one of two messages depending on how they respond to the question on the screen. If users pick any combination of incorrect choices, they will hear one message. If they pick all three of the correct choices and none of the incorrect choices, they will hear a different message.

To select between the two feedback messages, you will use the following Authorware features:

The *CorrectChoicesMatched* and *WrongChoicesMatched* variables.

288

A hot spot that's active as long as the user has not selected the three correct choices. When users click this hot spot, they receive one message.

A second hot spot that occupies the same location as the first hot spot but becomes active only if the user selects the three correct responses, and only those three. When users click this hot spot, they receive the other message.

The key to this approach is creating two hot spots in the same location on the screen. At any moment only one of these hot spots will be active because of expressions you create using the two variables. You'll enter these expressions in the Response Properties dialog box for each hot spot.

1] In the Design window, drag a map icon to the right of the Invoicing response icon and name it *Done (Wrong)*.

This will be the response icon that Authorware branches to unless users pick the three correct choices, and only those three. All other responses—including no response—will match this response icon because of criteria you will specify.

You need to change the Status setting for this new response icon.

2] Change the Status setting of Done (Wrong) by using Ctrl+click to remove the minus sign.

When the user clicks Done, Authorware will not count this response as correct or wrong.

3] Drag a map icon to the right of Done (Wrong) and name it *Done (Right)*.

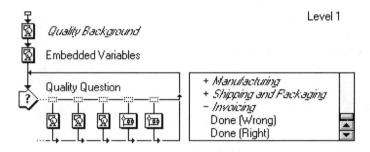

This will be the response icon that Authorware branches to only when users select all three correct choices and no incorrect choices.

The two hot spots will occupy the same location over the word *Done*. One hot spot will lead to one message. The other hot spot will lead to the other message.

4] Double-click the response type symbol for Done (Wrong) to open its Response Properties dialog box.

Authorware allows you to determine whether a response choice is available to users by entering an expression in the Active If box.

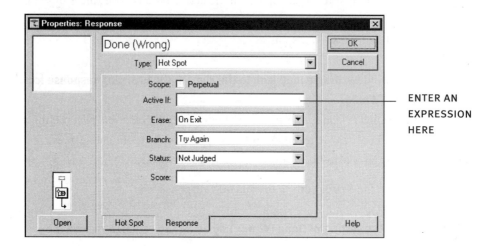

ENTER AN EXPRESSION HERE

5] On the Response tab, type the following expression in the Active If box:

WrongChoicesMatched>0 | CorrectChoicesMatched<3

WrongChoicesMatched is a numeric system variable that contains the number of wrong responses the user makes in the interaction.

CorrectChoicesMatched is another numeric system variable that contains the number of correct choices a user makes.

Notice that this expression includes the "or" vertical bar (|) between the two statements.

Using initial capital letters for words within a variable is not required. Initial capital letters make variables easier to read, but you can use no capitals or all capitals; Authorware will still understand the variable, as long as you spell it correctly. If you make a spelling error in typing a system variable, Authorware will catch it right away. Authorware won't tell you that you made a mistake, however. Instead, it will open the New Variables dialog box on the assumption that you've just created a custom variable. If that happens, check your typing for errors.

This expression makes the Done (Wrong) hot spot available if the user selects at least one incorrect choice or fewer than three correct choices. These are very broad conditions. In fact, selecting no response fulfills the second condition. Therefore, this hot spot will be active as soon as the user enters the interaction.

6] Select Exit Interaction as the Branch setting.

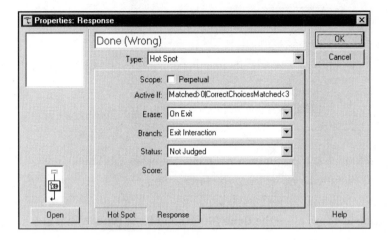

After users receive the feedback message, you want Authorware to leave the interaction.

7] Click OK to close the dialog box.

Now you'll set up the Done (Right) hot spot so it is available under a different set of conditions.

8] Double-click the response type symbol for the Done (Right) hot spot.

9] On the Response tab, type this expression in the Active If box:

WrongChoicesMatched=0&CorrectChoicesMatched=3

This expression uses the ampersand (&) to connect two conditions that must both be true. It says that this hot spot will be available to users only if they select all three of the correct responses and none of the incorrect responses. These conditions are much more exacting than the set of conditions you used for the Done (Wrong) hot spot. If a user fails to meet these conditions, the Done (Wrong) hot spot will remain active.

10] Select Exit Interaction as the Branch setting. Then click OK.

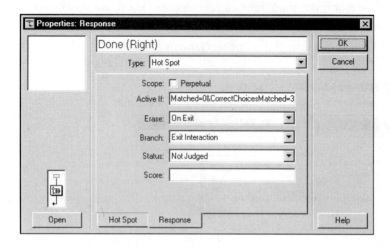

You're using the same Branch setting for both hot spots. Whether users make the right or wrong choices, clicking Done will end the interaction.

11] In the Presentation window, align the Done (Right) and Done (Wrong) hot spots over the word *Done*.

Both hot spots should have the same size and location.

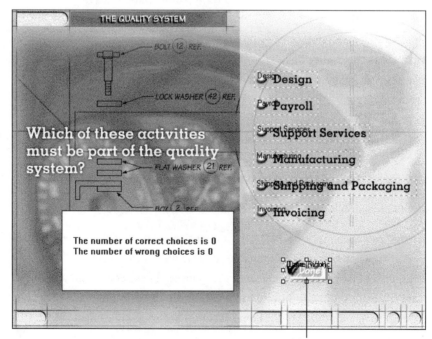

BOTH HOT SPOTS IN THE SAME LOCATION

12] Save your work.

You've set up the expressions that will determine which of the two feedback messages Authorware will provide users, and you've placed the hot spots where users will click. Next you'll add the two different messages that appear when users click Done.

ADDING TWO FEEDBACK SOUNDS

In this task you'll complete the interaction by adding a graphic and sound to each of the two Done hot spots.

The graphic will display checkmarks beside the correct choices on the screen, and the sound file will provide feedback—different feedback, depending on which Done hot spot is active when the user clicks.

1] Double-click the Done (Wrong) map icon to open its window.

You'll add two icons from the library.

2] Drag the Answers display icon to the flowline in the Done (Wrong) window.

This display icon contains check marks that will appear next to the three correct choices.

3] Drag the Although quality... sound icon to the flowline below the Answers display icon.

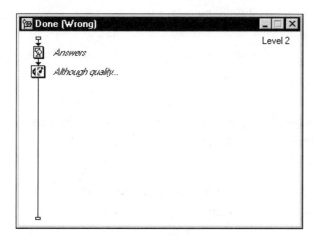

This sound icon contains the sound of a narrator explaining the correct answers.

4] Close the Done (Wrong) window and open the Done (Right) map icon.

You'll add the same display icon but a different sound icon for this map icon.

5] Drag the Answers display icon to the flowline.

Even when users make the correct choices, it's still good to provide an extra visual reminder of what those choices are.

6] Drag the Right! sound icon to the flowline below Answers.

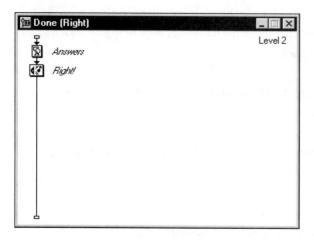

The Right! sound icon contains a slightly different message from the sound icon used for the Done (Wrong) response. This message congratulates the user for choosing correctly and then reviews why those choices are correct.

You're ready to try out the interaction.

7] Close the window and restart the piece. Try choosing the three correct choices: Design, Manufacturing, and Shipping and Packaging. Then click Done.

You should hear the voice saying, "Right!…"

What makes the Done (Right) hot spot active is the ongoing count of correct and wrong responses that Authorware is tracking. Each time you select one of the choices, Authorware adds one to the total of either correct or wrong responses. The expressions you entered in the Active If boxes for the two Done hot spots respond to the two totals. Depending on the values of the two variables, either one hot spot or the other is active.

In this case, you selected no incorrect choices and three correct choices. Until you selected the third correct choice, the Done (Wrong) hot spot was active. As soon as you clicked the third correct choice, the Done (Wrong) hot spot became inactive and the Done (Right) hot spot became active.

When you click Done, you're actually clicking the Done (Right) hot spot, which leads the flow to the sound icon that begins playing, "Right!..."

8] Restart the piece again and try any other choices before clicking Done.

You should hear slightly different feedback that begins, "Although quality..."

This time the Done (Wrong) hot spot stayed active throughout the interaction. Remember that this hot spot is automatically active as soon as you enter the interaction because of the expression in the Active If box: *WrongChoicesMatched>0 | CorrectChoicesMatched<3*. As soon as you enter the interaction, the number of correct choices is less than 3. If you make a single wrong choice, this hot spot remains active even if you select all three correct choices after the one wrong choice. Similarly, if you select no wrong choices but only select two out of the three correct choices, this hot spot still will remain active.

When you click Done, you're actually clicking the Done (Wrong) hot spot, which leads the flow to the sound icon that begins playing, "Although quality...."

9] Delete the Embedded Variables display icon from the flowline.

This step is optional. In a real-world project, you would remove this display icon before packaging a piece. In this case, you can leave the display icon in your piece if you want as a reminder of how embedded variables can be useful in authoring.

10] Save your work.

In this lesson you've used variables to control which of two messages plays in response to users' correct and incorrect choices in a hot spot interaction. In your own projects you'll have many opportunities to use variables in creative ways to provide capabilities that make your pieces valuable to users.

DEBUGGING TIPS

In this lesson you embedded two variables to make visible some of the work that Authorware performs behind the scenes. Embedding variables is one common debugging technique that will prove useful in your projects. Following are more suggestions for finding and resolving problems in your Authorware pieces.

Trace the flow. Many times a problem occurs because Authorware follows a different flow from what you intended. To see exactly what icons are executed while a piece runs, open the Control Panel and click the Show/Hide Trace button (Lesson 1). The Trace window displays a list of icons in the order that Authorware encounters them.

Check icon settings. Check the settings used for the icons involved in a section of the piece that isn't working properly. You may discover that an icon is set differently from how you intended, and changing one setting can sometimes resolve a problem.

Use the start and stop flags. When you think you know the section where a problem is occurring, use the start and stop flags to identify that section. Keep moving the flags until you isolate the section. (You'll use the start flag for the first time in Lesson 14.)

Re-create the section. In a new file, re-create the sequence of icons contained in a section that has problems. If your new version doesn't work properly, there's probably something wrong with the logic. If the new version works, compare it to the original to see how they differ. You might want to copy the section into the original piece and see if that fixes the problem.

Make one change at a time. When you make changes to fix a problem, make one change and see if it solves the problem. Then change it back and try something else. If you make several changes before trying out what you did, it's hard to tell which change solved the problem.

WHAT YOU HAVE LEARNED

In this lesson you have:

- Loaded a custom palette that includes the specific range of colors required for the graphics in a piece [*page* **274**]
- Created a hot spot interaction with three correct and three incorrect responses [*page* **276**]
- Used the Correct Response and Wrong Response Status settings to track a user's success in an interaction [*page* **279**]
- Used the system variables *CorrectChoicesMatched* and *WrongChoicesMatched* and the Active If property to create two hot spots that branch to two different feedback messages [*page* **288**]

digital movies

integrating

LESSON 14

Including digital movies in an Authorware piece is easy. Integrating movies with text, graphics, animations, and interactivity is more challenging. In this lesson you'll incorporate a movie in a project and then build a sequence of sounds and images that complement and expand the communication that the movie begins. You'll align the movie so it blends seamlessly against a background image. You'll produce smooth transitions between two images. You'll also use wait icons to control the timing

THE QUALITY SYSTEM

Digital movies play within a rectangular window, but they don't have to look that way. For example, the narrator in **Starting the QS-9000 Process** *appears to be speaking from within an automobile dashboard. In this lesson you'll use several techniques for integrating movies with other media to produce effective multimedia communication.*

relationship between sounds and their related images. If you would like to see the final result of this lesson, open the Final Files folder and play 14_Final.a5p.

WHAT YOU WILL LEARN

In this lesson you will:

- Mark the starting point of a flowline segment that you want to run instead of running the entire piece
- Add a digital movie to a piece
- Align a movie in the Presentation window so it blends seamlessly with background art
- Assemble graphics and sounds that complement and continue the message contained in the movie

APPROXIMATE TIME

It usually takes about 1½ hours to complete this lesson.

LESSON FILES

Media Files:
Your Files\Quality Project\Intro.a5l
Your Files\Quality Project\Quality Media
Beginning File:
Beginning Files\14_Begin.a5p
Completed Project:
Final Files\14_Final.a5p

SETTING UP FOR THIS LESSON

To prepare for using a movie, you'll open the Authorware file you used in the last lesson and use the **start flag** to set a starting point on the flowline for the work of this lesson. Then, on the flowline, you'll place the artwork that will be the background for the movie.

1] Open 14_Begin.a5p in the Beginning Files folder and save it as *14_Quality.a5p* in the Quality Project folder.

Alternatively, you can use the file you worked on in the previous lesson and save it as *14_Quality.a5p*.

2] Group the icons from the previous lesson into a map icon.

To do this, choose Edit >Select All (Ctrl+A). Then choose Modify > Group.

3] Name the map icon *Question*.

4] Open the Intro.a5l library.

This library is in the Quality Project folder. It contains the graphics and sounds you'll use in this lesson.

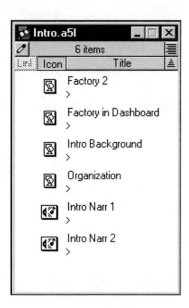

5] Drag the Intro Background display icon from the Intro.a5l library to the flowline below the Question map icon.

This image is a full-screen photograph of an automobile dashboard. It will serve as the background for the movie and graphics you'll work with in this lesson.

In previous lessons you attached groups of icons to a Temp. Storage decision icon to keep the icons off the main flowline while you developed new content. This time you'll use a different approach to setting up your workspace in the Design window. You'll leave the map icon from the previous lesson on the main flowline and place the start flag below that map icon. Then you'll use the Restart from Flag command to begin running the piece after the start flag.

One advantage of using the start flag is that whenever you want to run the entire piece from the beginning, you can use the normal Restart command. Using the start flag also lets you quickly change the starting point as you make changes to your piece.

6] Drag the start flag from the icon palette to the flowline between the Question map icon and the Intro Background display icon.

Authorware also provides a **stop flag**, which stops the flow at the point on the flowline where you place it. You can use the start and stop flags separately or together to indicate a section of the flowline that you want to run. Note that the icon palette contains only one start flag and one stop flag. When either flag is placed on the flowline, it's missing from the icon palette, unlike the other icons in the palette, which are available in unlimited numbers.

After you place the start flag on the flowline, you'll use the Restart from Flag command instead of the normal Restart command whenever you want to run the piece from the start flag.

tip   *If you forget to remove the start or stop flag from the flowline before packaging a piece, don't worry. Authorware ignores the start and stop flags in a packaged piece.*

7] Choose Control › Restart from Flag (Ctrl+Alt+R, or press 4 on the numeric keypad) to run the piece from the start flag.
You should see the full-screen image of the dashboard, which so far is the only media element that follows the start flag.

8] Save your work.

Now you're ready to add a movie to this piece.

USING A MOVIE

In this task you'll load a digital movie into the digital movie icon and select several options to control the way it plays.

1] Drag a digital movie icon from the icon palette to the flowline below the Intro Background display icon. Name it *Intro Movie*.

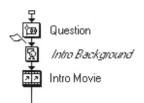

Question

Intro Background

Intro Movie

2] Double-click the movie icon to open the Movie Icon Properties dialog box.

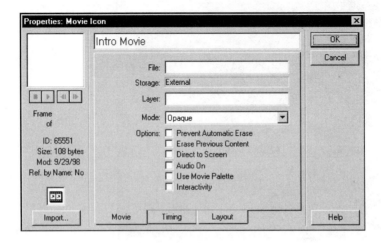

You'll use the options in this dialog box to control the way the movie plays. First you have to load the movie.

3] Click the Import button. Locate the Intro.avi file in the Quality Media folder.

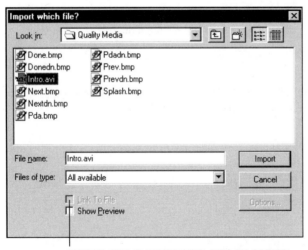

LINK TO FILE IS AUTOMATIC, NOT AN OPTION

Intro.avi is in the Video for Windows format. This is one of several digital movie formats that Authorware can play.

Notice that the Link to File box is inactive. The check box is inactive because Video for Windows movies are always linked externally rather than imported into the Authorware file; you can't import these movies into the piece. Using movies as external media keeps the size of pieces smaller and saves you the trouble of reimporting movies whenever you make changes to them. However, when you distribute a piece, you must also distribute a copy of the movie and the Video for Windows movie **driver**—the software needed to play the movie. The driver must be located in the same folder as the runtime for the packaged piece.

4] In the import dialog box, click Import.

Authorware creates a link to the movie file and displays information about it, including the location of the movie file. If you later make changes to the movie, make sure you put back the revised movie in the same location because Authorware will look for it there. Alternatively, you can reload the movie into the movie icon from its new location.

LOCATION OF MOVIE FILE

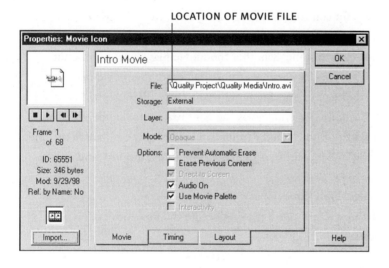

You can set several options to control movie playback.

For external movies, the Audio On and Use Movie Palette options are selected by default.

5] Click the Timing tab.

SET CONCURRENCY

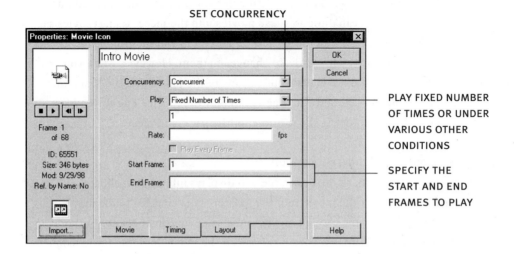

PLAY FIXED NUMBER
OF TIMES OR UNDER
VARIOUS OTHER
CONDITIONS

SPECIFY THE
START AND END
FRAMES TO PLAY

You have several options for controlling timing. The Concurrency setting determines whether the movie will play completely before the flow moves to other icons on the flowline. The Play setting determines whether the movie plays a set number of times until a condition you specify becomes true, or whether the movie play is controlled by various other factors you can build into a piece. By default, Authorware displays a *1* in the Start Frame box and leaves the End Frame box empty. If you don't enter a number for the End Frame, Authorware will play the movie to the end. To play part of the movie, specify different values for Start Frame and End Frame.

6] For Concurrency, select Wait Until Done.

This setting means the movie will finish playing before the flow moves down the flowline to the next icon.

You'll accept the rest of the default settings.

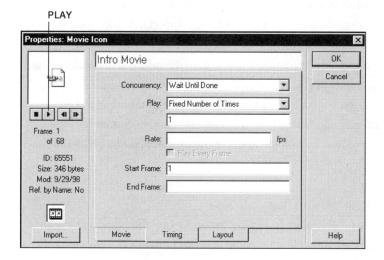

PLAY

7] **Click the Play button to preview the movie in the Presentation window.**

You may need to move the dialog box to one side to see the movie in the Presentation window.

8] **Click OK to close the dialog box.**

After you align the movie over the Intro Background image, the narrator will appear to be speaking from a gauge in the dashboard.

9] **Save your work.**

ALIGNING THE MOVIE AND BACKGROUND GRAPHIC

In this task you'll play and stop the movie several times as you make adjustments to its position in the Presentation window. Whenever you import a movie, you must align it with other images on the screen. When the movie blends with the background instead of occupying a rectangular frame on the screen, the task is more challenging. Instead of simply nudging the rectangular movie to fit within a rectangular viewing window, you must position it so that the portion of the background image shared with the movie is perfectly aligned with the background graphic. Sometimes this process takes several attempts in which you move the image, pixel by pixel, into its correct position.

1] Restart the piece from the start flag.

To do this, choose Control > Restart from Flag (or press 4 on the numeric keypad). When the movie begins playing, notice how far it is from its correct position in the dashboard image.

2] Pause the piece.

To do this, choose Control > Pause (Ctrl+P, or press 2 on the numeric keypad).

3] In the Presentation window, click the movie to select it.

You'll see handles around the movie, indicating that it is selected.

HANDLES

4] Drag the movie to its correct position.

Don't drag the movie by its handles.

The movie should play so that the narrator is speaking from within the RPM gauge of the dashboard. Move the movie as close as you can to its correct position and be prepared to make further adjustments after restarting the piece.

5] Restart the piece from the start flag.

When the movie starts to play, closely watch for any disparity between the background graphic and the portion of the background included in the movie.

Notice whether the image in the movie jumps up, down, left, or right. In most cases, you'll notice a combination of vertical and horizontal movement. Notice also whether the movement is a few pixels or more.

You may have correctly positioned the movie on your first try. If not, you'll need to repeat steps 2 through 5 until the movie is perfectly aligned with the background.

tip *Drag the movie if the distance is greater than a few pixels. Nudge it a pixel at a time by pressing the arrow keys if you need to move it only a short distance.*

Keep repeating this process until there's no jump when the movie begins. You'll use this procedure many times as you develop multimedia projects. With practice, you'll get better at judging how many pixels you need to move a movie to have it match the background art.

In the next task you'll continue building the sequence of media for this lesson by erasing the movie and introducing a new image.

ERASING THE MOVIE AND ADDING ANOTHER IMAGE

In this task you'll add an erase icon after the movie, followed by a display icon containing a new image that will appear for a few seconds in place of the narrator's face.

1] Drag an erase icon to the flowline below Intro Movie and name it – *Movie*.

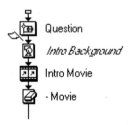

2] Restart the piece from the start flag. When the Erase Icon Properties dialog box opens, click the Icons tab if it's not already in front. In the Presentation window, click the image of the narrator.

The Intro Movie icon appears in the list of icons to erase.

note *You cannot apply transitions to external movies.*

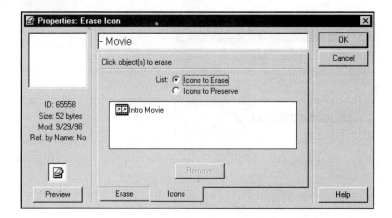

3] Click OK to close the Erase Icon Properties dialog box.

Next you'll add an image that will replace the narrator's face in the dashboard.

4] Drag the Factory in Dashboard display icon from the library to the flowline below the erase icon.

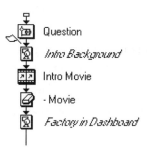

This display icon contains a photograph that fits into the RPM gauge in the dashboard, replacing the narrator's face. Because the artwork was created to align with the dashboard, you won't have to align it. You will apply a transition to the image, however, to enhance the way it appears on the screen.

5] Open the Transition dialog box for the Factory in Dashboard display icon.

To do this, with the display icon selected in the flowline, choose Modify > Icon > Transition.

6] Under Categories, select Dissolve. Under Transitions, select Dissolve, Pixels Fast. Then click OK.

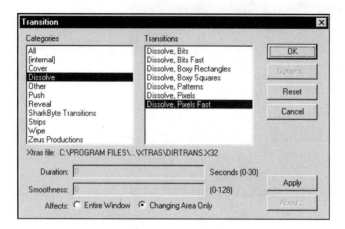

This setting produces a quick, finely textured transition.

7] Save your work.

In the next task you'll continue building the sequence of images and sounds.

SEQUENCING IMAGES AND SOUNDS

In this task you'll add, on the flowline, a sound icon that contains the narration that accompanies the Factory in Dashboard image, and you'll add a wait icon to hold the image on the screen for the appropriate length of time during the narration. Then you'll erase the Factory in Dashboard image and replace it with a new image that appears while the narration continues.

1] Drag the Intro Narr 1 sound icon from the library to the flowline below Factory in Dashboard.

This sound icon contains narration that accompanies the Factory in Dashboard image and an image that's displayed after it.

2] Double-click the Intro Narr 1 sound icon to open its Sound Icon Properties dialog box.

All the sound icons in the library have already been set up for this lesson. You'll just review the settings for this icon.

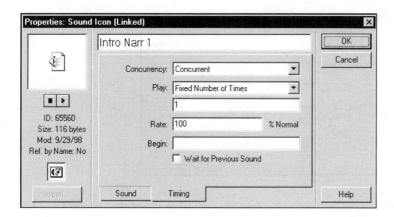

Notice that on the Timing tab, Concurrency is set to Concurrent. That way, the narration will play while Authorware moves down the flowline to the wait, erase, and display icons that follow it.

3] Click Cancel to close the dialog box.

4] Drag a wait icon from the icon palette to the flowline below the Intro Narr 1 sound icon.

You'll use this wait icon to pause the flow—as the sound continues—so that the Dashboard in Factory image remains on the screen for 2½ seconds before being erased.

5] Open the Wait Icon Properties dialog box. Click the Key Press and Show Button boxes to remove the checkmarks.

You'll enter a variable to make it easier to set and fine-tune the length of the pause that this wait icon will produce.

6] In the Time Limit box, enter _IconTitle_.

The _IconTitle_ system variable contains the name of an icon that appears in the title box and on the flowline. By using _IconTitle_ for the duration setting, you give yourself greater flexibility in adjusting the duration of the pause without having to open this dialog box again.

7] Type _2.5_ as the title of the wait icon. Then click OK.

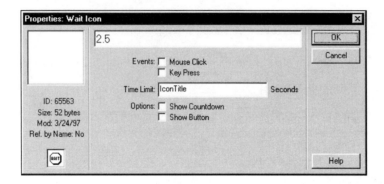

This wait icon will pause the flow for 2½ seconds before Authorware executes the next icon. This will not affect the playback of the sound icon, which will continue playing during the pause.

Now you'll place an erase icon after the wait icon to erase the Factory in Dashboard image.

8] Drag an erase icon to the flowline below Factory in Dashboard. Name it _– Factory in Dashboard_.

You'll erase this image and then use the same transition to display a new image on the screen. Using the same transition to erase one display icon and display the next display icon produces **cross fade**, in which two transitions act as a single transition, erasing one image and displaying the other.

9] Restart the piece from the start flag. When the Erase Icon Properties dialog box opens, click the image of the factory in the dashboard to select it for erasing.

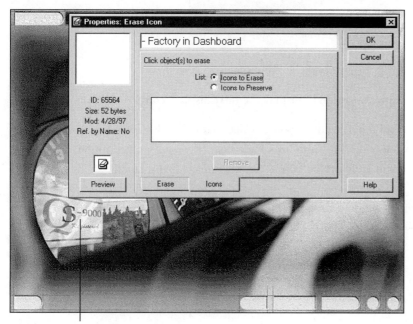

CLICK THIS IMAGE

10] On the Erase tab, click the Transition button to open the Erase Transition dialog box.

11] Under Categories, select Wipe. Under Transitions, select Wipe Right.

12] Type .5 in the Duration box. Then click OK.

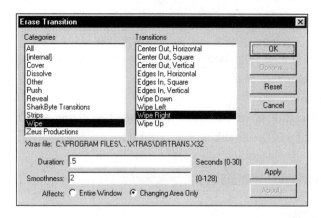

You'll use this same transition to display the next display icon.

In the Erase Icon Properties dialog box, notice that if you don't want cross-fade to occur, you can select the Prevent Cross Fade box. If you select this option, the first image will be completely erased before the next image is displayed.

13] In the Design window, drag the Factory 2 display icon from the library to the flowline below the erase icon.

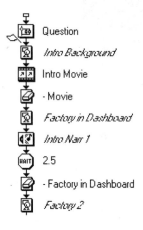

Question

Intro Background

Intro Movie

- Movie

Factory in Dashboard

Intro Narr 1

2.5

- Factory in Dashboard

Factory 2

14] Open the Transition dialog box for Factory 2.
To do this, choose Modify > Icon > Transition.

You'll use the same transition and duration to display the new image as you selected to erase the previous image.

15] Under Categories, select Wipe. Under Transitions, select Wipe Right. Type .5 in the Duration box. Then click OK.

You've created a seamless sequence of images. See how it looks so far.

16] Restart the piece from the start flag.

The Intro Background appears, and the movie plays. The movie is erased, and it's replaced by the image of the factory as the narration plays. After 2½ seconds, the image of the factory is erased with a wipe transition, and the Factory 2 image appears. Because the two images share the same transition, the effect is a smooth transition between the two images.

17] Save your work.

In the next task you'll continue building this sequence.

COMPLETING THE SEQUENCE OF IMAGES AND SOUNDS

To complete the work for this lesson, you will use another wait icon to hold the Factory 2 image on the screen before an erase icon removes it using a transition that cross-fades into the final image. Finally, you'll add a sound icon containing the final segment of narration that accompanies the final image.

You'll start by enlarging the Design window to make room for additional icons.

1] Drag the bottom of the Design window downward to enlarge it.

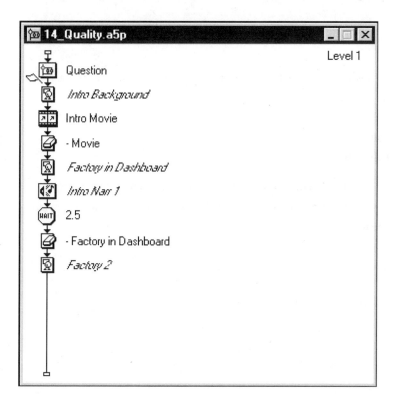

2] Select the wait icon you placed on the flowline earlier.

It has the icon title *2.5*. Copying this icon is the easy way to add a new pause. It has the settings you want. Moreover, because the icon title contains its duration, you can easily change the duration to what's needed for the new image.

3] Copy the wait icon.

To do this, choose Edit > Copy.

4] Click the flowline below the Factory 2 display icon.

Clicking the flowline positions the paste hand to indicate where you want to paste the copied wait icon.

5] Paste the wait icon.

To do this, choose Edit > Paste.

The wait icon appears on the flowline. You'll change its duration to create a longer pause—long enough for the sound file to play completely before the image is erased and a new image appears.

6] Enter *5.5* as the title for the new wait icon.

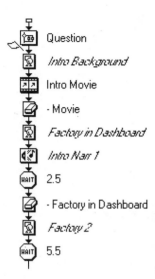

The flow will pause for 5½ seconds—long enough for the narration to finish playing—before moving to the next icon you put on the flowline. This next icon will be an erase icon to erase Factory 2.

7] Drag an erase icon to the flowline below the 5.5 wait icon. Name it – *Factory 2*.

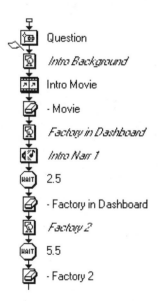

You don't need to run the piece to select the display icon to be erased. You just need to display its image in the Presentation window.

8] In the Design window, double-click the Factory 2 display icon.

The image appears on the screen. Now you'll open the Erase Icon Properties dialog box and select this image to be erased.

9] In the Design window, double-click the – Factory 2 erase icon.

First you'll select the transition. Then you'll select the image you want to erase.

10] On the Erase tab, click the Transition button.

The Erase Transition dialog box opens.

11] Under Categories, select Dissolve. Under Transitions, select Dissolve, Bits. Enter *1* in the Duration box. Then click OK.

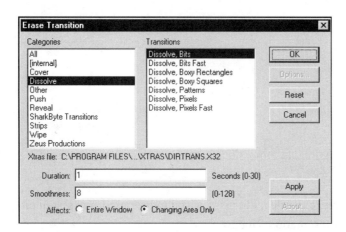

12] Click the Icons tab. Then click the Factory 2 image in the Presentation window to select it for erasing.

The image on the screen dissolves, and the icon title appears in the list of icons to be erased.

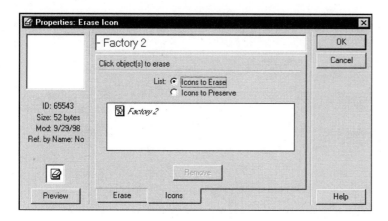

13] Click OK.

You've erased Factory 2. Now you'll add the final image, using the same transition.

14] Drag the Organization display icon from the library to the bottom of the flowline. Then open the Transition dialog box for this image.

To do this, choose Modify > Icon > Transition.

This is the final image in this section of the project and will be displayed using the same transition you used to erase the Factory 2 image.

15] Under Categories, select Dissolve. Under Transitions, select Dissolve, Bits. Enter *1* in the Duration box and click OK.

Now you'll place the final sound icon for this section on the flowline.

16] Drag the Intro Narr 2 sound icon from the library to the bottom of the flowline.

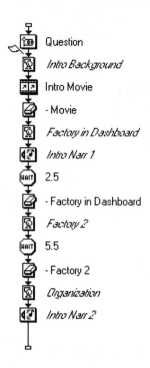

This narration will play as soon as the Organization image appears. Now it's time to check out what you've done.

17] Restart the piece from the start flag.

It works! The Intro Background photograph of the dashboard is displayed, and then the movie begins. When the movie—set to Wait Until Done—completes, it's erased. Immediately, the Factory in Dashboard image appears and is held on the screen for 2½ seconds by a wait icon. Then it's erased, and the Factory 2 image appears. During this time, the Intro Narr 1 narration is playing. Another 5½-second wait icon holds Factory 2 on the screen, and then it's erased. Then the Organization image appears, and the accompanying Intro Narr 2 sound begins to play.

In your own projects, you will need to experiment and adjust the durations used for wait icons to produce a smooth, comfortable flow of images and sounds that users will enjoy.

18] Save your work.

WHAT YOU HAVE LEARNED

In this lesson you have:

- Used the start flag and the Restart from Flag command to run one portion of a piece that you're working on [*page* **302**]
- Incorporated an external digital movie [*page* **303**]
- Aligned the movie in the Presentation window so it blends seamlessly with the background graphic [*page* **308**]
- Used display, sound, and wait icons to present a coordinated sequence of media elements that complements the movie [*page* **310**]

introducing frameworks

Paging structures are common in interactive media. Allowing users to move forward and backward among a series of screens of information is a familiar method of navigation for most people. Authorware's **framework icon** and **navigate icon** make it simple to create paging structures as well as more complex forms of navigation. By attaching icons to a framework icon, you create a **framework**—a series of pages—that can form the basis of many kinds of interactive productions.

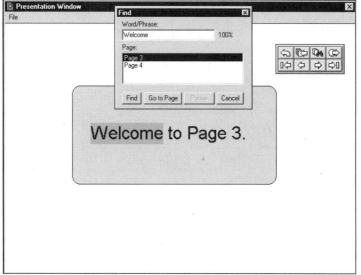

With Authorware you can create a simple paging structure in a few seconds just by attaching a few display icons to a framework icon— and that's what you'll do in this lesson. Even such a simple paging structure includes several navigation options, including the ability to navigate to a page by searching for a specific word or phrase.

In this lesson you'll use these icons to build a simple paging structure to see how Authorware's navigation controls work. In the lessons that follow, you'll create a more complex paging structure that includes a variety of media and interactivity. If you would like to see the final result of this lesson, open the Final Files folder and play 15_Final.a5p.

WHAT YOU WILL LEARN

In this lesson you will:

- Build a simple paging structure using Authorware's framework icon
- Use the default navigation controls to move to the next, previous, last, and most recently viewed page
- Navigate by selecting a page from a list of recently viewed pages
- Use the built-in text-search capability to navigate to a page containing the text you specify
- Explore how Authorware creates various navigation options

APPROXIMATE TIME

It should take about 30 minutes to complete this lesson.

LESSON FILES

Media Files:

None

Starting Files:

None

Completed Project:

Final Files\15_Final.a5p

STARTING A NEW FILE

In this task you'll begin a new file. Then you'll begin creating a paging structure by placing a framework icon on the flowline. Any icon you attach directly to a framework icon becomes a **page**. As you'll see, the framework icon includes a set of navigation buttons that let you move among the pages.

1] Start a new file (press Ctrl+N). Click None in the New File dialog box to close it without using a Knowledge Object. Then close the Knowledge Objects window.

2] In the Design window, drag a framework icon to the flowline. Name it *Practice Pages.*

The framework icon is the core of any paging structure you build in Authorware. As you'll see, the framework icon contains a group of navigate icons that give you the capability to move among a series of icons you attach to the framework to create pages.

3] Drag a display icon to the right of the framework icon and name it *Page 1.*

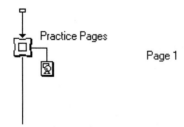

You attach icons to a framework icon the same way you attach them to interaction and decision icons.

4] **Drag three more display icons to the right of the Page 1 display icon. Name them** *Page 2*, *Page 3*, **and** *Page 4*.

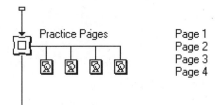

You've just created a paging structure with four pages. In a few moments you'll add content to each page, but first you'll examine what's inside a framework icon.

5] **Double-click the Practice Pages framework icon.**

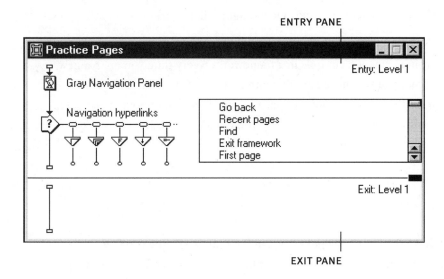

The inside of a framework icon resembles a section of the flowline that contains a perpetual interaction (Lesson 10). There are some important differences between the inside of a framework icon, however, and a normal section of the flowline.

One difference is that this perpetual interaction—a series of button responses with navigate icons attached—is perpetual only within the pages attached to the framework rather than throughout the entire piece. Thus, the navigation buttons are available throughout the pages in a framework but not elsewhere in a piece.

Another difference is that a framework icon is split into an Entry pane and an Exit pane. When a user navigates to any page attached to a framework, the flow of activity first passes through the Entry pane on its way to a page. When the user exits a page and leaves the framework, the flow passes through the Exit pane on the way out. This structure allows you to display images or play sounds on every page within a framework by placing icons for those elements in the Entry pane. Similarly, you can display images or play sounds that appear when a user leaves a framework from any page by placing display or sound icons in the Exit pane.

Another difference is that by default the navigation controls in a framework are set to **layer** 1. By default, each image contained in a display or interaction icon is normally set to layer 0. Images contained in icons that appear later on the flowline appear in front of images in earlier icons. If you need to make an image appear in front of other images regardless of where they occur on the flowline, you must assign the image a layer higher than 0—and that's what happens automatically to the Gray Navigation Panel display icon and interaction icon inside a framework icon. This makes the navigation buttons appear in front of whatever images you create for each of the pages—unless, of course, you assign a layer higher than 1 to any of those images.

The Gray Navigation Panel display icon, interaction icon, and eight navigate icons are the built-in navigation controls in a framework. Every time you open a new framework icon, you see these default controls. Each of the eight navigate icons is set up with a different navigation option. You can change or remove these default controls to suit the needs of your projects. You can also add other icons to the Entry pane and Exit pane.

tip *When you want your own text or graphics to appear on all pages of a framework, place the objects in the Entry pane and assign them to layer 1 or higher.*

6] Scroll down the list of navigate icons in the Practice Pages window.
Each navigate icon is set up for a different kind of navigation. For each navigation choice, users see a different button. In a moment you'll see the navigation panel and buttons that users will see.

CREATING CONTENT FOR PAGES

In this task you'll add text and a simple graphic to each of the four pages. Then you'll try out the navigation controls to move among the pages.

1] Close the Practice Pages window. Then double-click the Page 1 display icon to open it.

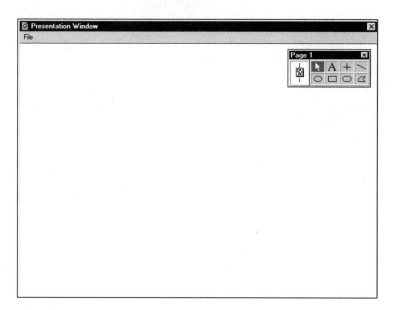

2] Use the Rectangle tool in the toolbox to create a rectangle on the screen.

Make the rectangle any size and color you want. You're building minimal content that you can see on each page as you navigate among the four pages. The dimensions and color of your graphics are not important. You just want a different image on each page so you can see how the navigation controls work.

3] Use the Text tool to create this text inside the rectangle: *This is Page 1*.

Use any font, point size, and color you want.

4] Use the Modes Inspector to make the text transparent.

To do this, choose Windows > Inspectors > Modes. Then select Transparent mode.

Your results should look similar to the following illustration.

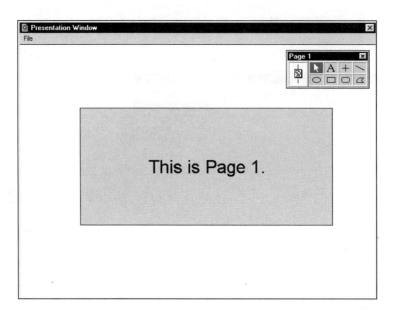

That's all the content you'll create for Page 1. Next you'll add a shape and text to the other three pages.

5] Switch back to the Design window. Double-click the Page 2 display icon.

6] In the Presentation window, use the toolbox to create another shape. Then use the Text tool to create this text: *This is Page 2.*

The idea is to create something different on each page. Don't worry about matching the following illustration.

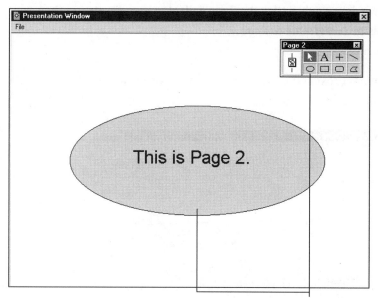

THE ELLIPSE TOOL MADE THIS SHAPE

7] Switch back to the Design window and double-click the Page 3 display icon. Create another shape and add this text: *Welcome to Page 3.*

It is important that you use the specified text here. You'll perform a search for this text later.

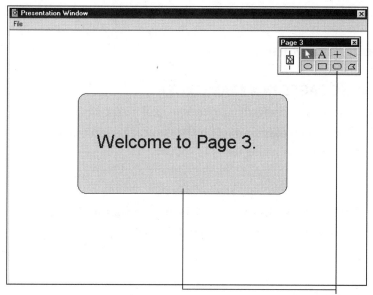

THE ROUNDED RECTANGLE TOOL MADE THIS SHAPE

8] In the Design window, double-click the Page 4 display icon. Create another shape and add this text: *Welcome to Page 4.*

Again, use the specified text.

You've created different text and images on each page. Now you're ready to run the piece and try out the navigation controls.

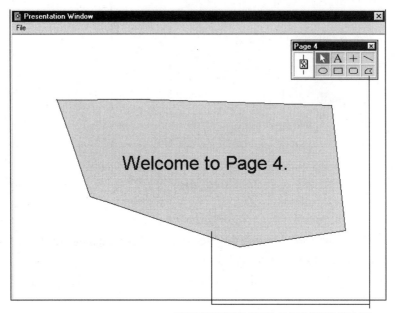

THE POLYGON TOOL MADE THIS SHAPE

9] Save your file as *15_Framewk.a5p*.

NAVIGATING AMONG PAGES IN A FRAMEWORK

In this task you'll use the default navigation controls to explore the simple paging structure that you've built. You'll page forward and backward, navigate to recent pages, and search for a page that contains text you specify.

1] Restart the piece.

The flow of activity first goes to the Entry pane of the framework icon, displaying the navigation controls, and then moves to the Page 1 display icon.

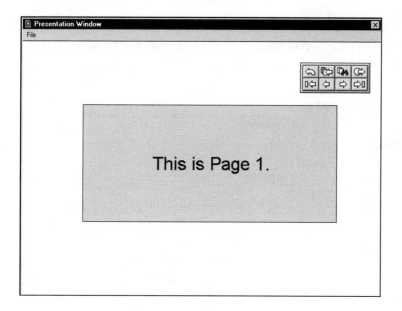

Each of the eight buttons in the navigation controls is connected to one of the navigate icons inside the framework icon.

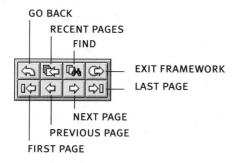

2] Click the Next Page button. Then click it again.

You should see Page 2 and then Page 3 appear on the screen.

3] Click the Previous Page button twice.

You'll move back to Page 2 and then Page 1.

4] Click the Last Page button.

This navigation control takes you to the last page in a framework—in this case, Page 4.

5] Click the Go Back button.

This navigation control takes you to the last page you viewed, wherever that is in the framework.

6] Click the Recent Pages button.

A list of recently viewed pages is displayed. To navigate to any page on the list, you double-click the name of the page.

7] Double-click Page 2 in the Recent Pages list.

The text and graphic you created for Page 2 appear on the screen.

To make this navigation device useful to users, you'll want to choose page names that describe the content of the pages, unlike the names you used here.

You can also navigate to a page by searching for a specific string of text.

8] Click the Find button.

This is the button with the binoculars on it. Click this button to display the Find dialog box.

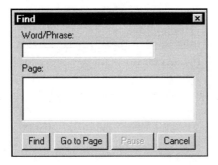

If text makes up a sizable portion of the content of a piece, providing text-search capability can be very helpful to users.

9] In the Word/Phrase box, type *Welcome* and then click the Find button.

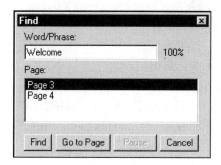

Authorware displays the names of the two pages that contain the text *Welcome*: Pages 3 and 4.

10] Select Page 3 and click Go to Page.

Page 3 is displayed with *Welcome* highlighted.

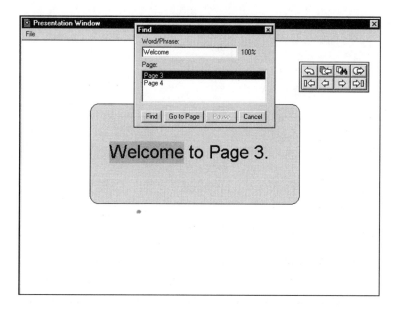

tip   *You can customize the Find dialog box to suit the needs of your pieces. You can change the name of the dialog box as well as that of every button and field that appears in the dialog box. To customize the Find dialog box, choose Modify > File > Navigation Setup.*

335

EXPLORING NAVIGATION OPTIONS

The navigate icon offers an array of navigation options. You've already seen a few of them. In this task you'll see how to set up navigation options.

1] In the Design window, double-click the framework icon to open it.

The symbol used for each navigate icon indicates its action. For example, the Go Back icon includes the upper corner of a page, and the Recent Pages icon includes the corners of three pages. As you use the navigate icons, you'll soon recognize the symbol for each kind of navigation.

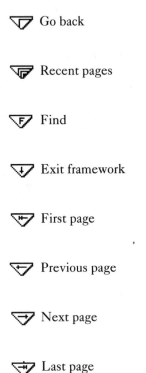

Go back

Recent pages

Find

Exit framework

First page

Previous page

Next page

Last page

2] Double-click the Go Back navigate icon.

The Go Back navigate icon is the first icon to the right of the Navigation Hyperlinks interaction icon. When you click the Go Back button, Authorware takes you to the last page you viewed, wherever it is in the file.

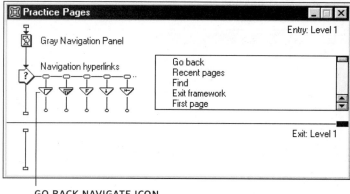

GO BACK NAVIGATE ICON

Double-clicking the navigate icon opens the Navigate Icon Properties dialog box. This dialog box contains the settings for all the types of navigation. You create each type of navigation by first selecting a destination type and then selecting from a group of options for that destination type.

The Go Back navigate icon is created by selecting Recent as the destination type and then Go Back for Page. The other option you have for the Recent destination type is to display a list of recently viewed pages.

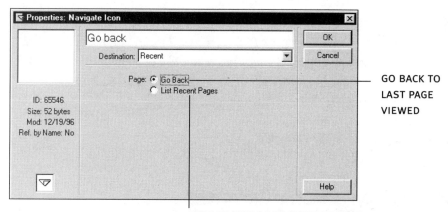

GO BACK TO LAST PAGE VIEWED

DISPLAY LIST OF RECENTLY VIEWED PAGES

Now examine a few more navigation options by selecting different options from the Destination menu.

3] From the Destination menu, select Nearby.

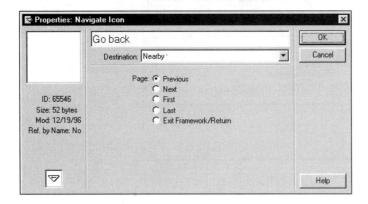

The Nearby destination type provides five navigation options, which are used to create five of the eight default navigation controls in a framework. The last option, Exit Framework/Return, is useful when users have navigated to a page from outside the framework. This option returns users to where they were before they navigated to the framework. For example, a user might click a button on the main menu of a piece to go to a page that's part of a framework. When the user is done viewing the page, he or she could return to the main menu by clicking the Exit framework button.

tip *You can place a navigate icon anywhere on the flowline, but its destination must be a page. A page is any icon attached directly to a framework icon. The only exception is a navigate icon set to Exit Framework/Return, which returns you to the point on the flowline from which you navigated. This works, however, only if you set the first navigate icon—the one that navigated to the framework—to Call and Return.*

4] From the Destination menu, select Anywhere.

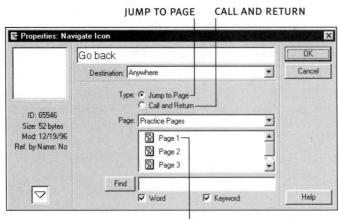

This destination type is very powerful because it lets you link a navigate icon to a specific page in any framework in a piece. You can even link a navigate icon in one framework with a page in a different framework. You'll use the Anywhere setting in later lessons.

Note that Anywhere is the default Destination type for a navigate icon you drag from the icon palette.

When you select Anywhere, you have the option of selecting either the Jump to Page or Call and Return option. Select Jump to Page to create one-way links and Call and Return to enable round-trip navigation, so users can return from a framework to the point on the flowline where they navigated to the framework.

5] Click Cancel to close the dialog box without changing the settings.

In this lesson you've created a simple framework and explored several ways of navigating among its pages. In the next lesson you'll build a paging structure that contains more complex content.

WHAT YOU HAVE LEARNED

In this lesson you have:

- Used the framework icon and a series of display icons to create a simple paging structure [*page* **326**]
- Used the default navigation controls to explore several kinds of navigation, including navigation to the next, previous, last, and most recently viewed page and to a page that you select from a list of most recently viewed pages [*page* **332**]
- Used the text-search capability to find a page containing the text you specified [*page* **334**]
- Examined several navigation options available with the navigate icon [*page* **336**]

framework pages

building

LESSON 16

In this lesson you'll convert the project you worked on in Lessons 13 and 14 into pages in a framework. Then you'll add a third page containing new content that you assemble from a library. Finally, you'll replace two of the default navigation buttons with custom buttons that were created to go with the artwork used in the *QS-9000* project.

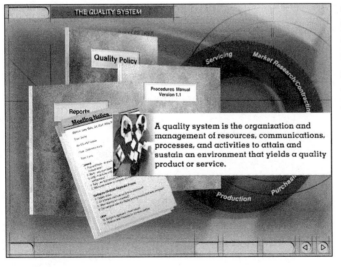

Authorware makes it easy to assemble text, graphics, sound, and movies into a paging structure that provides several kinds of navigation. In this lesson you'll assemble three pages of multimedia content and create two custom navigation buttons.

You'll start with the file you completed in Lesson 14. If you would like to see the final result of this lesson, open the Final Files folder and play 16_Final.a5p.

WHAT YOU WILL LEARN

In this lesson you will:

- Build a paging structure using a framework icon and the content from two previous lessons
- Add a new page to a paging structure by assembling a sequence of sounds and graphics
- Create custom navigation buttons that match the appearance of the background artwork

APPROXIMATE TIME

It should take about 1½ hours to complete this lesson.

LESSON FILES

Media Files:

Your Files\Quality Project\Compnts.a5l

Your Files\Quality Project\Quality Media

Beginning File:

Beginning Files\16_Begin.a5p

Completed Project:

Final Files\16_Final.a5p

SETTING UP A FRAMEWORK

In this task you'll open the file from Lesson 14 to begin work. Then you'll group the icons from that lesson into a map icon and open a library of media for this lesson. Finally, you'll place a framework icon on the flowline in preparation for creating the paging structure that you'll build in the rest of this lesson.

1] Open 16_Begin.a5p in the Beginning Files folder and save it as *16_Quality.a5p* in the Quality Project folder.

Alternatively, you can use the file you worked on in Lesson 14 and save it as *16_Quality.a5p.*

2] Click the icon palette where the start flag is normally located to return it to the palette.

You won't need the start flag in this lesson until later.

tip *When you want to use the start flag and can't remember where you last placed it on the flowline, click its place in the icon palette to return it.*

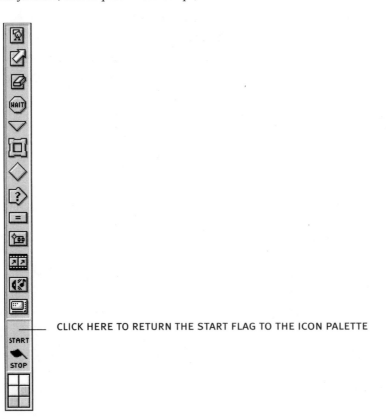

CLICK HERE TO RETURN THE START FLAG TO THE ICON PALETTE

3] Group the icons from Lesson 14 into a map icon.

To do this, marquee select the icons you used in Lesson 14. Then choose Modify > Group.

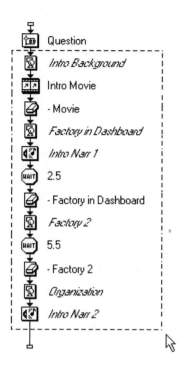

4] Name the map icon *Introduction*.

The flowline now contains the Question map icon you created in Lesson 14 and the new Introduction map icon. These map icons will become two pages in the framework you'll build.

5] Open the Compnts.a5l library in the Quality Project folder.

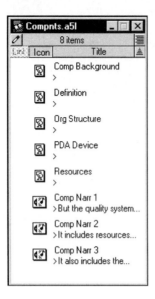

This library contains graphics and sound you'll use to create the third page of the framework. The library also contains one display icon that won't be used until Lesson 17.

6] Drag a framework icon to the flowline below the two map icons. Name it *Quality System*.

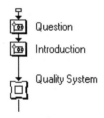

You'll create three pages, adapted from the *QS-9000* CD-ROM, that introduce and explain quality systems used in the automotive industry.

Any icon you attach directly to a framework icon becomes a page. The icon can be a single image or sound or a map icon containing a complex mixture of media and interactivity.

7] Drag the Introduction map icon to the right of the Quality System framework icon.
This movie and sequence of sound and graphics will be the first page in this paging structure.

8] Drag the Question map icon to the right of Introduction.

The question with three correct responses that you built in Lesson 13 will be the second page of the framework.

This is how easy it is to convert content into pages. Now check out what you've just accomplished.

9] Restart the piece.

The flow moves down into the framework icon and then immediately to the first page. This is what happens when the flow reaches the framework without a specific page as a destination. Because the navigation buttons are contained in the Entry pane, they appear on the screen first. Then the flow moves automatically to the first page, where the dashboard image—the first icon within this page—is displayed. Then the movie—the second icon in this page—starts playing. The other media elements appear in the order they were placed on the flowline. When all the media elements contained in the Introduction map icon have played, the flow stops. To navigate to another page within the framework, you need to use one of the navigation buttons.

10] Click the Next Page button.

Clicking the navigate icon connected to the Next Page button takes you to the top of the flowline in the Question map icon, which is the second page. The question you created in Lesson 13 is displayed, and Authorware pauses, awaiting your response to the question.

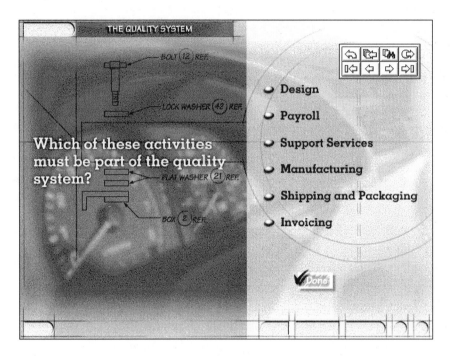

A framework erases the content of a page when you navigate to another page or leave the framework. You see only one page at a time. The only content that remains on the screen as you move from one page to another is what appears in the Entry pane of the framework—in this case, the panel of eight navigation buttons—and any content that was already on the flowline when the user entered the framework.

11] Choose File › Save All to save the piece and its libraries.

You've quickly converted two sets of content into pages in a framework. In the next few tasks you'll assemble additional media into the third page of this framework. Then you'll remove several of the default navigation buttons and replace others with custom buttons that you create.

CREATING ANOTHER PAGE

The third page of this portion of *QS-9000* will include sounds and graphics that explain the components of quality systems.

In this task you'll add a map icon to the paging structure and then begin to place content from the library along the flowline to create the new page.

1] Drag a map icon to the right of Question and name it *Components*.

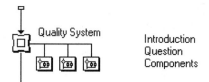

2] Double-click the Components map icon to open its window.

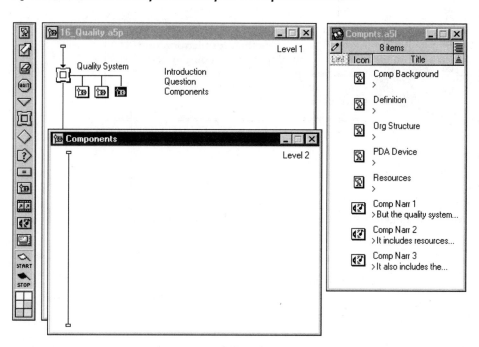

347

You'll arrange several display and sound icons from the Compnts.a51 library along this section of the flowline, sequencing narration with accompanying images. In Lesson 14, you used wait icons to hold images on the screen until they were replaced with other images, while the narration continued to play. In this lesson, you'll take a different approach. You'll use a series of three segments of narration, each contained in a sound icon set to Wait Until Done, to control the timing of the images. Before you start, you'll preview what you're about to assemble.

3] In the library, preview the contents of each icon.

To do this, right-click the icon. To stop the display of an image or the playback of a sound, click elsewhere.

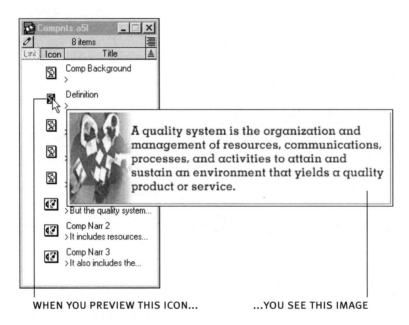

WHEN YOU PREVIEW THIS ICON...   ...YOU SEE THIS IMAGE

At this point you're acquainting yourself with the content before you assemble it into a sequence on the flowline. One display icon, PDA Device, won't be used until Lesson 17.

The graphics in this library have been prepared to appear in the correct position on the screen. You won't need to align the images as you did the movie in Lesson 14. Now you're ready to start putting this content onto the flowline.

4] Drag the Comp Background display icon from the library to the top of the flowline in the Components window.

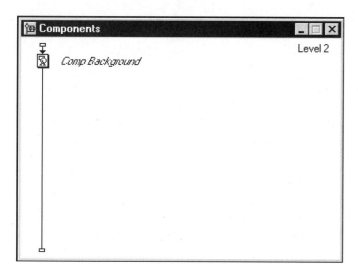

This is a full-screen image that will be the background for this page. Now you'll add a sound icon that contains the accompanying narration.

5] Drag the Comp Narr 1 sound icon from the library to the flowline below the Comp Background display icon.

This sound icon has been set up with the Wait Until Done concurrency setting. That means that only when the sound has finished will the flow move to the next icon on the flowline. This is what you want because this narration is meant to accompany the background image and introduce the next image.

6] Drag the Resources display icon from the library to the flowline below Comp Narr 1.

This next image will appear as soon as the narration in the first sound icon is complete. Next you'll place the second section of narration for this page on the flowline.

7] Drag the Comp Narr 2 sound icon from the library to the flowline below Resources.

This narration is designed to accompany the Resources graphic. You'll add one more image and one more sound to go with it, and then you'll see how the sequence plays.

8] Drag the Org Structure display icon to the flowline.

This image is a variation on the Organization image that appears on the Introduction page.

9] Drag the Comp Narr 3 sound icon to the flowline.

You'll place one last image on the screen—a text box containing a definition of *quality system* that appears after the narration ends.

10] Drag the Definition display icon to the bottom of the flowline in the Components window.

Now try out the sequence of images and sounds.

11] Place the start flag at the top of the flowline in the Components window. Then restart the piece from the start flag.

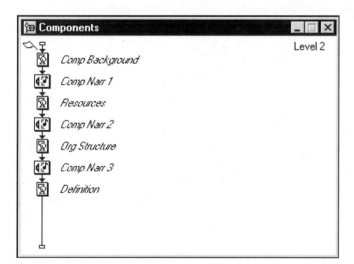

Although the start flag is placed at the top of the Components window, the flow actually begins in the Entry pane of the framework. Authorware first displays the two navigation buttons and then displays the Comp Background and begins playing the Comp Narr 1 sound. When the sound is done, the Resources image appears and the Comp Narr 2 sound plays. When Comp Narr 2 ends, the flow moves down to the Org Structure image and the Comp Narr 3 sound. Finally, after Comp Narr 3 is complete, the Definition image appears.

By breaking a sound into segments and placing those segments in different sound icons, you can coordinate narration with its related images.

12] Save your work.

In the next task you will enhance the sequence of images by adding transitions.

ADDING TRANSITIONS

To enhance the way each new image in this section appears on the screen, you will apply a transition to each image that appears after the Comp Background image.

1] In the Design window, select the Resources display icon. Then open the Transition dialog box.

To do this, choose Modify > Icon > Transition.

2] Under Categories, select Dissolve. Under Transitions, select Dissolve, Pixels Fast. Then click OK.

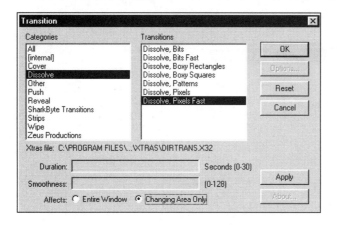

This produces a quick, finely textured transition.

3] Apply the same transition to the Org Structure and Definition display icons.

To do this, select each icon and then open the Transition dialog box and select the Dissolve, Pixels Fast transition.

> **tip** *Use restraint with transitions. You could pick a different transition for each visual element on this page, but it wouldn't be a good idea. Transitions are intended to highlight the visual or informational content, not draw attention to themselves.*

4] Restart the piece from the start flag.

Notice the difference now that you've added transitions for each new image. Each new image appears on the screen more smoothly than before.

> **tip** *Multi-icon editing, a new feature in version 5, lets you select several icons on the flowline and then apply the same property to them all at once. This feature can save you a lot of time. For example, instead of individually applying the same transition to the Resources, Org Structure, and Definition display icons, you could have selected them on the flowline and then chosen Edit > Change Properties. In the Change Icon Properties dialog box, you could then have selected the transition you wanted for all three icons and applied it to them at once. This feature might not make much difference when it affects only three icons. But imagine what a difference it could make if you needed to apply the same transition—or some other property—to 20, 50, or 100 icons.*

5] Save your work.

The final major task in this lesson is removing some of the default navigation buttons that won't be used and replacing others with custom buttons that will appear in the panel at the bottom of the screen.

CREATING CUSTOM BUTTONS

When you create a framework, you begin with the default navigation buttons that Authorware provides. For this project, however, you don't need all the navigation options provided by the defaults. In addition, the background artwork for this piece is designed to contain a set of custom buttons along the bottom of the screen that look quite different from Authorware's default buttons.

You won't be creating all the buttons used in the full *QS-9000* piece; some of the button locations at the bottom of the screen will remain empty.

In this task you'll remove the navigation buttons you don't need. Then you'll replace the other buttons with custom buttons, using artwork created for this project.

> **tip** *If you repeatedly use the same set of custom navigation buttons, you can replace Authorware's default navigation buttons with your own. See Authorware's online help for details.*

1] In the Design window, double-click the framework icon to open it.

You'll delete several components of the framework icon, starting with the rectangular panel behind the eight navigation buttons.

2] Select the Gray Navigation Panel display icon and then choose Edit › Clear or press Delete on the keyboard.

This deletes the Gray Navigation Panel display icon.

3] Delete the following navigation icons attached to the Navigation Hyperlinks interaction icon:

Go Back

Recent Pages

Find

Exit Framework

First Page

Last Page

To delete these icons, use the same procedure you used in step 2.

Now only two navigate icons remain attached to the interaction icon: Previous Page and Next Page. You'll keep these but replace their artwork with custom artwork that matches the *QS-9000* artwork.

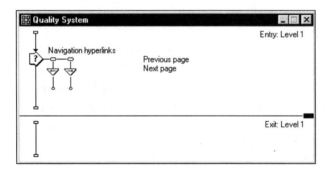

4] Double-click the response type symbol for the Previous Page button.

The Response Properties dialog box for this button appears.

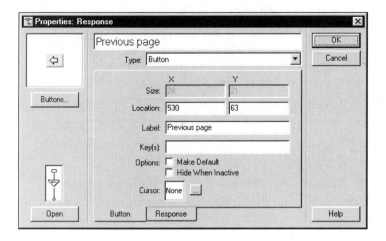

This is the first time you've worked with the button response type in this book. Buttons have many of the same options as other response types.

5] Click Buttons at the top left of the dialog box.

This opens the Buttons dialog box, which contains all the buttons available to this piece. This dialog box displays standard Windows and Macintosh buttons, check boxes, and option buttons. For each button used in a piece, Authorware displays the number of times it's used in the Uses field.

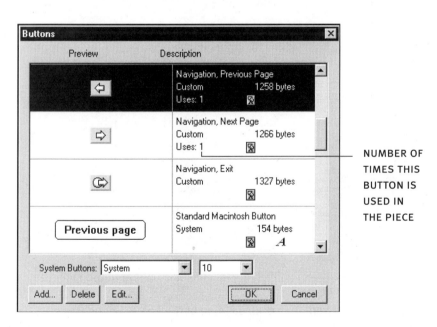

NUMBER OF TIMES THIS BUTTON IS USED IN THE PIECE

355

Standard buttons appear in the library with the label of the currently selected button. For example, if you select the Next Page button and then open the Buttons dialog box, the label *Next page* will appear on all the standard buttons in the library.

The default navigation buttons are custom buttons that are included with the framework icon. You want to replace the Previous Page and Next Page buttons with buttons that use artwork you'll import into Authorware.

6] Click Edit.

The Button Editor opens. By importing artwork and even sounds, you can create many different kinds of custom buttons. In this case, you'll import artwork for the normal up and down positions.

Notice that under Normal, Up is selected when you open this dialog box.

The Button Editor allows you to create a different image (and sound, if you want) for up to eight button states. The Up state is the way a button appears normally. The Down state is the way it appears while it's being clicked. If you want, you can create a different appearance for the Over state—the way the button looks when the cursor moves over it—as well as for the Disabled state—the way the button looks when it's inactive yet still visible.

In addition, you can create a series of images (and sounds) for the Checked states that are possible for check boxes and option buttons.

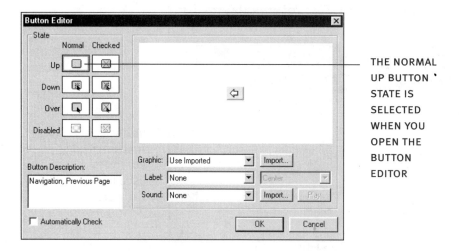

THE NORMAL UP BUTTON STATE IS SELECTED WHEN YOU OPEN THE BUTTON EDITOR

7] Click Import to import artwork for the up position of the new Previous Page button you're creating.

The import dialog box opens.

8] Select the Prev.bmp file and click Import.

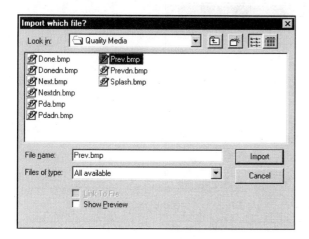

Prev.bmp is located in the Quality Media folder.

When you click Import, the image of a left-pointing triangle appears in the preview window, and the message in the Graphic box changes to "Use Imported." This is how the button will look when it's not being clicked.

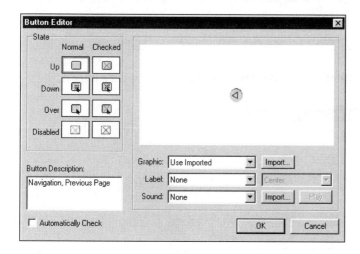

9] Under State, click Down in the Normal column.

SELECT DOWN

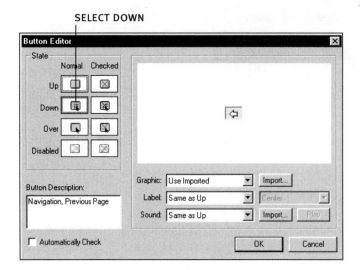

When you select Down, you have the option of importing the same artwork and offsetting it slightly for the down position. In this case, however, you'll import a different image for the down position.

tip   *To offset the artwork for the down position of a button, you click the image to select it (you'll see handles). Then you use the arrow keys to move the image 2 or 3 pixels down and 2 or 3 pixels to the right.*

10] Click Import. In the import dialog box, select Prevdn.bmp and click Import.

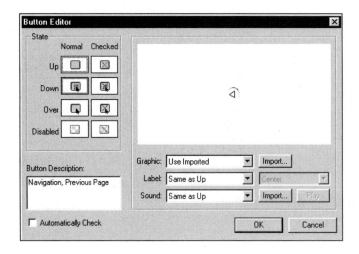

This is how the button will look in the down (clicked) position.

11] Click OK to return to the Buttons dialog box.

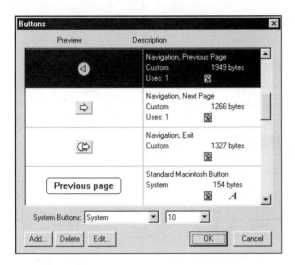

Your new custom button is selected in the list. When you click OK this time, the new custom button will replace the original button in the Authorware piece.

12] Click OK to close the Buttons dialog box.

The image of the new custom button appears in the preview window at the upper left of the Response Properties dialog box.

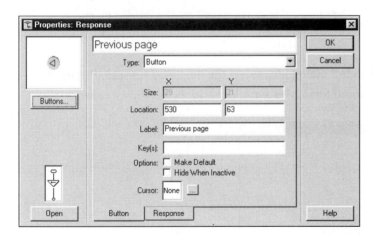

13] Click OK and save your work.

You've replaced one of the two navigation buttons. After replacing the Next Page button, you'll align both buttons so they appear in their proper locations at the bottom of the screen.

CREATING A SECOND CUSTOM BUTTON

In this task you'll repeat the same steps as in the preceding task for the Next Page navigation button.

1] In the Quality System framework window, double-click the response type symbol for the Next Page navigate icon.

The Response Properties dialog box opens for this button.

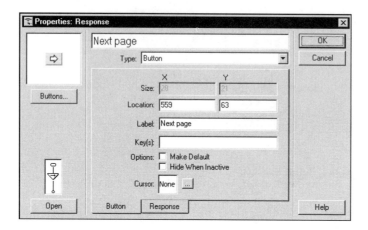

2] Click Buttons to open the Buttons dialog box. Click Edit to replace the artwork for this button.

The Button Editor opens. Again you'll import artwork for the normal up and down positions of this button.

3] Click Import. In the import dialog box, select the Next.bmp file and click Import.

The image of the up position for this button appears in the preview window.

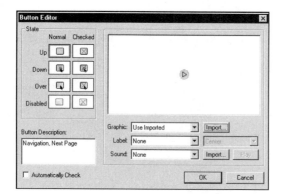

4] Under Normal, click Down. For Graphic, click Import.

Now you'll select an image of the same button in its down position.

5] Select the Nextdn.bmp file and click Import.

The image appears in the preview window.

6] Click OK to return to the Buttons dialog box. Then click OK to return to the Response Properties dialog box.

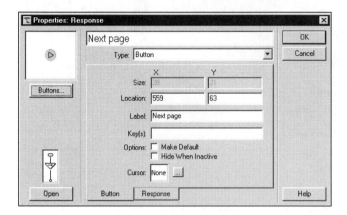

The preview window at the upper left displays the new custom button.

7] Click OK to close the Response Properties dialog box.

You've successfully created two custom buttons to replace the Previous Page and Next Page navigation buttons for this piece. Next you'll align the buttons with the artwork for the background.

ALIGNING CUSTOM BUTTONS WITH THE BACKGROUND ARTWORK

The background artwork created for this piece includes a panel for several navigation buttons at the bottom of the artwork. In this task you'll place two of the custom buttons for this piece in their proper positions over the background artwork. In the next lesson you'll add one more button.

1] Restart the piece from the beginning.

To restart from the beginning, choose Control > Restart (or press 1 on the numeric keypad).

The first page in the framework is displayed, and the movie begins playing. The two custom buttons appear, but they're definitely not in the correct location.

361

2] Pause the piece.

To do this, press 2 on the numeric keypad or press Ctrl+P.

3] Click the Previous Page button and drag it to the left circle in the panel at the bottom of the screen. Then drag the Next Page button to the right circle in the panel.

PREVIOUS PAGE BUTTON   NEXT PAGE BUTTON

Remember to use the arrow keys for precise adjustments.

When the buttons are where they belong, you're ready to try out the piece.

4] Restart the piece from the beginning and click the Next Page and Previous Page navigation buttons.

The flow moves to the framework icon, displaying the two navigation buttons, and then moves directly to the first page. When you click the Next Page button, its navigate icon navigates to the next page in the framework. When you click the Previous Page button, its navigate icon takes you to the previous page. Each time you click a navigation button, the flow first passes through the Entry pane of the framework on its way to the destination page, keeping the navigation buttons displayed on every page.

Notice that when you click the Next Page button on the third page, you go to the first page. Similarly, when you click the Previous Page button on the first page, you go to the third page. In Lesson 18 you'll prevent this wrap-around paging.

5] Save your work.

WHAT YOU HAVE LEARNED

In this lesson you have:

- Built a paging structure using a framework icon and content developed in two previous lessons [*page* **342**]
- Added a new page to a paging structure by assembling a sequence of sound and display icons from a library [*page* **347**]
- Replaced two default navigation buttons with custom buttons designed to match the appearance of the background art [*page* **353**]

navigating with hypertext

LESSON 17

Hypertext, which provides navigation by a click on a word or phrase, is one of the most common forms of interactivity. By combining two features—text styles and frameworks—Authorware makes it easy to create hypertext.

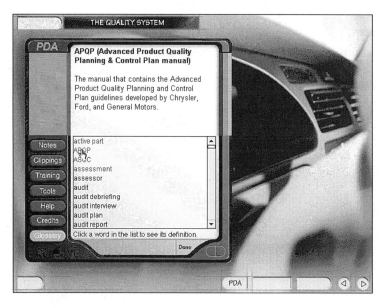

You can use Authorware's hypertext links to build a personal digital assistant, or PDA, in which users can click a term in a glossary to see its definition. The PDA you'll work on in this lesson is adapted from a device used in **Starting the QS-9000 Process.**

In this lesson you'll create a hypertext glossary that allows users to click words to see their definitions. You'll build the glossary as part of a perpetual interaction so that users can open the glossary while they're looking at the Quality System framework you built in the last lesson. The hypertext glossary is one component of a personal digital assistant (PDA) used in *Starting the QS-9000 Process* to give users access to additional information and capabilities. The glossary will be constructed using a framework in which each page contains the definition of one word in the glossary. For this framework you'll use a different navigation method than the paging buttons you used for Lesson 16. You'll define a hypertext text style and then use that style to create a link between each glossary term and the framework page that contains its definition. If you would like to see the final result of this lesson, open the Final Files folder and play 17_Final.a5p.

WHAT YOU WILL LEARN

In this lesson you will:

• Create a glossary of terms that's always available to users when they're viewing a piece

• Create custom buttons to display and remove the glossary

• Import text to create the list of glossary terms

• Use hypertext links so users can click a term to see its definition

APPROXIMATE TIME

It should take about 2 hours to complete this lesson.

LESSON FILES

Media Files:
Your Files\Quality Project\Quality Media

Beginning File:
Beginning Files\17_Begin.a5p

Completed Project:
Final Files\17_Final.a5p

PREPARING TO CREATE A GLOSSARY

In this task you'll open the project file and start assembling the components of the PDA Device, which will be used for a hypertext glossary.

1] Open 17_Begin.a5p in the Beginning Files folder and save it as *17_Quality.a5p* in the Quality Project folder.

Alternatively, you can use the file you worked on in the previous lesson and save it as *17_Quality.a5p*.

2] In the Compnts.a5l library, preview the PDA Device display icon.

To do this, right-click the icon.

This artwork depicts a personal digital assistant that users can display by clicking a PDA button that you'll incorporate in the panel at the bottom of the screen. In the full *QS-9000* product, the PDA provides access to several kinds of information and additional features. In this lesson, you'll create a highly abbreviated version of the PDA.

Now that you've seen how the PDA will look, you're ready to start assembling it.

3] In the Design window, drag an interaction icon from the icon palette to the flowline above the Quality System framework. Name it *PDA Interaction*.

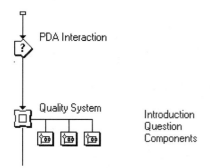

You'll attach one button to this interaction to allow users to open the PDA.

4] Drag a map icon to the right of the PDA interaction icon. In the Response Type dialog box, accept the default response type of Button and click OK. Name the map icon *PDA*.

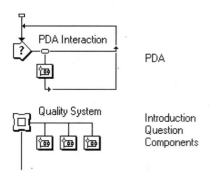

You'll build the glossary using a framework structure within this map icon.

5] Double-click the response type symbol for PDA to open its Response Properties dialog box.

To make the glossary available while users are paging through the other content in this piece, you need to make this interaction perpetual.

6] On the Response tab, click the Scope box to select Perpetual.

You'll also use the branching option you've used for other perpetual interactions in this book.

7] For Branch, select Return.

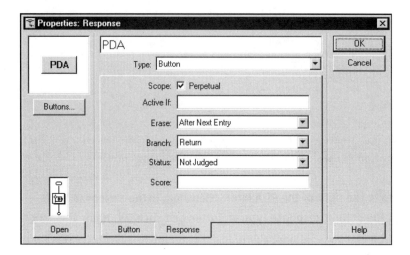

After users leave this perpetual interaction, Authorware will return them to the place on the flowline where they initiated the perpetual interaction. In other words, they'll be back viewing the page where they started in the Quality System.

When you select a button response type, Authorware automatically creates a standard button whose label is the icon title of the response icon. You'll replace the standard button with a custom button that fits into the button panel at the bottom of the screen like the other buttons you created for this piece in Lesson 16.

CREATING A CUSTOM BUTTON

In this task you'll replace the standard button with a custom button using artwork created for this project.

1] Click Buttons to open the Buttons dialog box. Then click Add to create a new custom button.

You'll import art for the normal up and down positions of the PDA button. In Lesson 16, you clicked Edit to replace the artwork for one custom button with artwork you imported. When you want to create a new custom button, you need to click Add.

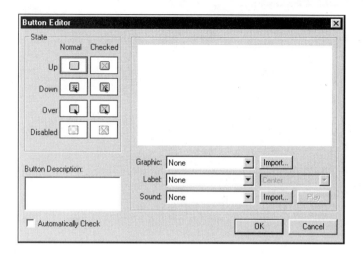

2] For Graphic, click Import.

The import dialog box opens.

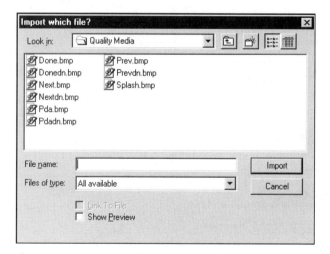

3] Select the Pda.bmp file in the Quality Media folder and click Import.

The image of the PDA button appears in the preview window.

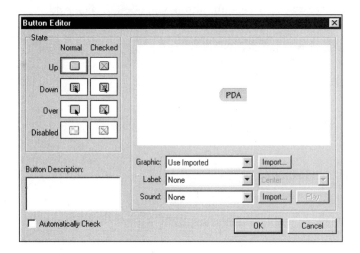

4] In the State section of the Button Editor, click Down in the Normal column. Then click Import again.

You'll import artwork for the down position of the same button.

5] Select the Pdadn.bmp file and click Import.

The image of the PDA button appears in the preview window.

6] Click OK to close the Button Editor. Click OK again to return to the Response Properties dialog box.

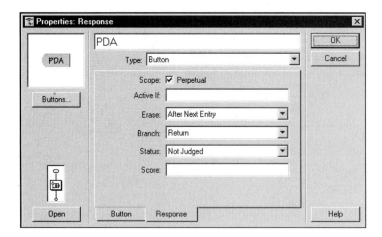

Now the image of the PDA button appears in the preview window in this dialog box.

7] Click OK.

You need to make one more modification to make sure the button is visible on the screen.

8] Restart the piece.

The PDA button appears on the screen before the background artwork, and then it disappears. The reason for this behavior is that Intro Background, a full-screen graphic, is displayed in front of the PDA button.

By default, every display and interaction icon is set to layer 0 in Authorware, and images in icons that come later on the flowline overlay those that come earlier. If you want an object that comes early on the flowline to be visible in front of other images, you must assign it to a layer higher than 0.

9] In the Design window, select the PDA interaction icon and choose Modify › Icon › Properties.

The Interaction Icon Properties dialog box opens. You'll enter a layer number for this interaction icon.

10] On the Display tab, enter *1* in the Layer box. Then click OK.

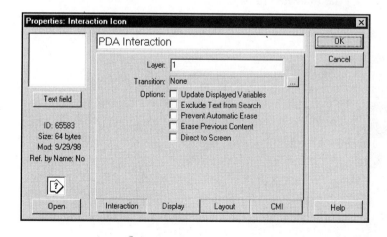

With all other display and interaction icons set by default on layer 0, a setting of 1 in this box will display the PDA button in front of the background artwork for the button panel.

> **tip** *A Layer setting of 1 is used by default for the navigation controls in a framework so that they overlay other visual elements on every page of a framework.*

11] Restart the piece.

This time the PDA button is visible on the dashboard image—but not in the right place.

PDA BUTTON

12] Pause the piece. Then drag the PDA button to the panel at the bottom of the screen.

Your screen should match the following illustration.

DRAG TO HERE

13] Save your work.

Now you're ready to build a framework that will contain the glossary.

SETTING UP A FRAMEWORK

In this task you'll assemble media and text from the library into a glossary in which users can click a word displayed on the PDA screen to see its definition.

1] In the Design window, double-click the PDA map icon to open it. Move the PDA window lower on your screen so you can see the main Design window while you work in the PDA window.

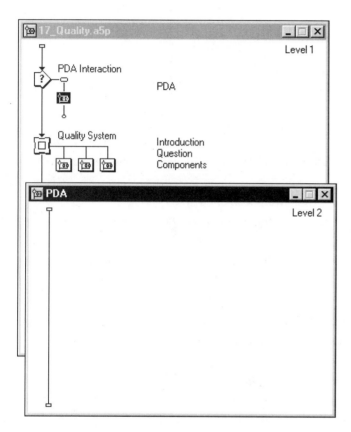

Next you'll start to assemble the glossary.

2] Drag a framework icon to the top of the flowline in the PDA window. Name it *Glossary Framework.*

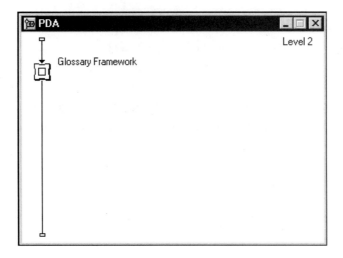

This framework will contain each definition of a term on a separate page. To prepare the framework, you need to strip out all but one of the default navigation controls.

3] Double-click the Glossary Framework icon to open it.
Users won't need to page through the framework pages or use other kinds of navigation. The only control they will need is the ability to remove the PDA when they're done using it. One of the navigation buttons, set to Exit Framework/Return, will do this.

4] In the Glossary Framework window, delete the Gray Navigation Panel display icon.
This contains the background panel behind the eight default buttons.

5] In the Navigation Hyperlinks interaction, delete all the navigate icons except Exit framework.
One way to do this is to first select the Exit framework icon by clicking its title in the scrolling list to highlight the icon. Then marquee select the icons on one side of the Exit framework icon and delete them. Finally, marquee select the icons on the other side of Exit framework and delete those.

374

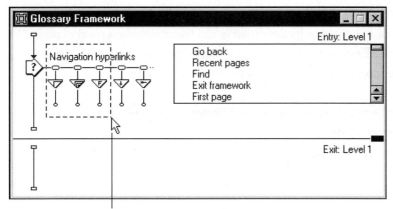

FIRST SELECT THE ICONS ON ONE SIDE OF THE
EXIT FRAMEWORK ICON AND DELETE THEM...

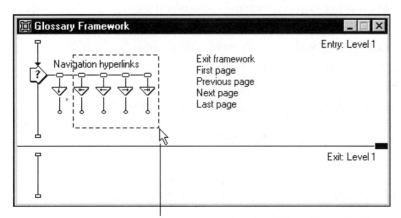

...THEN SELECT THE ICONS ON THE OTHER SIDE
OF THE EXIT FRAMEWORK ICON AND DELETE THEM

You're left with one navigation button. In a few steps you'll replace this button with
a custom button that matches the artwork for the PDA.

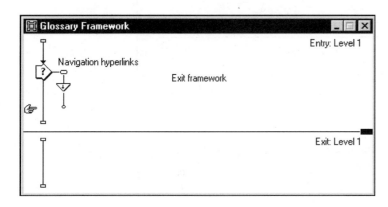

375

To make sure that the PDA and glossary terms remain visible after the user has clicked a word and navigated to its definition in the framework, you need to place those images in the Entry pane. Within a framework, the only images that are displayed on every page are those contained in the Entry pane.

6] Drag the PDA Device display icon from the library to the top of the flowline in the Glossary Framework window.

In the next task you'll create the list of glossary terms by importing a text file.

7] Save your work.

IMPORTING RTF TEXT

Although you can create text easily in Authorware, it often makes more sense to import a text file created in a word processing program—especially if the text has already been created for another purpose, so you can simply reuse it in a piece. In this task you'll import a text file that's been saved in a word processing program in rich text format (RTF). The benefit of importing RTF text is that you can import the text formatting along with the text itself. In this case the text file has been created in 9-point Arial, which will be readable and attractive when displayed as part of the PDA Device.

First you'll enlarge the Entry pane of the framework icon to make room for an additional icon.

1] Drag the pane divider downward to enlarge the Entry pane of the framework window.

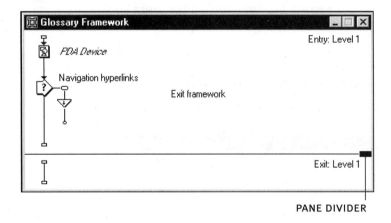

PANE DIVIDER

This will allow space for an additional icon that you'll add without the pane divider cutting off the bottom of the Exit framework navigate icon.

2] Drag a display icon from the icon palette to the flowline below the PDA Device display icon. Name it *Terms*.

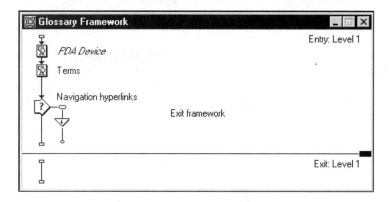

This display icon will contain the list of terms that users can click to see definitions.

3] Place the start flag at the top of the flowline in the Glossary Framework window. Then restart the piece from the flag.

The PDA Device appears, and then the piece stops at the Terms display icon. With the PDA Device displayed in the Presentation window, you can prepare the text field before importing the text so the text will fit within the dimensions of the PDA artwork.

4] Select the Text tool in the toolbox. Then click in the Presentation window on the left side of the PDA device, about halfway down the left side of its screen. (See the illustration below.)

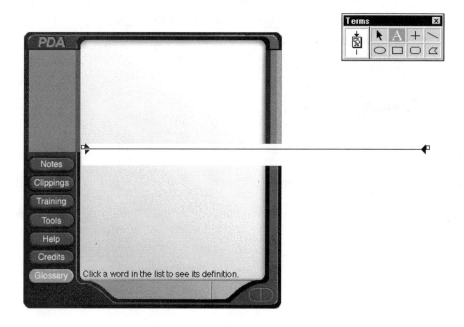

You're going to set the boundaries for the text you're about to import.

5] Drag the right end of the paragraph rule to the left to narrow the text field, so the right edge of the text will fit within the PDA Device screen. (See the illustration below.)

You're setting the boundaries for the text you're about to import. Don't worry if your screen looks a bit different from the illustration. After importing the text, you'll make fine adjustments to the text position and size.

6] Choose File > Import. Select the Terms.rtf file and click Import.
This file is located in the Quality Media folder.

When you click Import, the RTF Import dialog box opens.

You can choose to ignore page breaks or create a new display icon for each page break. In this case, it doesn't matter; the imported text is all contained on one page. Therefore, you'll accept the default, Create New Display Icon.

The second choice you have is whether to create a standard text object, which is the kind you've used so far, or to create a scrolling text object. You need to create a scrolling text object so that the list of glossary terms will fit into the PDA.

7] For Text Object, select Scrolling. Then click OK.

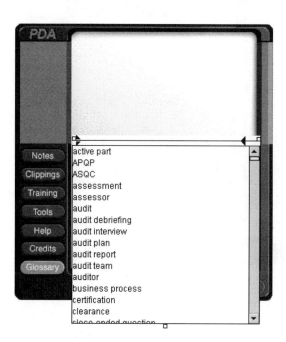

The text appears over the PDA image with a scroll bar on the right. Because you imported an RTF file, the formatting characteristics of the text (9-point Arial) were imported along with the words. You still need to make some adjustments, however.

8] Open the Modes Inspector and select Transparent.
To open the Modes Inspector, choose Windows > Inspectors > Modes. Then select Transparent in the Modes Inspector. Now you'll make the text fit the dimensions of the PDA.

9] Click the Pointer tool in the Toolbox. Then drag the handles of the text object to adjust its size and position to fit within the PDA.

The terms should start about halfway down the screen in the PDA because their definitions will appear in the top half of the screen.

When you're done, your Presentation window should approximately match the following illustration.

10] Save your work.

While the framework icon is open, you'll create a custom button to replace the default Exit Framework button.

CREATING A CUSTOM BUTTON

In this task you'll replace the Exit Framework button with a custom Done button that matches the artwork for the PDA.

1] In the Design window, double-click the response type symbol for the Exit Framework button.

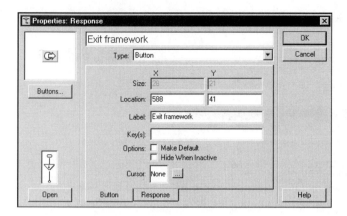

2] In the Response Properties dialog box, click Buttons. In the Buttons dialog box, click Edit.

You'll import artwork for the normal up and down positions of the Done button.

3] For Graphic, click Import. Select the Done.bmp file and click Import.

The Done.bmp file is located in the Quality Media folder.

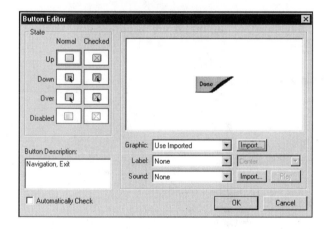

4] Under Normal, select Down. For Graphic, click Import. Select the Donedn.bmp file and click Import.

You're ready to save this new custom button.

5] In the Button Editor, click OK and then click OK again to close the Buttons dialog box.

The new custom button appears in the preview window of the Response Properties dialog box.

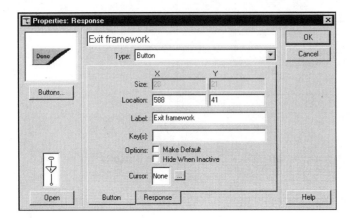

6] Click OK to use the custom button for this interaction. Then restart the piece from the start flag.

The PDA, list of terms, and Done button appear in the Presentation window. The Done button is not where you want it.

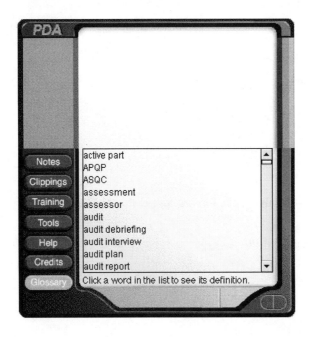

7] Pause the piece and then move the Done button so it's aligned over the artwork for the PDA.

Your screen should look approximately like the following illustration.

THE DONE BUTTON GOES HERE

8] Close the Glossary Framework window and save your work.

Now you're ready to create the series of definitions as pages in a framework. After you do that, you'll create hypertext links between four terms and the pages that contain their definitions.

IMPORTING AN RTF FILE TO CREATE FRAMEWORK PAGES

You'll import an RTF text file to set up four definitions of glossary terms as pages in a framework. After that, you'll link each definition with a word in the glossary using Authorware's hypertext links.

1] Drag a display icon from the icon palette to the right of the Glossary Framework icon. Name it *active part*.

The RTF text file that you'll import contains four definitions that will be broken into four display icons when the text is imported. Each display icon will be one page in the framework. The first display icon is named *active part* because the first definition in the text file is for active part, as you'll see in a moment.

2] Run the piece from the start flag.

The PDA Device is displayed, and then the active part display icon opens, awaiting content. Before importing the RTF text, you need to turn off the scrolling text setting and indicate where the text should be displayed.

3] Click the Text tool in the Toolbox. Then choose Text › Scrolling to turn off the scrolling text setting that remains from the last text you used.

4] Click in the Presentation window near the upper left corner of the PDA Device, approximately in the position shown in the illustration below.

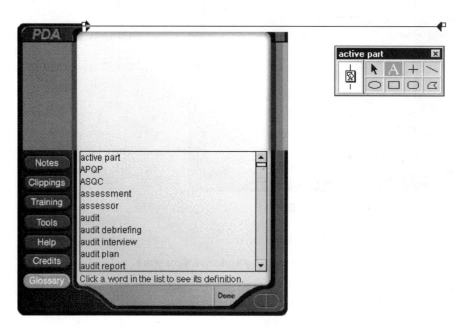

You need to make a narrower width for the text.

5] Drag the right end of the paragraph rule to the left, so the right end is within the borders of the PDA Device window.

Your screen should look approximately like the following illustration.

The placement and width of the text field determine where the imported text will appear on the screen.

6] Choose File › Import (Ctrl+Shift+R).

You'll import the Defs.rtf file, which contains four definitions in rich text format. Instead of always having to apply styles to text in Authorware, you can import an RTF file that you've formatted in a word processing program. You'll preserve the formatting and use an Authorware option that creates a separate page in the framework for each page in the RTF file.

7] Select the Defs.rtf file and click Import.

The RTF Import dialog box opens. This time you want to create a new display icon—which will become a separate page—for each hard page break.

8] Choose Create New Display Icon. Under Text Object, select Standard (not Scrolling) this time. Then click OK.

Authorware imports the text, creating a separate page in the framework wherever the text file contains a page break. The text field on each page has the same width and location. The text in each display icon contains the name of a term in boldface type, a line space, and the definition. Because you imported an RTF text file, all the formatting was imported.

Each page is a display icon containing a definition that users will see when they click a term in the glossary list. Notice that the three display icons created by importing the text file are named *: 2*, *: 3*, and *: 4*. To make it easier to link these definitions to the terms in the glossary, you'll rename each of these.

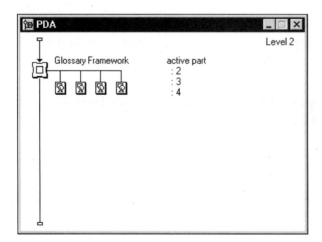

9] Select display icon : 2 and preview it.

To do this, right-click the icon. This is the definition for *APQP*.

10] Rename the icon *APQP*.

Renaming this display icon makes it simpler to identify it for linking to the glossary terms in a later step.

11] Preview icon : 3. Rename it *ASQC*.

12] Preview icon : 4. Rename it *assessment*.

13] Restart the piece from the start flag.

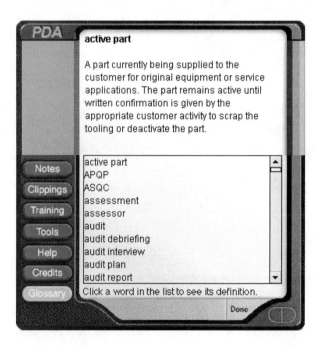

The flow moves into the framework icon, displaying the PDA artwork, list of terms, Done button, and first page in the framework. This definition is what users will see when they click the term *active part* in the glossary list.

14] Save your work.

In the next task you'll set up the links between the four terms and the pages containing their definitions.

CREATING HYPERTEXT

Authorware makes it easy to convert text into hypertext. In this task you'll define a text style that incorporates navigation. Then you'll apply the text style to the four glossary terms and create the link between each term and the framework page containing its definition.

1] Choose Text > Define Styles.

The Define Styles dialog box opens.

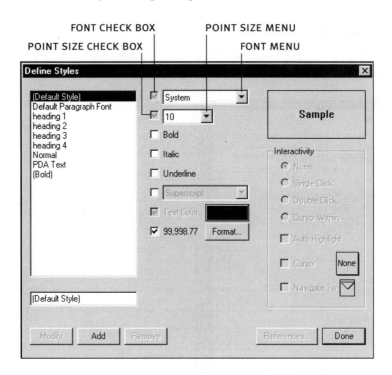

note *When you import RTF text into Authorware, you also import any styles that were present in the document you imported. In this case that's why you see style names listed in the Define Styles dialog box such as "heading 1" and "PDA Text," which you didn't create in Authorware. "PDA Text" was the style used in Microsoft Word to create text intended for use in the PDA Device.*

2] Select PDA Text in the list of styles.

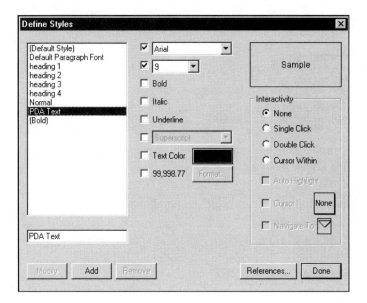

The hypertext style you'll create will use the same font and point size as PDA Text. By selecting a style that's close to what you want to create, you save yourself work.

3] Click Add to create a new style.

The term *New Style* appears in the list of text styles.

You'll change the color of the text style to make "hot," or clickable, words easy to distinguish on the screen.

4] Click the Text Color box to select it. Then click the color swatch to open the Text Color palette.

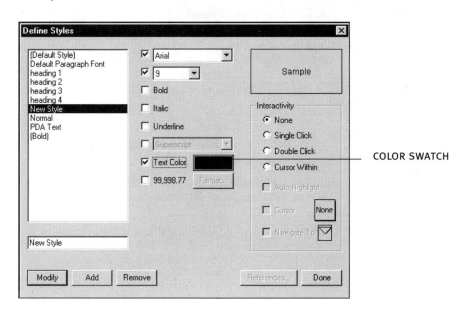

COLOR SWATCH

389

5] Select the bright red color in the bottom row of the palette and click OK.

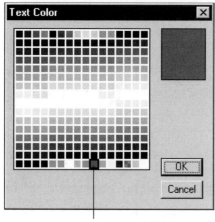

SELECT THIS COLOR

You've selected a look for the text style. Now you'll specify the kind of interactivity you want for the text style.

6] Under Interactivity, select Single Click.

Users will be able to click a word to see its definition.

Notice that when you select Single Click, other options become available. You'll select one of those options.

7] Click the Cursor box to select a custom cursor.

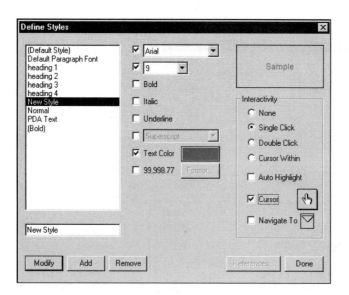

The hand-shaped cursor appears. You could select another custom cursor by clicking the image of the hand-shaped cursor to open a list of cursors, but this cursor is commonly used to indicate areas that a user can click.

You won't select the Navigate To setting. If you selected Navigate To, when users clicked any glossary term, they would go to a single destination. This kind of link is useful for some applications, but for a glossary you want each term linked to a different destination.

8] Select the New Style text in the box at the lower left of the dialog box. Then type *Glossary* as the name of the new style.

It's good to use a descriptive name for a text style because you might want to create more than one hypertext style in a piece.

9] Click Modify to save the name of the new style.

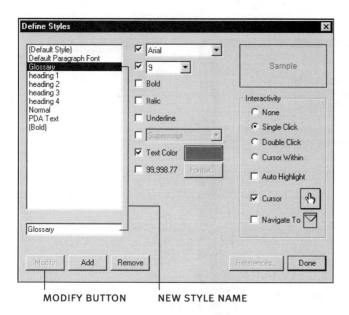

MODIFY BUTTON   NEW STYLE NAME

Notice that the Modify button is now inactive. As soon as you change any style settings, such as font or point size, the button becomes active again.

10] Click Done to close the dialog box.

You have saved the style as part of the Authorware file, ready to be applied.

11] Save your work.

You're ready to set up links between the words and their definitions.

CREATING HYPERTEXT LINKS

Of all the tasks in this lesson, this is one of the easiest. Now that you've set up a list of terms, a framework of pages containing definitions, and the Glossary text style, Authorware makes it very simple to link each word to the page that contains its definition.

1] Restart the piece from the start flag.

The flow begins within the Glossary window, moves into the framework, and displays the first page.

You see the first definition without clicking the word because Authorware automatically displays the first page of a framework when the flow enters the framework. In a few steps you'll insert an empty first page to resolve this.

2] Double-click the scrolling list of terms.

The Terms toolbox opens.

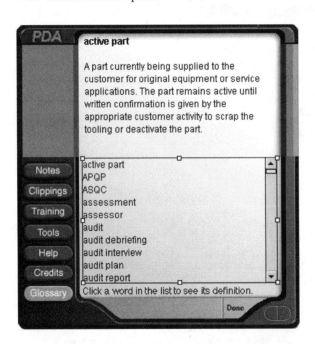

You'll apply the Glossary text style to each of the first four terms.

3] Select the Text tool in the toolbox. Then select the first term, *active part*, by clicking and then dragging through the two words.

When selected, *active part* will be highlighted.

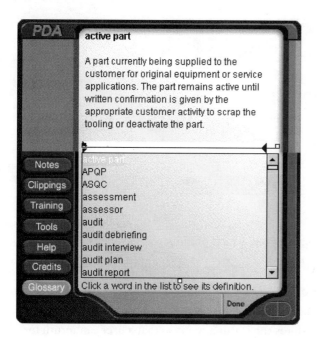

4] Choose Text › Apply Styles to open the Apply Styles window.

5] Click the Glossary text style in the window.

The Navigation Properties dialog box opens. You need to choose which page in the Glossary Framework you want to jump to.

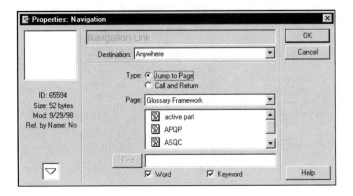

You'll use the Anywhere Destination type, which permits you to specify a different destination for each hypertext word.

Authorware provides two types of link: The Jump to Page option creates a one-way link that takes a user to the destination and stops there. The Call and Return option allows a round trip. Authorware stores the starting point so that a user can return to the place he or she started from when the link was originally clicked. Your glossary requires the Call and Return type of link.

6] Select Call and Return.

Now you'll select the page to which you want to link.

7] In the list of display icons, select the active part icon. Then click OK.

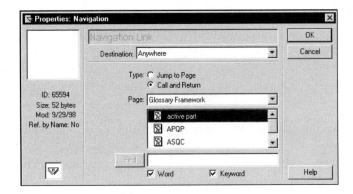

You've created a hypertext link. Now you'll perform the same operations for the other three terms.

8] In the Presentation window, select *APQP* by dragging through it or double-clicking it.

9] In the Apply Styles window, select *Glossary*.

10] In the Navigation Properties dialog box, select Call and Return for Type and select the APQP display icon in the list of framework pages. Then click OK.

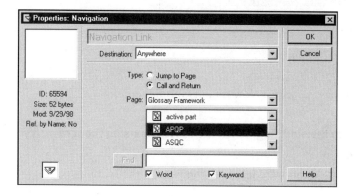

11] Select *ASQC* so that it's highlighted. Then select the Glossary style in the Apply Styles window.

12] In the Navigation Properties dialog box, select Call and Return and select the ASQC icon. Then click OK.

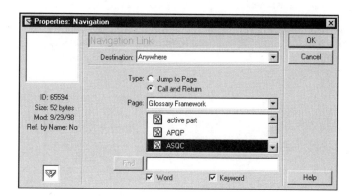

You'll finish by linking *assessment* to its definition.

13] Select *assessment* so that it's highlighted. Then select Glossary in the Apply Styles window. In the Navigation Properties dialog box, select Call and Return and select the assessment icon. Then click OK.

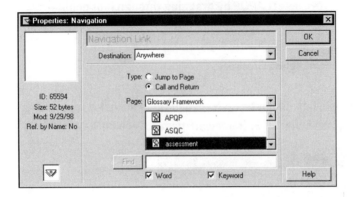

You've created four hyperlinked words. Now try out your hyperlinks.

14] Restart the piece from the start flag. When the PDA appears on the screen, try clicking each definition.

Each time you click a word, Authorware jumps to the page in the framework containing its definition.

WHEN YOU CLICK *ACTIVE PART* IN THIS DISPLAY ICON...

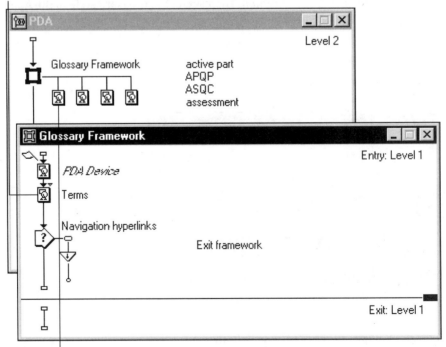

...YOU JUMP TO THIS PAGE IN THE FRAMEWORK

15] Save your work.

Notice that when the PDA appears, the definition for *active part* is displayed. That's because the definition is on the first page, and the flow automatically goes to the first page when it enters the framework. You don't want to display the definition for a term, however, unless the user clicks the term. There's a simple solution to this problem, and you'll apply it in the next task.

ADDING AN EMPTY PAGE

One brief task is needed to complete the PDA glossary. You need to prevent the first definition from appearing when the flow enters the framework.

1] In the PDA map window, drag a map icon from the icon palette to the immediate right of the Glossary Framework icon (to the left of the active part display icon). Name it *Empty*.

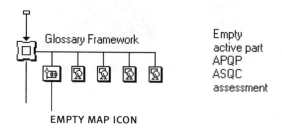

EMPTY MAP ICON

You're creating an empty first page for this framework. When the flow reaches the framework and automatically passes to the first page, no definition will appear.

2] Restart the piece from the beginning. After the movie plays, click the PDA button.

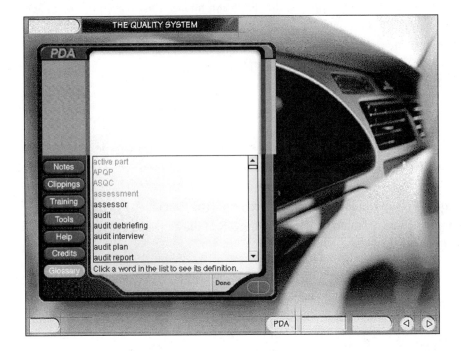

This time the upper half of the PDA screen, where definitions appear, is blank. The flow still goes to the first page in the glossary framework, but because that page is empty, nothing is displayed.

3] Save your work.

WHAT YOU HAVE LEARNED

In this lesson you have:

- Used a perpetual interaction to create a glossary that users can view from within the pages of a piece [*page* **366**]

- Created custom buttons to display and remove the glossary [*page* **368**]

- Used imported RTF text configured as scrolling text to create the list of glossary terms [*page* **376**]

- Used a framework icon and imported RTF text to create a separate page for each definition in the glossary [*page* **383**]

- Used a hypertext text style to link a term to the page in the framework that contains its definition [*page* **388**]

frameworks

enhancing

LESSON 18

Frameworks are remarkably versatile structures. You can use a framework to quickly assemble a simple series of pages, as you did in Lesson 15. At the other extreme, you can make a framework the core structure for delivering complex arrays of media and interactivity.

In this lesson you'll enhance and polish your work on the Quality piece. You'll improve the way the paging buttons work, avoid a potential conflict between the PDA (personal digital assitant) display and the movie, and create a progress indicator to tell users

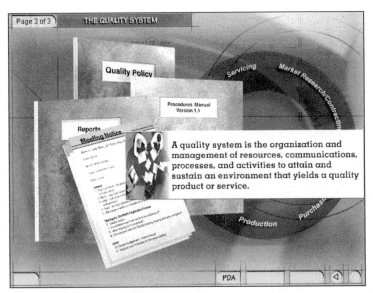

With Authorware it's easy to create a progress indicator to tell users what page they're on—one of the enhancements you'll create in this lesson. The project used for this lesson is adapted from **Starting the QS-9000 Process.**

what page they're viewing. Finally, you will create a smoother, more pleasing opening to the piece. If you would like to see the final result of this lesson, open the Final Files folder and play 18_Final.a5p.

WHAT YOU WILL LEARN

In this lesson you will:

- Use variables to prevent wrap-around paging
- Use a variable to make an interaction unavailable while a movie is playing
- Create a progress indicator that displays the current page in a framework
- Add an opening screen that produces a smooth beginning for the first page of a piece

APPROXIMATE TIME

It should take about 2 hours to complete this lesson.

LESSON FILES

Media Files:
Your Files\Quality Project\Quality Media

Beginning File:
Beginning Files\18_Begin.a5p

Completed Project:
Final Files\18_Final.a5p

USING A VARIABLE TO MAKE A NAVIGATION BUTTON INACTIVE

If you continue clicking the Next Page button in this piece, the piece wraps around from page 3 to page 1. Similarly, when you click the Previous Page button on page 1, the piece wraps to page 3. Wrap-around paging can be useful for some applications. For this piece, however, you want to make the Next Page button inactive on page 3 and the Previous Page button inactive on page 1. To accomplish this, you'll enter expressions in the Active If boxes for the two buttons.

1] Open 18_Begin.a5p in the Beginning Files folder and save it as *18_Quality.a5p* in the Quality Project folder.

Alternatively, you can use the file you worked on in the previous lesson and save it as *18_Quality.a5p*.

2] In the Design window, double-click the Quality System framework icon to open it.

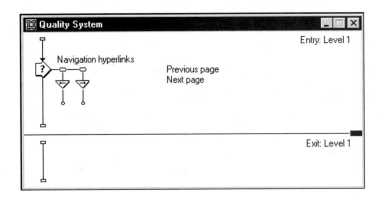

3] Double-click the response type symbol for the Previous Page button.

The Response Properties dialog box opens.

4] On the Button tab, select the Hide When Inactive option.

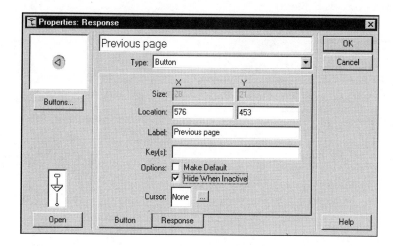

When the button is inactive, it will not appear on the screen.

tip   *If you don't want to hide a custom button when it's inactive, you can import art for the inactive state so the button will be visible but will have a different appearance than the active version. For standard buttons—the Authorware default buttons—the inactive state is automatically dimmed unless you select Hide When Inactive.*

5] Click the Response tab. Then click in the Active If box to prepare to enter an expression.

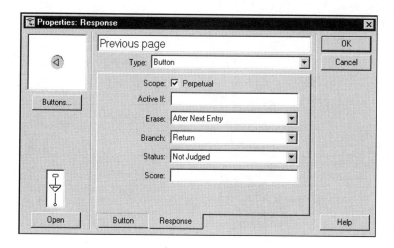

6] Open the Variables window.

To do this, choose Window › Variables.

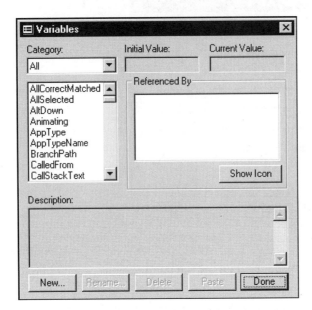

7] Under Category, select Framework. Then select CurrentPageNum in the list of variables.

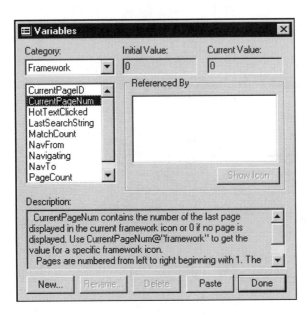

CurrentPageNum is a numeric system variable that contains the number of the page currently being viewed.

8] Click Paste and then close the Variables window.

If you have the screen space, you can leave the window open and move it to one side.

9] In the Active If box, type ›1 after CurrentPageNum.

The expression should now read as follows:

CurrentPageNum>1

If only one framework was in the piece, this expression would be sufficient. Because the glossary also uses a framework, however, you need to make this expression specify the Quality System framework.

10] Click between CurrentPageNum and ›1.

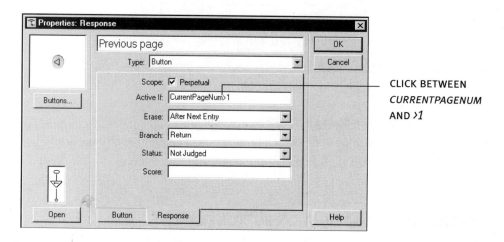

CLICK BETWEEN
CURRENTPAGENUM
AND *›1*

The flashing text editing cursor will appear between CurrentPageNum and >1. The expression you enter here will make it clear that you want this expression to refer to the Quality System framework.

11] Type this text: @"Quality System"

The @ symbol identifies the specific icon you want to associate with a variable. You'll use this for many expressions in your projects. The complete expression should now read

CurrentPageNum@"Quality System">1

Now the Previous Page button will be active only when the current page number of the Quality System framework is greater than 1. When the current page is 1, the button will be inactive. Because you selected Hide When Inactive, the Previous Page button will be hidden when page 1 is displayed.

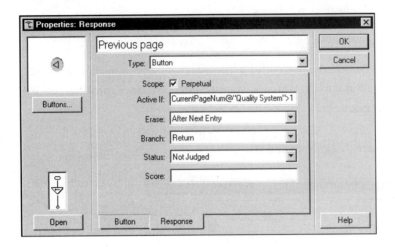

12] Click OK to close the dialog box. Then save your work.

You've set up the conditions under which the Previous Page button will become inactive. Now you'll use a slightly different expression to do the same for the Next Page button.

MAKING ANOTHER NAVIGATION BUTTON INACTIVE

You'll use the same system variable to make the Next Page button inactive. However, in this task you'll combine it with another system variable to create the expression you need.

1] Double-click the response type symbol for the Next Page button. On the Button tab, select the Hide When Inactive option.

Again, you'll make this button invisible when it's inactive.

2] Click the Response tab and click in the Active If box to prepare to enter an expression.

3] Open the Variables window. Select CurrentPageNum and click Paste.

Again, you'll specify the Quality System framework in the expression.

4] After CurrentPageNum, type @"Quality System".

5] Enter the < symbol after CurrentPageNum@"Quality System".

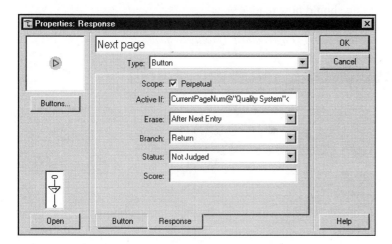

Now you'll paste a variable that you haven't used before.

6] In the Variables window, under the Framework category, select PageCount.

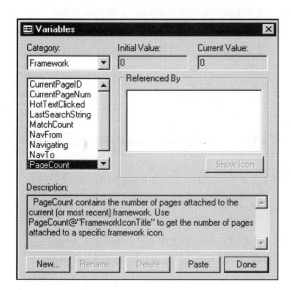

This variable contains the count of the total number of pages in a framework.

7] Click Paste. Then click Done to close the Variables window.

The expression should now read as follows:

CurrentPageNum@"Quality System"<PageCount

You also need to specify to which framework *PageCount* refers.

8] Add this to the expression in the Active If box: @"Quality System"

The complete expression should now read

CurrentPageNum@"Quality System"<PageCount@"Quality System"

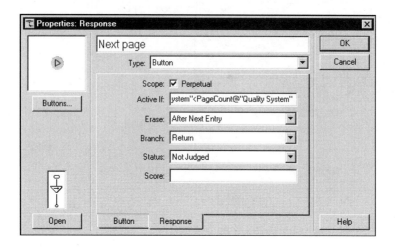

The Next Page button will be active only when the current page number is less than the number of pages in the Quality System framework. This means that on page 3, the Next Page button will be inactive, and because of the Hide When Inactive setting, it will also be hidden from view.

Now you can test your expressions by running the piece.

9] Click OK. Then restart the piece and click the navigation buttons to page through the piece.

The Previous Page button is hidden on page 1, and the Next Page button is hidden on page 3.

> **tip**   *Using variables instead of "hard" numbers can save you work and keep your expressions valid as your pieces change and grow. The value of a variable can change to meet changing conditions in a piece. For instance, the second expression will still work if it is written as* CurrentPageNum@"Quality System"<3. *However, if you add or delete pages, it will no longer work because page 3 will no longer be the last page. By using* PageCount *instead of 3, you make the expression flexible; it will continue to work properly in a framework of any size.*

10] Save your work.

In the next task you'll make a perpetual interaction inactive when you don't want users to have access to it.

MAKING A PERPETUAL INTERACTION INACTIVE

In your projects you will sometimes find that you don't want a given perpetual inter-action to be available throughout an entire piece. For example, if the information on a pull-down menu is relevant only in certain sections of a piece, you'll want the menu to be unavailable in any other sections. You can accomplish this by entering an expression in the Active If box of a perpetual response.

In this task you'll use this technique to make the PDA button inactive while the Intro Movie is playing. You don't want users opening the PDA while the movie is playing because an external movie always plays in front of any other images on the screen, so the movie would partially block the PDA. You'll start by viewing the problem.

1] Restart the piece.

The movie begins to play.

2] Click the PDA button.

The PDA opens, but it's partially blocked by the movie. Normally, any images in a perpetual interaction are displayed in front of all other images. In this case, however, the movie plays in front of everything else on the screen. No matter what layer you assign to the PDA interaction, the movie will be on top.

note *Digital movies in most formats always play in front of other images. See Authorware's online help for details.*

You'll use an expression in the Active If box of the PDA button to make the PDA unavailable to users while the movie is playing.

3] In the Design window, double-click the response type symbol for the PDA button.

4] In the Response Properties dialog box, select the Hide When Inactive option on the Button tab.
When the PDA button is inactive, it will not be visible.

5] Click the Response tab and then click in the Active If box to prepare to enter an expression.
You'll paste a variable using the Variables window.

6] Open the Variables window. Under the General category, select MediaPlaying.

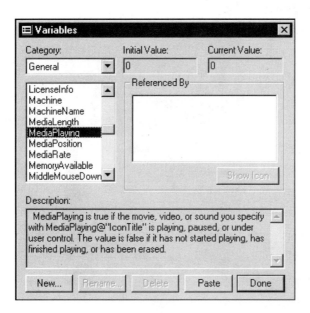

This is a logical variable, with a value of True or False. *MediaPlaying* is true when a movie, analog video, or sound is playing. You'll include a reference to Intro Movie with this variable to specify to which media you're referring.

7] Click Paste and then click Done to close the Variables window.
At this point you're setting up the button so it will be active when media is playing—but you want the opposite condition.

8] Insert the symbol ~ before MediaPlaying.

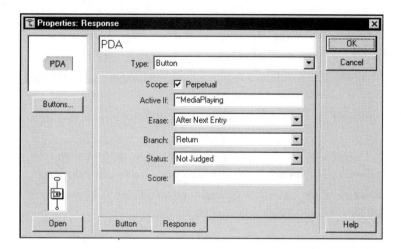

The tilde (~) means *not* in an expression. Now you'll specify which media should not be playing for this button to be active.

9] Enter this text after ~MediaPlaying: @"Intro Movie"

If you used a different icon title for the movie icon, use that title instead.

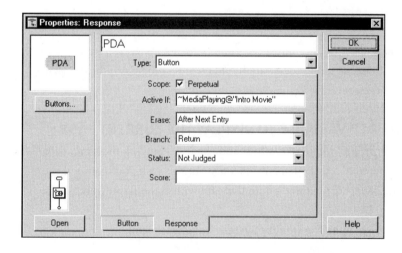

The expression should read as follows: *~MediaPlaying@"Intro Movie"*

Now the PDA button will be active only when the movie in the Intro Movie icon is not playing.

If you create an expression in the Active If box and need to close the dialog box to check the icon title to which you're referring, you don't have to press Cancel and lose your work. You can insert two hyphens at the beginning of the expression and then click OK. The two hyphens turn your expression into a comment, which is text that Authorware ignores when it reads an expression. The comment is saved when you click OK. You can then check the spelling of the icon title on the flowline, open the dialog box again, make the necessary changes, and remove the hyphens.

If you make a typing mistake when entering the icon title in the expression, an error message will appear. Authorware immediately warns you when you've incorrectly entered an icon title and will not accept an expression with an incorrect icon title. Even typing an extra space in the title will elicit the error message.

10] Click OK to close the dialog box. Then restart the piece.

As the movie plays, notice that the PDA button is hidden until the movie ends. Then the PDA button appears, and you can click it to open the PDA.

Authorware stores perpetual interactions in memory. Having a number of perpetual interactions active at one time can hinder performance. When a perpetual interaction is not needed in part of a piece, it's a good idea to make it inactive to free some memory for processing other elements in the piece.

11] Save your work.

In the next task you'll use an embedded variable to create a progress indicator that tells users what page they're viewing.

USING AN EMBEDDED VARIABLE TO DISPLAY THE CURRENT PAGE

Embedded variables can provide useful information to users such as the time, date, and length of an interaction and their scores on a test. In this task you'll embed the *CurrentPageNum* variable to show users where they are within the framework pages.

1] In the Design window, open the Quality System framework icon.

This window may already be open from previous tasks.

2] Drag a display icon from the icon palette to the top of the flowline in the Quality System window. Name it *Current Page*.

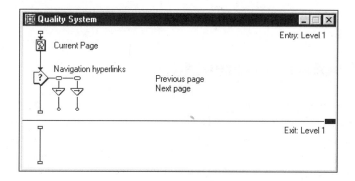

You'll embed the *CurrentPageNum* variable in this display icon. Because it's in the Entry pane, this information will be displayed on every page of the framework.

3] Double-click the Current Page display icon to open it.

4] In the Presentation window, select the Text tool. Select 9-point Arial. Make sure black is selected as the color and Transparent as the mode.

5] In the Presentation window, create this text: *Page {CurrentPageNum@"Quality System"} of 3*

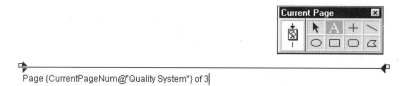

It doesn't matter where you type the text on the screen. In a few steps, you'll move it to its proper location.

Be sure to type curly brackets; they are needed for the value of the variable to be displayed.

To display this embedded variable properly, you need to adjust two options in the Display Icon Properties dialog box.

6] Choose Modify › Icon › Properties.

The Display Icon Properties dialog box opens.

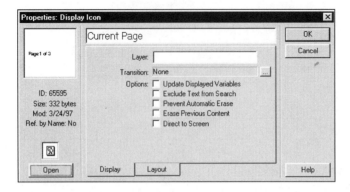

7] On the Display tab, enter *1* in the Layer box.

This layer setting ensures that the embedded variable will be displayed over other images on the screen. If you didn't change the layer, the embedded variable would be hidden behind the background artwork on each page of the framework.

The second option will ensure that the displayed value of the variable changes when the page changes. Normally, Authorware would display the value of the embedded variable only when the flow passed through the Current Page icon. You need to change that.

8] Click the Update Displayed Variables box.

Now every time the value of the embedded variable changes, Authorware will display the new value.

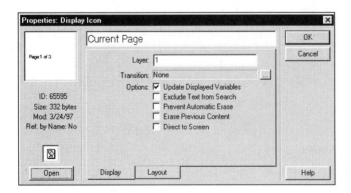

9] Click OK. Then restart the piece.

You should see "Page 1 of 3" appear on the screen—but not where you want it.

THE EMBEDDED VARIABLE MAY APPEAR IN THIS PART OF YOUR SCREEN AT FIRST

10] Double-click the text object in the Presentation window.

You should see handles around the text.

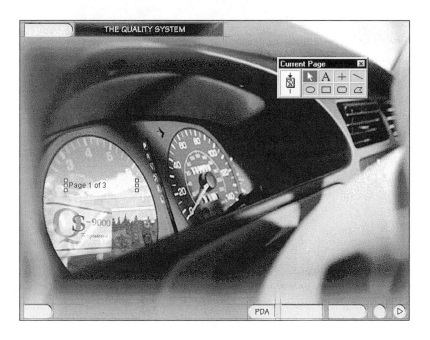

11] Drag the text object so that it's inside the blue area at the upper left.

415

Your screen should look similar to the following illustration.

If you're using a screen resolution of 640 × 480, you might need to turn off both the toolbar and menu bar so you can move the text object to its proper location. To turn off the toolbar, choose View > Toolbar (Ctrl+Shift+T). To turn off the menu bar, choose View > Menu Bar (Ctrl+Shift+M).

THE PROGRESS INDICATOR GOES HERE

Now you're ready to try out all the enhancements you've added.

12] Restart the piece. Try out the navigation buttons and the PDA.
The current page number is displayed at the upper left; however, the current page number is first displayed as 0 because the flow encounters the embedded variable before it encounters page 1 of the framework. There's also a delay at the beginning of the piece, during which the PDA button and navigation buttons appear before

they are hidden by the background artwork. This delay occurs because Authorware has to handle a number of preliminary tasks, including the loading of the digital movie driver. This isn't as nice a start as the piece should have.

13] Save your work.

In the next task you'll produce a smoother, more pleasing opening for the Quality piece.

ADDING A SPLASH SCREEN

You can improve the way the Quality piece begins by adding a **splash screen**—a full-screen graphic that is displayed at the very start of the piece and hides the various visual elements that Authorware assembles on the screen, such as the navigation buttons and background artwork. Just before the movie begins, the splash screen will be erased with a pleasant transition, providing a smooth opening for the first page.

In this task you'll import the artwork for the splash screen, add a wait icon to keep it on screen a second or so, and then place an erase icon just before the movie in the Introduction page of the framework.

1] In the Design window, drag a display icon from the icon palette to the very top of the flowline. Name it *Splash Screen*.

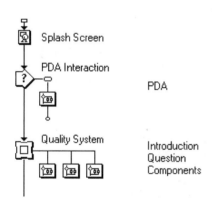

You'll import a full-screen graphic into this display icon that will open the Quality piece.

2] **Double-click the Splash Screen display icon to open it. Then choose File › Import and import the Splash.bmp file from the Quality Media folder.**

3] **Open the Display Icon Properties dialog box for the Splash Screen image.**
You need to set the layer for this artwork high enough so that it's displayed in front of any other images on the screen. Because you've already set layer 1 for the PDA buttons and other buttons, you need to use layer 2 for the Splash Screen image.

4] **On the Display tab, enter *2* for Layer. Then click OK.**

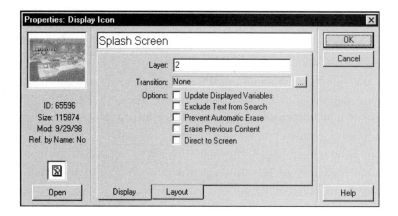

Next you'll add a pause to make sure the splash screen is on the screen long enough for users to read the title.

5] Drag a wait icon to the flowline below Splash Screen. Open its Icon Properties dialog box and click the boxes for Key Press and Show Button to remove the check marks. Enter a duration of *1.5* and then click OK.

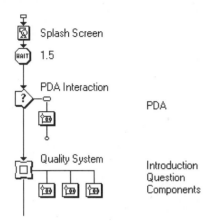

Alternatively, you can enter *IconTitle* for the duration and then enter *1.5* as the title.

Next you'll insert an erase icon to remove the splash screen just before the movie begins.

6] Double-click the Introduction map icon to open it.

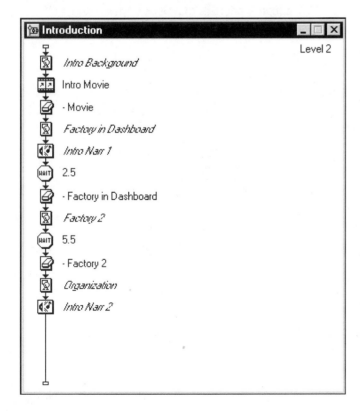

7] Drag an erase icon to the flowline between Intro Background and Intro Movie. Name it – *Splash Screen*.

INSERT AN ERASE ICON HERE

Intro Background

- Splash Screen

Intro Movie

- Movie

Factory in Dashboard

Intro Narr 1

2.5

- Factory in Dashboard

Factory 2

5.5

- Factory 2

Organization

Intro Narr 2

8] Restart the piece. When the Erase Icon Properties dialog box opens for the new erase icon, click the Splash Screen image in the Presentation window to select it for erasing.

9] On the Erase tab, click the Transition button. In the Erase Transition dialog box, choose any transition you like and click Apply to preview it. When you are satisfied with your choice, click OK.

10] In the Erase Icon Properties dialog box, click OK.

Now you'll see how well this enhancement works.

11] Restart the piece.

Authorware first displays the Splash Screen full-screen image. Because it's on layer 2, it's the only image visible while the flow passes through the icons for the PDA button, navigation buttons, and Intro Background image. The contents of these icons are displayed behind the Splash Screen image. When the erase icon removes the Splash Screen image, the Introduction page appears seamlessly on the screen.

12] Save your work.

WHAT YOU HAVE LEARNED

In this lesson you have:

- Applied variables to make the Previous Page and Next Page navigation buttons inactive to prevent wrap-around paging [*page* **402**]

- Used a variable to make a button for a perpetual interaction inactive while a movie is playing [*page* **409**]

- Embedded a variable in a display icon and selected the Update Displayed Variables option for the icon to display the current page number in a framework [*page* **412**]

- Used a full-screen image on layer 2 to hide visual elements at the beginning of a piece and produce a smooth opening for the introductory page [*page* **417**]

CONCLUSION

Congratulations on completing the lessons in *Authorware 5 Attain Authorized*. In this book you've created interactive pieces that include text, graphics, animation, sound, and a digital movie. You've used nine types of interactivity and created navigation structures that use a variety of navigation types. You've used Authorware variables to expand the capabilities of your pieces.

This book has introduced you to the basics of using Authorware to develop and distribute interactive information. Yet there's so much more to learn. Be sure to take advantage of the additional learning tools listed in Appendix B.

APPENDIX A

Authorware provides many shortcuts that make it easier to get your work done. Many are described in the lessons in this book. This appendix is a quick reference to all Authorware shortcuts.

NUMERIC KEYPAD SHORTCUTS

You can use the numeric keypad for several of the most common operations in Authorware. To use numeric keypad shortcuts, NumLock must be off.

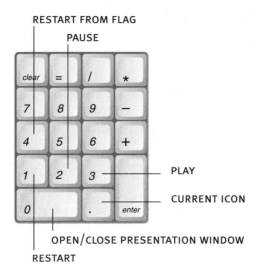

RESTART FROM FLAG

PAUSE

PLAY

CURRENT ICON

OPEN/CLOSE PRESENTATION WINDOW

RESTART

KEYBOARD SHORTCUTS

FILE MENU

Command	Shortcut
New › File	Ctrl+N
New › Library	Ctrl+Alt+N
Open › File	Ctrl+O
Close › Window	Ctrl+W
Close › All	Ctrl+Shift+W
Save	Ctrl+S
Save All	Ctrl+Shift+S
Import	Ctrl+Shift+R
Preferences	Ctrl+U
Exit	Ctrl+Q

EDIT MENU

Command	Shortcut
Undo	Ctrl+Z
Cut	Ctrl+X
Copy	Ctrl+C
Paste	Ctrl+V
Clear	Delete
Select All	Ctrl+A
Find	Ctrl+F
Find Again	Ctrl+Alt+F
Open Icon	Ctrl+Alt+O

VIEW MENU

Command	Shortcut
Current Icon	Ctrl+B
Menu Bar	Ctrl+Shift+M
Toolbar	Ctrl+Shift+T
Floating Panels	Ctrl+Shift+P

MODIFY MENU

Command	Shortcut
Image Properties	Ctrl+Shift+I
Icon › Properties	Ctrl+I
Icon › Calculation	Ctrl+= or Ctrl+0 (zero)

MODIFY MENU CONTINUED

Command	Shortcut
Icon › Transition	Ctrl+T
Icon › Library Links	Ctrl+Alt+L or Ctrl+Alt+double-click
File › Properties	Ctrl+Shift+D
Align	Ctrl+Alt+K
Group	Ctrl+G
Ungroup	Ctrl+Shift+G
Bring to Front	Ctrl+Shift+up arrow
Send to Back	Ctrl+Shift+down arrow

TEXT MENU

Command	Shortcut
Size › Size Up	Ctrl+up arrow
Size › Size Down	Ctrl+down arrow
Style › Bold	Ctrl+Alt+B
Style › Italic	Ctrl+Alt+I
Style › Underline	Ctrl+Alt+U
Alignment › Left	Ctrl+[
Alignment › Center	Ctrl+\
Alignment › Right	Ctrl+]
Alignment › Justify	Ctrl+Shift+\
Apply Styles	Ctrl+Alt+Y
Define Styles	Ctrl+Shift+Y

CONTROL MENU

Command	Shortcut
Restart	Ctrl+R
Stop	Ctrl+J or Ctrl+1
Play/Pause	Ctrl+P
Step Into	Ctrl+Alt+right arrow
Step Over	Ctrl+Alt+down arrow
Restart from Flag	Ctrl+Alt+R

WINDOW MENU		HELP MENU	
Command	**Shortcut**	**Command**	**Shortcut**
Control Panel	Ctrl+2	Help	F1
Inspectors › Lines	Ctrl+L	Help Pointer	Shift+F1
Inspectors › Fills	Ctrl+D		
Inspectors › Modes	Ctrl+M		
Inspectors › Colors	Ctrl+K		
Presentation	Ctrl+J or Ctrl+1		
Functions	Ctrl+Shift+F		
Variables	Ctrl+Shift+V		
External Media Browser	Ctrl+Shift+X		

DESIGN WINDOW SHORTCUTS

Many shortcuts are available within the Design window for common operations. This section lists the shortcuts available in the Design window.

To do this . . .	do this
Open an icon's Properties dialog box	Alt-double-click the icon (Double-clicking also produces the same results for most icons)
Open an icon's Properties dialog box without opening the Presentation Window	Ctrl-double-click the icon
Open a calculation window	Double-click a calculation icon
Open a map window (sublevel flowline)	Double-click a map icon
Open the Response Properties dialog box	Double-click a response type symbol (use Control-double-click to keep the Presentation window closed)
Open the Response Type dialog box	Ctrl-Alt-double click a response type symbol
Preview an icon's contents without opening the Presentation window	Right-click the display, interaction, sound, or digital movie icon
Preview the first object in an erase icon's list	Right-click the erase icon
Preview an icon to be animated	Right-click the motion icon
Cycle through response branching options	Control-click the branch path in the flowline or toolbox
Cycle through response status options	Control-click to the left of the response type symbol title
Select the next icon on the flowline	Press Tab or Enter
Select the previous icon on the flowline	Press Shift-Tab or Shift-Enter
Open a Framework window	Double-click a framework icon
Open an attached calculation window	Double-click the calculation symbol above an icon
Open the Library Links dialog box	Ctrl-Alt-double-click an icon linked to a library
Open the Decision Path Properties dialog box	Double-click a decision path synbol

PRESENTATION WINDOW AND TOOLBOX SHORTCUTS

This section lists the shortcuts available in the Presentation window and toolbox.

To do this . . .	do this
Display the contents of a display or interaction icon in the Presentation window	Double-click the icon
Display an icon's contents in addition to the current or previous Presentation window contents	Shift-double-click the icon
Select all objects in the current icon	Double-click the icon in the toolbox
Select objects not contained in the current icon	Control-click the object
Open the Modes Inspector	Double-click the Pointer tool
Open the Lines Inspector	Double-click the Line tool
Open the Colors Inspector	Double-click the Ellipse tool
Open the Fills Inspector	Double-click the Polygon tool
Nudge a selected object by 1 pixel	Press an arrow key to move the object in the desired direction
Draw a square, circle, or perpendicular line	Shift-drag with a drawing tool
Constrain an object to its original aspect ratio when resizing	Shift-drag
Deselect all objects	Press the spacebar
Select the next object in the current icon	Press Tab

PRINTED

- *Using Authorware 5 Attain*, the printed documentation included with Authorware.
- *The Official Guide to Authorware 5 Attain*, by Nick Roberts and Joe Ganci, Macromedia Press.

ONLINE

- The Authorware 5 Attain Help Pages, included with Authorware. The online help system for Authorware provides procedures, reference information, and links to Macromedia Web learning resources.
- Show Me examples, provided on the Authorware 5 Attain CD-ROM. Provides Authorware pieces that demonstrate solutions to common Authorware challenges, with flowline logic you can paste into your own pieces.

WEB

- Authorware 5 Attain Developers Center, located at the Macromedia Web site (*http://www.macromedia.com/support/authorware*), accessible from the Help menu in Authorware. Regularly updated information includes how-to articles, in-depth coverage of programming issues, and new Show Me examples.
- TechNotes, accessible from the Help menu. Contains answers to numerous questions. You can search to find relevant TechNotes for your issues.
- Authorware Discussion Group, in the Authorware Developers Center.
- AWARE list, an Internet mailing list in which users post questions and answers to a wide range of Authorware questions. To subscribe, send an e-mail message to *LISTSERV@CC1.KULEUVEN.AC.BE* that says *SUBSCRIBE AWARE <your name>*. Warning: Subscribing to the list means you'll start receiving 50 to 100 e-mail messages almost every day.

index

R

Macromedia tech support number: 415-252-9080

LICENSING AGREEMENT

The information in this book is for informational use only and is subject to change without notice. Macromedia, Inc., and Macromedia Press assume no responsibility for errors or inaccuracies that may appear in this book. The software described in the book is furnished under license and may be used or copied only in accordance with terms of the license.

The software files on the CD-ROM included here are copyrighted by Macromedia, Inc. You have the non-exclusive right to use these programs and files. You may use them on one computer at a time. You may not transfer the files from one computer to another over a network. You may transfer the files onto a single hard disk so long as you can prove ownership of the original CD-ROM.

You may not reverse engineer, decompile, or disassemble the software. You may not modify or translate the software or distribute copies of the software without the written consent of Macromedia, Inc.